MW00564653

THE
METH
LUNCHES

THE
METH
LUNCHES

FOOD AND LONGING IN AN AMERICAN CITY

KIM FOSTER

ST. MARTIN'S
PRESS
NEW YORK

"The Meth Lunches: The Care and Feeding of a Drug Addict" was first published as an article in Nevada Public Radio's *Desert Companion* magazine, July 1, 2017.

First published in the United States by St. Martin's Press, an imprint of St. Martin's Publishing Group

www.stmartins.com

Designed by Steven Seighman

The Library of Congress Cataloging-in-Publication Data is available upon request.

ISBN 978-1-250-27877-7 (hardcover)
ISBN 978-1-250-27878-4 (ebook)

Our books may be purchased in bulk for promotional, educational, or business use. Please contact your local bookseller or the Macmillan Corporate and Premium Sales Department at 1-800-221-7945, extension 5442, or by email at MacmillanSpecialMarkets@macmillan.com.

First Edition: 2023

10 9 8 7 6 5 4 3 2 1

To David.
Everything good in my life is because of you. I totally married up.

I was reminded how expensive it was to be poor. Lise's thin-walled, roach-infested apartment cost more than I paid for my four-bedroom foursquare in Ann Arbor. For what she paid in rent she could've gotten her own house, or at least rented a place that was clean. But she had debt, student loans, and bad credit, and a more affordable place would not have her. "I just don't make food here," she said as she flipped on the kitchen light and the cockroaches scuttled under the fridge, annoyed.

—Claire Vaye Watkins, from *I Love You But I've Chosen Darkness*, on her sister's apartment in Las Vegas

CONTENTS

FROM THE AUTHOR

This book is true.

But as my seventeen-year-old daughter, Lucy, reminds me: "You can write my story, but everyone needs to know it's your take on my life. It's not actually my life."

She's spot-on, of course.

I've made some moves while writing this book—I've played with time occasionally, changed names, combined two people to form one character. Some names are real, others not. I've sometimes changed appearances or personalities or location to give people cover.

I made choices creatively that I hope show my respect and love for the people I've written about.

When you are reading this book, know that this is my take on other people's stories, on the research, on our culture and our communities, on food, the absence of food, on my family and on myself. It will always have the veneer of me and my thoughts and experiences, biases and blind spots.

That doesn't mean it isn't true.

Just that there are many truths. This is one.

Thank you so much for reading.

1

THE CARE + FEEDING OF A DRUG ADDICT

"CHARLIE IS DEAD in the backyard!" our ten-year-old daughter Edie is screaming. She is running across the backyard.

"He's dead! There's a dead body!"

She is beside herself. Tears on her cheeks. She flies into my arms. I rub her head, pulling her in so she can't see whatever is out there.

We've been in Las Vegas a few months, after leaving New York City, a place we never imagined leaving. Already, we have a dead person lying in our small backyard casita.

David runs out there.

From where I am standing, with Edie bunched up into my waist, sobbing, I can see our meth-addicted handyman on the floor. He is still. David checks him. He gives me the sign that he is breathing. He tries waking him up. But Charlie is out cold. David sweeps his mouth for obstructions. He tries to rouse him. Charlie is lead.

We leave him there.

This is the first time Charlie's addiction is noticeable to the kids.

While he sleeps on the cement floor of the casita, we eat lunch on the patio.

This should be weird. It's remarkably not.

The kids eat their sukiyaki noodle bowls. Their favorite, a treat they used to order in a Japanese restaurant back East. A reminder of their old life inside their new one.

David and I are eating a pan of bacalhau no forno à portuguesa, salt cod baked on top of thin wafers of potato, onions, peppers, briny olives, blistered cherry tomatoes, and charred lemon halves that get squirted warm and tart over the fish. We eat and talk about this dude like he isn't passed out in our backyard.

We talk about firing him.

We talk about what is good for us and what is enabling.

We talk about boundaries. How I struggle with mine. How David has them drawn in great, bold, permanent strokes around him and us.

We talk about Charlie's work pace. How it is suffering. How Charlie is suffering. We talk about how we can't fix him and have to protect the kids. And ourselves. We talk about how we just want the work in the casita done, and how we want Charlie to finish.

We wonder whether we should ever have invited him to lunch.

* * *

It's a late fall day in Las Vegas, Nevada.

The sky is clear.

It's seventy-two degrees, which is like a small miracle if you are from the East Coast. My husband, David, and I and our daughters, Lucy, eleven, and Edie, ten, moved here from Manhattan. David is a show producer—circus, comedy, cool multimedia shows—some productions on the Strip, some in cities around the world. Someone called him an "experience creator" once, and this seems to describe his work best.

But then he started doing a show on the Strip in Vegas.

The New York to Vegas, Monday to Thursday commute was getting grisly. We missed him. He missed us. So, we moved together across the country. This move feels like a fresh start we didn't know we needed.

Will it be forever? Only for a few years? Will we hate it?

We don't know.

But it's an adventure for sure. We leave our opinions open-ended.

Here in Nevada—a state pronounced Ne-VA-da, not the fancier sounding Nev-AH-da, a mistake that gets you outed as a noob or a tourist—I am cheating the hell out of winter. The girls are in shorts and eating on the back deck while the Northeast is frozen under the polar vortex.

Honestly? I barely miss New York City.

It shocks me to even write this. I expect the pangs of my city calling me back.

But nothing.

I'm bare-armed and my face is full of sunshine. I'm not looking behind me.

Downtown Vegas is like 1990s New York, except with big open skies that turn shockingly, brilliantly pink and violet at twilight. New York and Vegas are weirdly similar—our landscapes dictate our lives. Both the sardine tin–packed city and the oppressively baked city can be hard and extreme. And exciting.

They dare us to live there.

* * *

I want to say that Vegas is easier and kinder than New York. But when I check out our downtown neighborhood grocery store, a large Smith's, I get educated about the local ways of urban Vegas living.

It makes me nearly giddy to see a '70s-era Elvis impersonator, complete in a white pantsuit, with lamb chop sideburns, and a red shopping basket over his arm, pondering the tomato sauces. Or the grandpas hitting the slots at the front of the store while their wives do the weekly shopping unfettered.

There are also the drug addicts clustered in corners. Homeless folks all along the edges. You can't hit a downtown grocery store without being accosted by unhoused people hoping for spare change. Or a young mother who tells me, with teary eyes, how short she is at the end of the month, and could I buy diapers for her baby?

It is not easier and kinder for a lot of people.

And there's a shitload of meth. Meth is everywhere here.

I don't really get meth. I never noticed it in NYC quite the same way I do here. It's everywhere. I drive down the street and see a young man hanging off a lamp post. His face cracked apart. Older than his years. His teeth are missing. His face is caving in on itself.

The meth in the New York we left must be hidden away, in abandoned tenements and alleys. Or in secret apartments, where no one is watching.

Or maybe it is everywhere, but New York is so segregated into neighborhoods that I barely notice. The only whisper that meth might exist is that I couldn't buy multiple cold medications at our local Duane Reade.

But still, meth didn't feel close to us in New York.

But in downtown Vegas, it's at the supermarket and the corner store. It's in the neighborhood. You can't walk a mile without seeing someone with the telltale hollowness etched into their sucked-in faces. Downtown Vegas feels like the old New York my friends back home whine about and long for—gritty and real, unrelenting, exciting and unforgiving. High highs, low lows. The beautiful and the ugly. The easy and the impossible, all plastered together in one glossy, well-lit city.

Maybe this is why I am falling in love with Las Vegas.

It's New York the way I remember it when I first arrived there. It's how everything is pulsing and vibrating and teetering on the thinnest of edges.

We live here only two weeks before we meet Charlie, the first of many meth-addicted friends. It doesn't take long for meth to become a huge part of our everyday lives.

* * *

Our little bungalow, in the Huntridge section of downtown, is ancient by Vegas standards, built in 1944.

It predates even the Strip.

Some of the neighbors who grew up around here refer to it as "the Snow-White House" because of all the ivy and the big, leafy green tree in the front yard. We buy the house because of that mulberry, pretending we don't see the bleached-out naked skeleton branches on top.

Those telltale jutting white bones.

As soon as we move in, the local NPR tree guy, who passes out gardening wizardry on the radio, tells us that the tree is a goner.

Months later, David will pull it out, trunk and roots and soil and bugs, and say goodbye to the leafiness, the very thing that makes the house like a cottage in the desert. David embraces the Mojave. He plants a fast-growing Tipu right where the mulberry used to be. He rips up every inch of grass.

Grass is the enemy of the waterless.

He adds a California pepper, a nod to me and my love for long, stringy-branch trees that bend and weep and get all dramatic. He adds plants that can live on drips and be in permanent states of thirst, like lantana, Australian racer, yellow bells, thick, spiky agave, and bougainvillea, which grow into long tendrils of green limbs, sprouting Corvette-red flowers. I buy small citrus trees and put them in giant planters on the patio. Next door, there are olive trees and pomegranate, and down the street, lemon trees.

I have a fantasy about having trees that make us breakfast. This is the West, where all the things are possible, right?

The house is a disaster, and we fill a dumpster with all the sad debris of other people's lives. Old tables, a dead cactus, little bits of dirty, forgotten toys, a tipped-over side table with a broken leg, cracked plastic plant pots with clumps of petrified dirt inside, and a TV still hoisted onto the stained walls of the bedroom, like it was in a hospital ward.

Cockroaches, the big ones that look like tiny puppies and run really fast up the walls, have taken residence. I find a pissed-off mouse in my sink. And the outside of the house is covered in empty cicada shells, which the girls collect and keep in tin cans, and store everywhere in the house, much to my consternation.

It is the most depressing house I have ever been in.

Is Vegas a mistake?

My mood quickly absorbs all the sadness left behind, and I teeter from being obsessed with the vermin to being sucked down the black hole of sadness. I am either searching the walls frantically for imaginary roaches that might be scuttling about or slumped into myself, bleak and worried about our choices.

David responds to my plummeting mood and strange obsessions by doing two things: He (1) gets me to a doctor, who puts me on antianxiety meds, and (2) paints. These help immensely. As the Lexapro settles into my system, and David and I paint a crisp white over the asylum green, I start to see how this house can change, how it can be ours.

We hire an exterminator. We buy two excruciatingly beautiful antique couches, a gloriously battered farm table from the 1800s and a primitive-style chipped and peeling sideboard, a couple battered chandeliers.

We are giving up on our IKEA period. This helps my brain.

We start to plan, to look forward to whatever new incarnation is next for the Snow-White House.

But what we need is a handyman with some skills.

This is where Charlie comes in.

* * *

The Day Laborers Office is an ingenious project.

It's a place that matches workers with people who have work for them. Cash for work. No taxes. No waiting for a paycheck.

Many of the folks who come to the Day Laborers Office are immigrants, as many as 94 percent of them, according to *The Nevada Independent*. Others are felons. They are people between careers or new transplants looking to get some footing. Some are itinerant and use day work to stock up on cash for their gambling, or for nursing their drug and alcohol addictions.

Before such offices existed, day workers gathered at Lowe's or Home Depot, on street corners. And still do. Often they got into the back of a stranger's pickup, negotiated a job and payment, and took their chances getting paid fairly.

Things often went wrong for the workers.

"They don't always pay what they promise," Enrique told me. He was a day worker who laid some stone for us. Enrique was not unskilled, just undocumented.

"I worked for this guy who said he would pay me $200 for a walkway, and he told me at the end, he didn't have the money."

The guy shoved whatever cash he had into Enrique's hand. He walked with his tools for hours to get back home.

"I worked all day," Enrique said.

That day, Enrique made $40 for nine hours of hard work. That's a little more than $4 an hour.

This is how day workers find themselves making poverty wages. There is no safety net. No union. And if you are here illegally, the last thing you want is to call the police and draw attention to yourself.

Enrique lived with other Mexican workers in small apartments dotted throughout the city. They worked, saved, and returned to their families and communities in Mexico a couple times a year with cash, and to rekindle their lives and get to know each other again.

He showed us the photos of his wife and small daughters. His whole life is missing them and supporting them from afar.

The Day Laborers Office tries to create some protection for workers like Enrique. The office works on the idea that the people who are doing the labor are often treated with the least humanity.

In *The Nevada Independent*, writers Luz Gray and Michelle Rindels interview the founder of the National Day Laborer Organizing Network, who is also a former day laborer himself, Pablo Alvarado.

"If they accept the fruits of undocumented people's labor, they should accept their humanity," Alvarado told them. "And accepting their humanity means giving them their rights, recognizing who they are, protecting them when they are in the workplace, making sure that institutions that are supposed to administer justice are accessible to them."

The office is set up to take some of the hardship and uncertainty out of waiting on street corners near Lowe's, and parks and street corners, to pick up day work. The space is comfortable enough. But bland, a blank canvas, for sure. They supply hot coffee and a stream of home and garden TV shows while people wait for calls.

Workers jokingly, and sometimes critically, refer to it as a "day residence" for workers because often there are more workers than calls for work, and folks end up hanging out all day, sleeping, drinking coffee, smoking, waiting.

What the office does well is make sure people get paid the agreed-upon amount, with a minimum starting hourly of $10. If they do get the call, and their skills match the job, they are told the requirements, the number of hours (at least four), and the hourly wage. They can decide to take it or not.

When we begin hiring day workers, we find they need lunch, too. They often don't have vehicles, so it's not easy for them to run out and grab food or drinks.

Could we run out and buy them some fast food? Sure. And we have done that, too.

But why wouldn't we invite people to come eat at our table if we are cooking food and sitting down to eat?

We pay them $25 an hour, plus lunch, an infinite supply of ice-cold water, and a ride home if they need it.

David calls the office.

We ask people to come to our house and jackhammer in 107-degree heat.

And we meet Charlie.

* * *

Edie passes a platter of yakitori-style chicken skewers to Charlie.

Thigh bits swim in soy sauce, fish sauce, lime, garlic, ginger, rice wine, some cilantro, and a few chopped-up Thai chilies. We fell in love with yakitori when we were in Tokyo the month before with one of David's shows. I made a silent promise that yakitori, in one form or another—particularly grilled, heavily salted, crunchy chicken skins—would become a staple.

I throw all the thighs on the grill, on skewers. I like a hot fire and my chicken bits slightly blackened and grilled up crunchy, but still soft and supple on the inside. I like to smell the last steak I made on the grill infused into my chicken.

Edie takes a large spoonful of jasmine rice and ignores the salad, just simple greens that I quickly toss with lime juice, olive oil, salt, a handful of cilantro, and chopped spring onion.

There are wedges of fried-up scallion pancakes. Charlie puts three on his plate, heaped with all the chicken and veg. He doesn't think you can get scallion pancakes anywhere but at a Chinese restaurant. He thinks it must've taken me hours in the kitchen.

I want him to continue on with his fantasy, but I can't help it—I can never keep anything food-related to myself—and I tell him how easy it is to make scallion pancakes, and the three ingredients required, and how anyone with half a cerebellum and a hot plate can do it.

David, hell-bent on cutting carbs, ignores the pancakes for salad and chicken. We talk about the work Charlie is doing in the casita.

Charlie and David are transforming the casita from a dirty, overrun garage into a light, airy studio, one that will house David's work, and mine as a writer, and the children as constant makers of one thing or another.

There will be windows that let in light. And French doors that open into what will be the garden, currently a patch of dusty dirt. There will be a small bathroom and a tiny kitchen.

It's David's ideas and Charlie's hands that will make it happen.

They talk about the inner workings of a miter saw. I pretend to listen while Charlie fills his plate again.

Then he tells us, kind of abruptly, that he hasn't heard from his wife, Tessie, today. She is a meth addict, too. He knows what phone silence means. That little sign—her simply not picking up the phone for several hours—is a bomb that flattens him. We see it land, all except the kids, who are joyful and clueless.

She has started using again.

It's what always happens.

In just three months, we have seen Charlie and Tessie through a lifetime of crises—temporary sobriety, meth binges, two stints in jail, three moves, one eviction, several religious, end-of-the-world texts on our phones, a dozen different phones and phone numbers (meth addicts go through "Obama phones" like packs of cigarettes), and a stay in a psychiatric hospital. Every day brings some kind of cruel surprise, some hardship that would pummel me. But it is just business as usual for them.

Their lives are a tedious wreckage. And it never becomes clearer than when we eat lunch together. It's like sitting around the table forces us to look at everything. See it up close.

Charlie is quiet about Tessie in front of the kids. I watch his face and wonder if he is more scared of Tessie being high or Tessie pulling him back into his own high, which she always does.

Maybe both.

What I know is that when he leaves our house, he will run straight to her. He will say he is going to rescue her, but they will drown each other. They will get high together. He will pillage the four sober days he has under him.

On the weekends, when David is home and the girls are out of school, we all eat lunch together. During the week, when Charlie works a full day, I make him a lunch he eats alone at the same table on our back deck.

I don't set the table or put out bowls. I make a plate, a big one, with several servings of each food, usually leftovers from the night before. I put out a cold glass bottle of water and a glass. He prays over the food. I go back inside, writing or washing dishes. When he finishes, he brings in a neatly cleaned and scraped plate and drops it into the sink. He thanks me profusely and swears I am a brilliant cook.

I don't mind hearing this at all.

When we are all there, and Charlie is working on the house, we all eat together. One big happy, weird, extended family that isn't a family.

And meth is always there.

I no longer ask myself why there is a meth addict eating with us, at our table. Next to our children. Eating our grilled chicken thighs. But that wasn't always the case.

In the beginning, there were a lot of questions.

* * *

We roasted pork butts the day before in coals in the backyard.

I have one butt left over today for bo ssam. This is our first of the lunches with Charlie.

I warm it in the oven and tear off warm, smoky chunks of meat. I set the pork out on the table with little bowls of quick pickles, pickled watermelon rind, homemade radish kimchi, rice, a honey-sweet but face-melting ssam sauce, and ginger scallion sauce. It takes fifteen minutes to pull together the leftovers and set it all on the table on the patio.

I call everyone to lunch, including Charlie. He is surprised.

What I don't know is that meth addicts often don't eat. Not really. Meth is a stimulant, and it removes the desire to eat. Charlie is lean, muscled from physical work, not a bit of paunch on him.

We dig in.

Charlie is silent.

He is sort of looking around like he doesn't know how to raise a fork to his lips.

He sits there looking at us, looking at his empty plate. I shove a platter of food in his hands and tell him to take what he wants and pass it along. He forces himself to be polite, but he's a great actor—addicts are—and it doesn't register with me that he is resisting the food, at first.

Charlie is in his thirties, boastful, blond, darkly tanned from sleeping in the desert for the last three months with Tessie. He works relentlessly, as if he is proving how tough he is, how hard he can work. He loves the jack-hammering the most, and he guts the concrete that used to be a driveway inside of a day. He rarely takes breaks. He is from Texas and has big Texas manners. I am Ma'am and always will be.

Charlie talks about cooking with his wife, as he forks food into his mouth.

He talks about his love of Chinese food. He talks about dan-dan noodles. He is an extroverted guy, and once he starts talking, there is no stopping him. This is part Charlie, part meth.

Charlie tells us about his family, his wife, Tessie, and their five boys. Two are hers from a previous marriage, two are his from a previous marriage, and one is theirs, together. He talks about working in his father-in-law's plumbing business. He talks about love and staying together.

And Jesus.

He talks about God a lot.

All of this makes me wonder how he ended up as a day laborer. How he came to be jackhammering in our backyard in the Vegas summer. I wonder if it's the economy. Had the business gone belly up? Had he simply been downsized? It could easily have been the economy. Vegas was decimated and underwater during the 2008 financial collapse. It was one of the hardest-hit housing markets in the country.

Charlie talks so intimately about his children and his wife. Like that time they took the kids hiking in Zion, scrambling over boulders and wading in knee-high water through narrowly cut canyons. He tells us about wrapping the kids' Christmas presents to go under the tree. How he and Tessie stay up all night getting everything done, until they are bleary-eyed and the kids rouse them.

I pass around the sauces wondering why a young-enough white man with a young family and lots of building skills is taking on day work.

How the hell does he end up here?

Later, after the lunch is done and the dishes are drying in the racks on the sink, he tells me.

Charlie is in the backyard, bent over. Crying. Hysterically crying, in the way that makes your whole person shudder. He tells me that seeing Lucy and Edie hanging out, everyone eating together, reminds him of his kids. He tells me their names are Brandon, Jackson, Justin, Daniel, and Cade. They were taken from him and Tessie by Child Protective Services (CPS) in Texas.

He is sobbing so hard the words cannot come out.

He buries his face in his hands.

"I haven't seen my kids in months," he tells me.

The kids are in Texas with Tessie's uncle. A pastor and his wife.

He tells me that he is so fucked up on meth that he barely thinks of them. That they are some intangible whisper of smoke in his head. Two-dimensional cardboard dreams of kids he once knew and loved and worried about, and now he doesn't remember how their hair smells after a bath or the sound of their little voices saying prayers at their bedside.

"Seeing you and David and the girls, remembering what this feels like," he says.

"Having a family around a dinner table, talking about normal things, passing plates . . ." His voice trails off. Charlie rubs his hands through his hair.

"God, what have I done?" he asks the sky. He asks his God.

There is no answer.

I see how much he has lost.

He sees how much he has lost.

Charlie leaves our house and gets high.

It's the only thing he can do.

* * *

Charlie's entry into drug use happens in that slow dribble of time that Stephen King and Peter Straub call "slippage" in their horror novel *Black House*.

They write about a solitary house that sits alone. Unseen by travelers. Slowly decaying and falling into disrepair over days and weeks and months, until it collapses into something much more dark, and hostile, and fragile.

I think about slippage a lot—how things and people invisibly, over long lengths of time, slide into states of decrepitude. Of the way five pounds here and five pounds there becomes thirty pounds over the slow compounding of months. Of the way depression covers you in gray blankets, which get heavier and heavier, until, months later, they are smothering you in total, mind-fucking blackness. Or the way we just get older, slowly. One bad knee, some cracking joints, a disease and then another, something chronic and insidious that we think we can survive, but instead it chips away at our strength, breaks down the body further.

Slippage is everywhere.

And it's also how people become addicts.

It's how Charlie describes his fall into addiction.

"Beers. Too many beers," he tells me.

It started there, and then with liquor. Blurry nights. Some of them delightful and filled with laughter. A job injury that requires pain pills. More pills. He needs to up the level of blurriness and numbness. Then it escalates to doctor shopping. Then dependency, a boulder running downhill, piling up momentum. Slippage.

He brought Tessie in. He gave her pills. No one wants to destroy themselves alone. And when that supply dried up, they switched to cheap street drugs.

"I needed relief from myself," he tells me.

"It's like one day we don't take the kids to school, or to a doctor's appointment, we stop making them take baths." Their world closes into their four walls.

"Those really normal day-to-day things just get lost because the focus is getting drugs, having drugs, taking drugs, being on drugs."

Slippage.

And then, one day, the cars roll up. CPS comes for the kids.

Losing the kids is huge. It triggers a kind of landslide, the loss of work, the loss of their home. There is no reason to fight when there are no kids to fight for. More drugs to cover the loss of the most important things in their lives. The kids go to various family in Texas and Vegas. It's like once the kids are gone, there is no structure, nothing to tether Charlie and Tessie to their lives.

"I need structure, a framework to be in," he tells me.

"Or I'm lost."

They decide to come back to Vegas. Tessie has family here. But there is a shitload of everything they are running from in Vegas. There is no treatment plan in the desert.

Charlie and Tessie cook in the Mojave. They sleep under the stars. They do their drugs.

More slippage.

Tessie and Charlie go to the desert to kill themselves.

* * *

I make dan-dan noodles.

And I blow Charlie's ever-lovin' mind.

I make the noodles from scratch this time, the chili oil–based sauce, crumbles of pork, preserved mustard greens, Sichuan peppercorns. A dusting of minced scallions.

It's September. Charlie is coming to work nearly every day now.

David gives him a chore list. I ignore him, except for bringing him lunches.

He is always busy and moving, but sometimes not really doing anything. His pace is frantic. A shark in open water. He might take an hour to build himself a worktable to cut something. Or a podium out of leftover wood for his list and his pencil. He is engrossed in menial tasks that he needs to get done, in his brain, so he can get to the real task.

He's a talented carpenter, tile layer, plumber, and handyman. But his mind is hopelessly addled. This is something he will have to live with, his Swiss cheese brain. Because meth can be, is often, a lifelong affair. The success rate for getting off meth is dismal.

Meth is special in what it does to the brain. It's a neurotoxin and can deplete as much as 90 percent of the user's dopamine. Dopamine is a messenger that makes the brain feel pleasure, joy, euphoria. Meth sucks out all the dopamine. This lack of dopamine drives the user into bouts of severe and painful depression and anxiety. To combat this, meth users push more of the drug. More meth means more nerves getting fried. It burns out the nerve endings.

It can take two years for the fried nerve endings to come back again, so that the person can feel joy again. It takes that long for recovery. This is why the drug is so awful. This is why recidivism is so high.

Meth thwarts all attempts to get off it.

And this is the story of an older, less lethal kind of meth. A chemical made in small batches in home cook laboratories. A process made famous in the TV show *Breaking Bad*. A dude in an RV that smells like rotten eggs, out in the desert tweaking ephedrine molecules, surrounded by empty boxes of spent Sudafed.

In his book *The Least of Us: True Tales of America and Hope in the Time of Fentanyl and Meth*, Sam Quinones explains how the old system worked.

"Hell's Angels cooks took three days to make five pounds of meth,"

Quinones writes in an excerpt in *The Atlantic*. "Mexican crews soon learned to arrive at cook sites like NASCAR pit crews, with premeasured chemicals, large vats, and seasoned workers. They produced 10 to 15 pounds per cook in 24 hours in what came to be known as 'super labs.' Soon the biker gangs were buying their meth from the Mexicans."

The new meth uses something called the P2P method. It doesn't require ephedrine, but a wide array of chemicals that are also used in mining, photography, perfumery, and car racing. So many industries that there is no way for the government to regulate their use. Any chemist worth their salt can also produce the chemicals, making it infinitely generative.

By 2012, meth coming into the United States was pretty much all new meth, according to Quinones, and it felt immediately different, especially to longtime users. The manufactured euphoria of old meth is now replaced with intense, debilitating paranoia. Hallucinations, delusions, conspiracy theories, memory loss, disordered speech. Outright psychosis. Longtime users called it "weirdo meth." Then new meth labs popped up in the West, and the price dropped by 90 percent. This made the barrier to entry very low.

So much so that even the East Coast feels it. Longtime opioid users, who traditionally came to drugs for different reasons than meth users, start using Suboxone to stave off their cravings and turn to the new meth to pair it as a stimulant. So now, even opioid users are using the new meth.

It's everywhere in Vegas.

It's devastating to see it up close.

Charlie knows the statistics are against him. He talks about it openly at lunch. He tries to stop. He never stops trying. He's the rat on the wheel.

The wheel keeps spinning.

It works this way: He comes to work disgusted with himself that he did meth. But he's better on meth. At first. He works harder. He's happier. He has less drama in his life. Meth takes away all the pain, the turmoil. He talks fast, a machine gun of words and ideas.

This time, it will work, he tells us.

This time, he won't do meth again. This time, everything is different. There are grand plans. The grandest. Because he feels good. Because he is high.

He's on the wheel.

He disappears for the withdrawal. The withdrawal is hard. Lots of paranoia, fights, jealousies, real and perceived. Sickness, both in the brain and the body.

But after a week or so, he comes back to life. He reappears. I make him an omelet with baby arugula, from a small pot I hope will be my garden someday. I add goat cheese. He watches, and something about the simplicity of the omelet makes him want to cook. Lots of questions. He borrows David's Jeep to go to Walmart for groceries. He is trying to find normal again. And cooking for himself seems like something sane, non-tweaking people do.

Drug addicts do not keep a full pantry or fresh herbs in the fridge. He wants to be the kind of person who has fresh herbs on hand.

I teach him how to make the omelet—the heat, the butter, the flipping, the spectrum of ingredients, the-anything-you-have-in-the-fridge no-rule of making an omelet.

This cooking soothes him.

He starts cooking for his wife and his friend Salvador, a meth addict who also has zero days clean and lives with them in a pay-by-the-week apartment, known as a weekly, in the drug alley that is East Fremont Street. The weekly is its own fresh hell. A transient place, where the drugs and accompanying dysfunction are plentiful. But it's better than the desert. And better than a tent city. He is not homeless, and that feels like something.

The rat wheel turns.

When he gets a few days clean, Charlie buys scallions. And salt. And cream cheese. And hot sauce. He cooks and feels the old life coming back into him. He feels like he can do it this time. I believe him. Because I'm stupid, and I have no idea this is the pattern. The endless, circuitous pattern, where all hope is false hope, and addicts have good intentions, but horrendous rates of success.

He tells me what he cooks. Salmon over greens. Noodles with shrimp. He asks about Chinese black vinegar. His interest grows as sobriety takes hold. For a couple of days, it's like having a toddler in the house, exclaiming joy at every color. Every ray of sunshine. Every tiny blessing.

Then he and Tessie have a fight. Or they just watch TV and are bored. Or whatever else triggers them into using. He uses. And he feels like a god for a couple days. Then he tumbles into the dark hole of withdrawal. A shell again. Then the toddler named Charlie, ogling at the world, is back.

Over and over.

He burrows into his head. Nothing he says makes sense. He is making wood boxes and tables for sawing for hours. He mutters. He rails at the world. He stays up for days. He sleeps for days.

And then Edie finds him in the casita.

Passed out cold.

We wonder if we will still make the lunches.

* * *

David wakes up Charlie at 9 p.m., hours after Edie finds him.

We tell him Edie found him. He immediately gets where this is going.

He is sobbing and remorseful.

We double-cop him. David goes stern and hard. Pissed-off Dad. No tolerance. I go soft and tell him we want him to be okay, and we want to support him, but not this way.

We explain it to the kids, all of it: What meth is. How to tell if someone is on meth. Why Charlie and Tessie lost their children. Why we gave him a job—because he is talented in areas we needed, and to give him a chance.

I see they are imagining themselves there, in the shoes of Charlie's kids, thinking about what it must be like to lose their parents. They ask a barrage of questions.

"Have you done meth?"

"What makes them leave their kids?"

"Are their kids okay?"

Then, when we have fed their curiosity, and they are quite sure this isn't going to happen to them, they bounce off to their bedroom. I hear them laughing. They are fine.

Charlie is remorseful. He is a sobbing mess. But just like a switch has been thrown, he brightens and tells us he has news.

Great news.

News that will change everything.

News that will make him quit drugs.

News that is a blessing from his God.

He tells us Tessie is pregnant.

* * *

Charlie looks bleary-eyed. Hunched over.

It's October. He shaves his head. He cuts off his beard.

He doesn't come through the house anymore to get to the casita. No more stopping in with the day's news. Or problems. Or drama. Now he goes through the side gate and never tells me he's here. He's late some days, and often cryptic about when he's coming in. He works, but barely. He is moving things around.

David is getting more and more disgruntled with his progress. Charlie moves like a ghost in the backyard. There, but not there. Some days he never shows up at all. He's largely unreachable by phone or text.

He tells me he's doing meth, which I know. Of course.

I'm like a meth expert these days.

He says Tessie is gone, disappeared. Last time he heard, she was living with a guy in a different shitty weekly apartment on Fremont.

"Using and she's pregnant?" I ask. I can't hide the disdain I feel.

He nods.

"Did she use with your last baby?"

"For six of the nine months."

"Fix the problem, Charlie," I say.

I'm hard and unyielding. He has drained the compassion from my body so that I am stone, hardness.

"You and Tessie have to go to rehab. Get a counselor. Stop white-knuckling. Fix the pain," I tell him, as if lecturing him will make a difference.

At the word "pain," he cries.

It's a flood. He crumples in on himself.

He tells me about the pain.

How his dad sexually abused him and how he had, in turn, sexually abused his sister. And how he would never abuse this baby. He would never. Not this time. Things are going to be different. The words come out in jumbles. I follow it and then lose it. I pick up the conversation in bits behind tears and animal wails and his body rocking back and forth.

"I look in the mirror and can't stand myself," he stutters.

He does everything he can to fix this problem on the most superficial of levels. He changes his hair. His clothes. He shaves his beard. He grows his beard. He wears a cap. He takes it off. He shoots more meth into his veins. He is a dopamine grifter, looking for it wherever he can find it. He tries to be the person he isn't. But he's always there in the mirror, this person he hates. This human with no paths to redemption.

And the wheel keeps turning.

Sometimes, when I make Charlie lunch, I think that it's no wonder he is a drug addict. It's no wonder he turns to something that sublimates, drowns, exterminates the crushing amounts of shame and self-hatred he feels. I'm not sure anyone can hold all of it every day, like a great iron balloon, without being crushed, obliterated by it.

Of course, he uses.

Meth takes away all the pain. Which is why, in that moment, filling his plate with food, I become sure that Charlie is lost forever.

He will never quit meth.

* * *

Charlie finishes off the shaking beef at lunch.

I give him thin wisps of chuck, grilled, crunchy and rare, and tossed in a mixture of Thai chilies, garlic, fish sauce, oyster sauce, soy sauce, lime, and sugar, served on watercress tossed with a light vinaigrette.

He leans in and tells David and me he has something to tell us.

It's November and we have heard all the new pronouncements and resolutions. These announcements are wearing us to the bone. Turns out his friend Salvador shows up at the apartment with drugs and a pocket full of works and wants to get high. Charlie smiles and tells us he told his friend "No," that they would not do drugs.

Salvador breaks down and tells him about the voices he hears. How the voices have been with him since he was a kid. How he was almost pulled under the bed by spirits. How the whispering monsters kept him company as a boy, whether he wanted them or not. How no one believed him. How a shrouded figure follows him around. It always has. It still does.

How meth makes the shrouded man disappear.

But then Charlie talks to Salvador about Jesus and his plan. He convinces him to not get high. Salvador agrees.

"Best night of my life," Charlie tells us.

He stabs at the drunken slabs of beef with his fork and smiles.

Salvador relapses the following night.

Charlie stays clean for another week.

* * *

I'm making steamed pork, with shiitakes, ginger, and salted fish.

It's a Charles Phan recipe that has come to be an easy lunch staple. A crowd-pleaser. I put out some sushi rice. A few leftover, cold imperial rolls. I quick-sauté some bok choy with bits of garlic and fish sauce. My friend and cookbook author Kian Lam Kho calls this dish "Chinese meatloaf," which reminds me that, like dumplings and meatballs, nearly all cultures have their types of ground meat in the shape of some kind of loaf.

I get everyone to the table.

I ask Charlie about the baby that's coming. It's December. He hasn't been working for us as much. A few days a week. David gives him very specific projects with lots of limits. He can no longer focus in a meaningful way. But the bathroom in the casita is almost tiled. We want to see it done.

I wonder about this baby. If she will be fucked up in utero. Or be born into all this chaos and heartache with her fucked-up parents.

Of course she will be fucked up.

* * *

This triggers something. Gets me thinking. I talk to David again about becoming foster parents.

We have had this conversation before. Actually, more than a conversation. We started the process to foster in New York City. We went to an orientation meeting that happened to coincide with the 2010 earthquake in Haiti. The big room was packed. Over two hundred people. Most were Haitian. They came to take in orphaned members of their extended families.

Caseworkers could hardly process the number of people.

This wasn't the time.

We went home. We shelved the idea. We lived our lives.

The next time we tried, the class was tiny. Six people stuck together in a cramped beige and maroon conference room. One of the women there—white and middle-aged—in a wheelchair, was looking for a child that might help her be more functional and ambulatory.

"I'm interested in an older child," the woman said when the caseworker mentioned that this was not the place to come looking for babies.

"Old enough to go to the store and pick up my meds," she added.

The caseworker frowns. This woman wasn't getting a junior maid.

But what about us? We lived in a three-bedroom apartment on 145th Street and Frederick Douglass Boulevard. On the bigger side for NYC. We were open to taking sibling groups. Older kids.

We followed up. They called back, promised to set up the next steps, never did. There were more phone calls. They stopped. We followed up. More of the same. Crickets.

It wasn't the right time.

We lived our lives.

But here in Vegas? Maybe it's time to think about fostering again.

* * *

I put out the Chinese meatloaf for lunch.

Charlie is talking, rattling on. He is a child, we realize, like our own. And we know innately that he is high again.

"Tessie is home," he tells us. She has stopped sleeping around with other dudes.

Charlie sees clear sailing ahead.

Instead of concerns, he talks about marriage. Vows on a beach in Florida. He has elaborate fantasies. He will be barefoot in khaki pants. She will be in a sundress. Flowers braided into her hair. All of us will be there. It will be warm and salty and we will all feel their love. Our girls will carry flowers and they will be barefoot, too. It's all romance.

David takes a full bite of that gingery, fishy pork, and says nothing. He doesn't engage in the crazy.

Charlie talks of wanting to throw Tessie a baby shower. He hopes I will throw it. He doesn't say it but leaves the thought out there hanging in the air, in hopes I will jump up and take it. I am the shower-thrower type, for sure, but I can't bring myself to touch this. There is so little to celebrate here.

He keeps going. His plans. His dreams. How he will rent a house for the three of them. How he will get the other boys back, even though they have long been adopted. How this baby is a gift from God, a sign to him that everything will be okay.

He doesn't seem concerned that Tessie is probably five months along. That she has used meth all of her pregnancy and has not been to a doctor.

I become so angry with Charlie, I stop cooking for him.

I stop making the lunches.

We stop inviting him to join us for meals.

I cut him off without explaining why. I use food as a weapon.

Not that he notices. He's too deep inside the addiction to notice.

* * *

Ephedrine-based meth, or the old meth that Quinones writes about, is the meth of euphoria.

The whole reason to take meth is to be with other people, to be social, to be more confident and full of life. Old meth was a huge part of the gay party scene, hookups and staying up all night dancing. Bikers loved the old meth. Not only cooking it to sell, but also using it to party. That meth made you love everyone and feel good.

In his book Quinones writes about the change. This is a controversial take. There are no studies at this writing that support what he witnessed on the ground, but his depictions resonate with what I have seen in Charlie and Tessie.

In an interview with *Los Angeles Magazine*, Quinones says:

But starting around 2009, the meth effectively changed. It seemed to have a different and much darker impact on the people who were using it. One of the first people to clue me into this was a veteran meth user named Eric, who lives in L.A. He'd been using for almost a decade, and for several years he held his life together—you know, he had a job, he had a girlfriend, a car. I mean, his life wasn't great; he was constantly making up excuses for why he had to come in late to work and that kind of thing. But he wasn't on the street.

. . . It was not the same drug. It was a drug that had him going crazy. He was imagining his girlfriend hiding men in the apartment, in the mattresses. And he began to stab the mattresses with a butcher knife. He went out of his mind. No more euphoria; now it was intense paranoia. And he never got back to that euphoric meth again.

Finally, his life just completely crashed. He told me he stayed using it for the next four years, during which time he was gradually alienated from everybody. Eventually, he ends up homeless.

Quinones writes about how Eric got help through the VA. He was diagnosed with schizophrenia, and he stopped using. But his sanity returned slowly over time, and he no longer suffered from delusions, hallucinations, psychosis, and paranoia. His doctors dialed back his diagnosis.

He is no longer diagnosed with schizophrenia.

I see Charlie take tools apart and put them back together. Apart and together. Over and over. He is erratic. Unhinged. He scowls. He bangs things. He grunts when he pushes the wheelbarrow or hammers the nail. Mutters to himself.

He can't keep his stories straight.

His paranoia about Tessie is intense, all-encompassing. It borders on compulsion. He blurts out too-personal accounts of sex and intimacies.

But she is doing divisive things, too. Or maybe Charlie is imagining them? I can't tell.

Tessie moves another addict into their studio apartment. Charlie gets pissed and borrows our Jeep and moves his stuff out. Charlie isn't afraid to be unhoused.

"She is jeopardizing my sobriety with this guy," he says.

He lives in tent cities. Flops on strangers' couches. Lives packed, like small oily fish, inside a weekly apartment, with a crowd. Everyone gets high together. They drop in and out. And when they are together, he and Tessie panhandle the highways.

"I put Tessie out front because they give her money," he says.

"I hide in the bushes."

Everything they say is as impermanent as steam. One minute they are madly petting each other like teenagers. The next, they are screwing other people. Breaking bonds like toothpicks. Strangers wander in and out of their lives, and their beds. They lose one apartment and find another. They lose their phone, get another number, lose that phone, get another number. They go days without anyone knowing where they are. A phone that goes unanswered means someone is high again or dead or passed out. As a couple, Charlie and Tessie find the soft spot in the other and poke at it until it ruptures and abscesses and bleeds.

They cannot be housed. Or employed in a meaningful way. Or have any hope of a typical, functioning life. Because the meth scrambles their brains.

"I'm leaving Tessie," he announces one day at work, after a litany of deceptions and betrayals.

Then, two days later, I see Charlie and Tessie walking into the backyard, holding hands.

"Tessie is going to help me work," he says brightly.

I stop listening. I turn into David, which I should've done long ago. When Charlie speaks, it's like a lonely, clueless wind in David's ear. This is harder for me because I want to connect, ask questions. I like the drama, too. I like to be pulled into these crazy worlds because I have tendrils of my own crazy that need to get out and be exercised.

And I get to feel like the sane one. The one who has her shit together.

But I'm over that now. This is too much even for me.

Charlie whispers to me that Tessie's uncle just died in rehab. Her eyes are ringed red. I pull her in and hug her, hard. She is uncomfortable and wiggles out of my grasp. She laughs nervously. I make a mental note about being too touchy-feely with her.

Tessie, mostly, watches him work. She calls me "Mrs. Foster," which makes me feel old and matronly. She smokes cigarettes and sweeps a little to busy her hands. Her belly is huge, like a giant wasp hive protruding from her pencil body. She has all kinds of social anxiety. Her leg jackhammers fast, always. She is not comfortable here.

Tessie is in her mid-thirties, sickly pale. Like the color of dumpling skins. I can tell she was once pretty, but the meth has gotten to her face. She looks hard and jagged. Beaten up. And I know she is empty inside. This is why she keeps her distance from me. She is so empty that anything alive and warm is terrifying.

I decide to break my no-cooking-for-Charlie streak. I might be mad at them, but I can cook for the baby.

I make a quick salad—greens with pear slices, cilantro, olive oil, lime, and salt. Catfish, marinated in tequila and lime and dredged in potato starch and fried in oil. Slices of hard goat cheese. A quick garlic, sriracha, and lime aioli for dipping the catfish. I plate it and set it on the table outside. It's Tessie's first meal here, out on the patio, in the cool night air, twinkle lights above their heads like they are in a Sandra Bullock rom-com.

After they eat and David and I struggle through the girls' homework, Tessie brings in their empty clean plates and stands in my kitchen, asking me about the catfish, how I make it. If the cooking is expensive. She wants to know if they can make it in the tiny kitchen of their weekly.

Then she hugs me. Deeply. Much more so than I expect.

"My mother never hugged me as hard as you did," she says.

It's the saddest thing I've ever heard.

* * *

Las Vegas is breaking eighty degrees. It's February.

Uncommonly hot, even in the desert.

I think of those people in New York, with their below-zero wind chill and feet of snow. The gray cloud blanket that will hover over them until sometime in April. The thick stews and hearty soups they are making and posting online.

And there's us in the desert. I'm barefoot and grilling the shit out of everything.

Our windows and doors are thrown open, sun everywhere, so much light. I revel in the light. I make the food Australians are making now, because it's summer there, and David is Australian, and I swear it's summer here, too. I'm making seared nubs of negi maki, alongside lightly charred lemongrass pork skewers, and chili and lime–grilled prawns with a tub of romesco for dipping. It's all finger food. I don't even want to look at a fork.

We are into the yakitori again, too. Oysters, chicken livers, necks, gizzards, hearts, and skin, pork belly, cow tongue, and stuff from the dirt—shishitos, scallions, shiitakes. I throw them on the heat and let the smoke and flame rip into them.

I'm not feeding Charlie anymore.

Not because I am still angry on behalf of their unborn child. We just want the casita done. Charlie is a goner. We have no more investment. We are exhausted by him. He is exhausted by himself.

My girlfriend Adrienne, who was once married to a heroin addict, is, like, "Duh," when I tell her this. I see it now so clearly. Everything she had told me about her marriage, how investment, even in its most remote, seemingly safe form, is stupidity.

I get it.

I really, really get it.

Lunch is stupidity.

David says he has never seen Charlie this bad. He is shooting up right before coming to work. His thoughts are disordered and chaotic. He forgets what he is saying mid-thought. Sometimes he cannot speak at all. He is emotionally fragile and so exposed and sore and openly wounded that he breaks down in even the most casual conversations. He doesn't stay at work long enough—when he comes—to eat anything anyway.

He is almost no longer there.

He is present in the way zombies are present in the make-believe apocalypse—stumbling around, but dead inside.

There are no lunches. So, there are no connections.

And without connections, there is no recovery.

I find out from Facebook, there has been an intervention. Tessie's family gives her an ultimatum, like she's on an episode of A&E's *Intervention*. They offer her treatment. Again. And tell her if she doesn't take it, they will refuse her help with the baby. They tell her they have readied the nursery not because they are excited another grandchild is coming, but because they know if they don't take her, this baby will be taken away by CPS.

Their responses are cold. Hard. Unrelenting. And necessary.

Family fights break out on Facebook. I secretly stalk them and watch what unfolds. It's a clusterfuck. I eat crunchy little pork empanadas at the counter, crumbs falling on the keyboard, completely weirded out, yet fascinated, by this soap opera.

We Fosters are a messy people, but this is otherworldly messy shit. I'm enthralled and horrified. I cannot look away. I'm not proud of this. It is simply the truth.

Charlie refuses treatment. On Facebook.

"It's not my thing," he writes. "Too rigid."

He writes that he needs to move, be physical, use his hands. They shut him down, humiliate him. He quotes Scripture. He invokes Jesus. He says he must follow his own path. His using, meth-addict friends tell him to keep going on his own path.

"Stay with the Lord," one writes. "Jesus will get you clean."

Charlie does not think Tessie will go to treatment.

"This child will make us different," he says. But his voice is weaker and weaker in her ear. Tessie has moved out again. He can only access her on Facebook.

Then Tessie does the unthinkable.

* * *

Tessie gets on the bus and goes to Texas, to a special house for pregnant women.

Some of the women are drug addicts, but mostly they are girls who are lost, kicked out, abandoned, alone in the world, except for their big bellies.

Tessie begs Charlie to get treatment. She messages me and asks me how he's doing. But the more sober she gets, the more tired she is of his excuses. She blocks him. Her family blocks him. She refuses his phone calls.

This makes him crazy. He sinks into meth even more. He stays high all the time. He doesn't sleep. He is ragged and deranged.

"I have to buy a birthday present for my son," he tells me, "and send it to Texas—"

"Wait," I interrupt. "Didn't you buy him a present last week after you got paid?"

"No."

"You told me you did."

"I lied. He never got a present from us for his birthday."

"Where were you?"

"Using. But I'm a good dad. No matter what Tessie says," he tells me, and wipes away the tears.

"I'm a good dad."

But he cries because he knows. We both do. He isn't a good dad. He isn't a dad at all, really. His kid didn't get a birthday present because Charlie was high. His kid doesn't have a father because Charlie was high.

David calls the Day Laborers Office. We get a new laborer to finish the casita. We let Charlie go.

Lunch doesn't save a life.

* * *

Charlie is high.

He blows his one week clean in March.

He doesn't work for us anymore, but he is doing work on the house next door, which is for sale, and the landlord gets a desperate deal from Charlie.

Sometimes he stops over and says hi.

He is a mess. All over the map. He is going back to Texas to be with his family, he says.

He isn't going back to Texas, because Jesus has a plan for him.

He is going to find a program five hours from where his sons live.

He is not going to go to a program because he has Jesus, and Jesus will save him.

He is going to go to college to be a pastor.

He is going to run a ministry.

He is going to run a ministry on Facebook.

His addiction goes from drugs to Facebook, where he posts persistently about Jesus, and his mistakes and his triumphs, to inspire other people to get clean, all while he is using. He doesn't see the contradiction. He writes long, too-intimate public missives to Tessie on Facebook, and because she has blocked him, she doesn't see them.

He writes them to whomever will listen and agree. It's pitiful and hard, even for a stalker like me, to watch.

Then the landlord lets him move into the house next door while he fixes it.

"It's a sign from God," he tells me. "Everything will be all right."

Then he asks if we want to get together and grill something for dinner. Like we are neighbors.

But meth has broken our connection.

We decline.

* * *

Do the lunches matter?

Do the lunches make everything worse?

What does lunch mean to an addict? What should it mean to us?

I think a lot about how Charlie's addictions played out around our table. How his family and all their trauma became intertwined in our family and our experiences, because of the intimacy and repetition of sitting and eating together.

The food made space for the dysfunction.

I already think about food as a conduit for connection—it's a cliché now. "Food brings us together" and "Food connects us." The messages are everywhere. A sea of perfectly constructed social media food images floods my feeds daily. It's all beautiful, heavily curated, intentional, and privileged. The people eating are happy, smiling, and having a ball. It's a monoculture of food happiness. I am a contributor to this culture. I like a good dish shot as much as anyone.

But food is also a conduit for disconnection, stress, family trauma, and workplace abuse.

Eating with Charlie and Tessie makes me rethink everything.

In families, the table, the eating together, the passing of plates may hold discomfort, anxiety, and anger. It brings up things that can, in other environments, be let go. For others, the table holds scarcity, an annihilating reminder of their poverty. While others have food on their table, but no one sitting next to them to share it.

Food can be a weapon. Food can be a way to control. And punish. And abuse. And force people to conform. The Meth Lunches with Charlie get me thinking about the severely wounded people in our new community and what food means and doesn't mean to them.

I think about hoarding food. And giving food. And accepting food.

And having no food at all.

Food is a litmus test, I think. It must be. What we are eating and how we are eating tells us something integral about how we are doing, what our lives are like.

Are we okay?

I'm not sure.

But I want to know.

* * *

I'm growing a garden on the side of the house. Trying to, anyway.

It's spring now. I have herbs and greens growing on the side of the house next to where Charlie is working and living for the next month.

"She won't talk to me. Her family won't talk to me," he complains over the fence while I am planting a shiso cutting into a pot.

I'm excited to grow the shiso. I have whole wok-fried snapper with shiso and lemon in my head, and screaming-rare, grilled New York strip underneath a melting chunk of shiso-shallot butter. I'm cooking them already in my imagination.

"It's unfair to take all my support away," he says, blinking into the sun.

"They want me to have a year clean before I can see her or the baby when she is born. It's wrong."

"Charlie, she is saving herself," I say. "Let her save herself."

I go back into the kitchen and bring out a plate of Chinese-fried eggs, eggs poured into scalding oil and fried so quickly the outside is puffy and crunchy, and the inside is runny as all hell, and served with stripes of oyster sauce, and bits of Thai chilies and scallion. I make it for myself, but he is grateful to eat it. It is the tiniest of Band-Aids on a problem unfixable by food. Or gathering together. Or cooking.

He eats, standing at the fence, and we talk about lighter things. The grain of the wood on the walls of the casita, the way the new window lets the sun in, how everything about that little house has changed.

How everything has changed. And nothing.

David comes home, the Jeep doors snap open, and the kids pile out of the car.

There is chatter, and Lucy is talking wildly and loudly. Edie follows behind her, occasionally whispering in her ear. Charlie shows David his work on the house next door. He hands me back his empty plate, scraped perfectly clean as always.

He goes back to painting something. To his thoughts. To his mind buried in meth. To his zero days clean.

I walk away from the fence. Let that go. I want to talk to David about foster parenting. Maybe it's time to take the first orientation class? I know the idea is warming in him. My man is always up for a new adventure, and this is one of the things that make me love him so madly.

I forget about Charlie. And meth. And his abandoned kids. The baby who's going to be born into all of it. I wrap myself around David. I catch up with him and the kids, and all the things I've missed.

I revel in them.

Everyone is hungry, so I head to the kitchen to make supper. I have chicken wings marinating in mirin, soy, and fish sauce. They are ready to coat in cornstarch and deep-fry.

I make lunch for the people who matter. And for whom lunch matters.

We sit together.

Pass plates.

Everything is so fucking normal, it's beautiful.

2

SURVEILLANCE OF HUMANS + THEIR FOOD

DESTINY MIDDLETON IS getting scammed.

She has no idea that the rented house she's living in—with her four-year-old son, Joseph—is not actually the one her cash is paying for.

She is squatting. And she has no idea.

For the first time in a long time, Destiny feels like she is getting ahead in Vegas. She is saving money, making strides.

Her sister, Deandra, invited her to come out here. To start a new life away from their hometown of Detroit. But when she got here, Deandra had no patience for her or helping with Joseph. Old family disputes and grievances surfaced. There was tension. Arguing.

It got ugly.

Destiny worried how Joseph was being treated while she was out looking for work.

"She used to shame him if he wet his pants," Destiny says. Deandra put him in the corner when he had accidents.

"You don't shame a little boy for having an accident. That's crazy."

Then, she came home from a job interview to find Joseph on the sidewalk. Sitting on a pile of his toys and clothes and luggage. He was alone.

He was three years old.

"She threw my son out while I was looking for work," she told me, exasperated. "Family, not family, you don't do that to my kid."

The sibling war boiled over. There were words. And then fists. And then a street-style, hair-pulling beatdown on the Las Vegas Strip, in front of Planet Hollywood. Part of it is Destiny's fierce attachment to Joseph taking over. A genetic uprising that pushes mothers to fight for the survival of their babies. But it is also the way she was raised. Destiny is prone to fight because she had to. She had to look out for herself and her own. Joseph is her one and only.

Spectators on the Strip called for the police. Destiny was arrested on a misdemeanor. She skipped court, amassed fines she couldn't pay. And as is the case in Nevada, a warrant for her arrest was issued.

That warrant is a bear-trap that lurks dangerously underfoot. For Destiny, it is nearly forgotten. She has more immediate concerns.

Destiny moved out of Deandra's house. She took Joseph to a shelter. She told no one. But to get them out of the shelter, she had to make fast money. She turned tricks at Treasure Island casino. She is not a sex worker by trade. But like just about every mom I know, she would do whatever is necessary to take care of her kid.

And it's only temporary, she thought.

She wasn't planning to do it for long. She focused on her endgame. Survive now. Thrive later.

Destiny spent years of her childhood in foster care and group homes. Her parents have since died. Her sister is her nemesis, her frenemy. They are the very definition of bad blood. Her other siblings, all in Detroit, and all struggling to stay afloat in their own lives, are in and out of hers. She can depend on no one.

In every sense of the word, she was alone.

"Just like I've always been," she tells me, with just a touch of sadness and pride.

It wasn't easy. It took months. She saved all her money. She meets someone with a house for rent. She gives him all her cash. She signs a bogus lease. She gives him nearly everything. But it's worth it—she can plan for the future.

Destiny is focused on the prize, a good safe daycare for Joseph just around the corner, a market in walking distance, a nail store, a beauty shop she can walk to. Dinners around the table, just her and Joseph doing things their way. She decides she will try for a job at a supermarket or a dollar store.

This is the beginning of a new life in Vegas.

Destiny Middleton has plans. And dreams.

She does this and everything for Joseph.

He is the reason.

Her son is the reason.

* * *

"I have a cute little guy here," Jada tells me on the phone. Since we became foster parents, Jada is our favorite placement worker.

"He's pretty scared. Come down and visit with him," she says.

I turn off the heat on the stove. I boiled off some pork belly and am caramelizing brown sugar into oil in my wok. I motion to David.

"His name is Joseph. It's all we know about him," Jada says. "That and his age. He is three and a half."

* * *

The job of getting kids into the right homes is handled by placement workers, like Jada.

Their job is complicated and difficult. They have to manage both the foster parents' expectations and the welfare of the child and probably a hundred other issues. They assess kids coming into care, figure out what they might need with limited information. They get them into homes where they can heal and be loved until it's time for them to go back to their families or other caregivers.

Their superpower is making those matches.

Foster parents often call placement workers the used-car salespeople of social work. Sometimes a placement worker, desperate to place a child in a family, will get a little loose with the facts. But not Jada. If she thinks a child will do well with us, they probably will.

Joseph is currently at Child Haven, a large residence campus that can house up to ninety kids, from newborn to eighteen. The kids have been removed from their family's care, or been abandoned, and are housed in cottages by age and gender. Child Haven keeps kids from sleeping under the desks of social workers. It gives kids a place to be.

For kids in foster care, Child Haven is the physical hub of CPS. It's where we have supervised visitation with the children's biological families. Juvie is there. Along with family court. There are resources for parents, like

Peggy's Attic, which provides clothes, toys, diapers, and hygiene products to biological and foster families.

And in my experience, Child Haven is populated with workers who care deeply for kids. But it still has a *Lord of the Flies* vibe to it. It isn't a home. It's an institution.

No one wants to see kids stay at Child Haven for long.

* * *

We had a few different kids placed in our home.

And the truth is, we are thinking we might not be cut out for the job. The boys we just dropped off with their dad—Jaden, five, and Tyson, three—came to us a few days before Christmas, after their mom was jailed on a drug charge. It was a short but intense stay.

Jaden, angry, nonverbal, and on the autism spectrum, cleaned the bookshelves of books. He ran his hand down shelf after shelf, laughing as they tumbled to the floor. He tipped over chairs and benches. He hit the dogs—three pugs—with sticks and threw toys at their heads. He crushed antique glass ornaments under his little slippered feet. He screamed and hit for reasons we couldn't figure out. His body was dysregulated the entire time he was with us.

Their behavior made sense.

A strange new place, with new people, away from family and friends, inundated with toy after toy—a garbage bag full of presents, gifted by corporations. It was so much for them to process and handle.

We had to stop Christmas.

Which was not popular with Lucy and Edie.

We hadn't learned yet what parents of neuro-diverse kids know by heart—holidays can bring a particular kind of chaos that is epic and all-consuming. Kids who struggle this way need schedules and more rigid guardrails to feel safe.

David took the boys to a playground because they were smashing the girls' presents, heaving their corporate toys at each other. Lucy and Edie took their gifts and locked themselves in their room. Our house was a dump. Upside down. Chaos and anger everywhere.

The boys stayed until their dad got an expedited court appearance. He got them back.

We are happy for them. I bring the boys, their clothes, diapers, supplies, and the corporate toys to Child Haven. I pack everything in the red duffel bags they come with, except for the toys, which are in garbage bags. Dad is young and quiet. He barely speaks to me. I have the stink of child removal on me. He is taking the bus with the kids and he can't take their things. I offer him a ride to wherever he needs to go in Vegas, but he just wants to get his kids and get the hell away from the system.

I get it.

Along with Jaden and Tyson, our foster care journey includes taking in a sibling group of sisters whose mom was in the hospital on suicide watch. And a boy whose mom died suddenly. He spent an entire night alone trying to wake her in their bed.

He was the saddest boy I have ever met.

Our house is a mess. We are wondering how the hell people do this work. The toll on Lucy and Edie is more severe than we anticipated. Biological siblings are on the front lines of lots of unhealthy behaviors. Lucy spends a lot of time in her room alone. And Edie boils over with anxiety and frustration because the littlest kids—who also happen to be the most adorable—are taking her place as the baby.

Fostering is a slog. A blur of broken children that leave as quickly as they come to us.

I don't know how long we can do this, or why it even matters.

* * *

After Tyson and Jaden left a few days before the New Year, we skipped town.

We got cheap, last-minute flights to San Francisco. A hotel near Union Square. The four of us walked the streets. We ate porky ramen noodles in Japantown. The girls hung off the sides of cable cars. We ate steamed black cod in banana leaf, fried chicken, and imperial rolls at Slanted Door.

It's everything we needed as a family. The return of "the original four" as the girls like to call us.

We ran away from being foster parents.

* * *

Back at home, we are better. But we still wonder why the hell we are doing this.

Jada is still on the phone.

"Seriously, you want to meet this kid," she urges. "You all will do well together."

I turn the stove back on so the wok gets good and hot. In a clean wok, I add ginger, garlic, scallions, and star anise. Some soy sauce, Shaoxing wine, the pork cubes, and water. I let everything braise for a couple hours.

We put the car seat in the car only as a precaution. Edie gives us the stink eye when we leave.

"Don't worry, we're just going to meet him."

She doesn't believe us. Nor should she.

At Child Haven, we meet a three-and-a-half-year-old boy coiled in Jada's arms. He wears diapers under shorts and a T-shirt. He is scared, and only peeks out one eye to look at us.

"A guy dropped him off with nothing, no possessions," Jada says. "His mom is in jail."

I reach out to him.

"Hi, sweetheart," I say gently.

"Shut up!" he screeches at me from Jada's shoulder.

"He only says two phrases," Jada says.

When David says "Hi" to him, he says the other phrase.

"I hate chu!" he says, his face screwed up into a defensive grimace.

Jada tells us the people who dropped him were babysitting for Mom. They didn't want to keep him any longer.

"They were off to California," she tells me, shrugging.

The man who drops him says Joseph is hyper, largely nonverbal, and not potty-trained.

Next thing we know, we are strapping his angry body into the car seat.

Joseph is muscly for a little kid. Thin, but strong. His hair is in braids. He is stereotypically handsome. His skin is russet and brown. He does not talk to new people easily. He says "shut up" and "I hate chu" to everyone. He hates cops. He bristles at the sound of police sirens.

Things we find out about Joseph: he is potty-trained; when he has an accident, he punishes himself. He hits his head with his little balled-up fist;

he puts himself in the corner when he makes a mistake. He is whip-smart and not at all hyper. And he is profoundly talkative. He knows many more than two phrases.

* * *

We start at the McDonald's across from Child Haven.

He opens his Happy Meal carefully and snags a French fry before racing off to the Play Place. He comes back and forth. Eyeing us. Eating a bite. Running with kids. Coming closer. He takes a bite of burger. Pops it in his mouth. Smiles. Then back to the slide.

I tell him our names, Kim and David, but almost immediately I am "Mommy Kim" and David is "Daddy David." This is not a sign he loves us, or we are taking over Mom's role in his life. Instead, he understands our roles as mom and dad of the household, supplier of food and hugs and chicken nuggets and bedtime stories.

He throws his head back and laughs when we play tag around the play area. A good sign.

David texts Edie that we have him.

"OMG, you can't say no to these people when they call!" she yells at us by text.

Lucy is just mad that we aren't getting girls.

"You said 'no boys, no babies,'" she texts.

We did say that. We are licensed for girls, ages four to ten. The universe has other ideas, though.

At home, we settle Joseph in. Give him a bath, show him his room, put on cartoons. My thoughts turn to Mom a lot. She'll be in jail for at least four months.

That's a long time to not know where her son is.

Dinner is largely inaccessible for a three-year-old, but I started it, so I keep going.

The girls come out of their rooms for the red-cooked pork belly on just-steamed lotus buns, with cucumber quick pickles, wads of radish sprouts, and dribbles of sriracha. And to meet Joseph.

I offer to make him a quesadilla or grilled cheese. But he has his eye on a bun, so I make him his own and hand it to him. He looks it over, and then eats while keeping his eye on the cartoon playing on the TV. He will go on to devour three of them.

The cuteness wins Lucy over. Edie hangs back. But later, when he hops off a stool, she reaches out instinctively to guide him. That's Edie—deep, deep feelings. Big heart. Raging worry that he will take her place in the family.

"We are not adopting him," she tells me. It's an order, not a question.

"No, baby, we aren't adopting him," I say, shifting the hair off her cheek. "He has a mama who loves him."

"Good," she says adamantly, and turns on the ball of her foot and walks away.

Edie will be the hardest one to win over, but when it happens, he will feel that love the most.

We put Joseph in the fresh jammies that come in the red duffel bags from Child Haven. CPS gives you a couple outfits, new sneakers, and jammies in case there is no time to shop.

David picks him up, and Joseph folds into him. He walks the floor holding him, rocking him. Singing in his ear. Then Joseph sleeps, his head on the pillow of David's shoulder. His belly full of McDonald's and pork belly.

For the longest time, I watch them. David still does that thing I love—when he carries a baby and instinctively rocks side to side. You can be away from babies for years and that memory in your body will always come back.

The sun has barely set behind Mt. Charleston, and we've already begun to love Joseph.

And when you love a kid, you do everything you can for them.

* * *

Does she lie awake in jail wondering where her son is?

Is it a dull ache, like something is missing? Or is she gutted? Maybe she's okay during the day, keeping herself busy. But at night, in the silence and the dark, her mind panics.

It is easy, as a foster parent, to keep the blinders on. People are well-intended when they say you're a saint.

"I could never do it," they say.

"I could never give a child back," they say. "I would love them too much."

The realities are much more complex. Children in foster care come to us and we get to parent them, but we are not their parents. Not at first. Maybe never. They belong to their own people.

I think back to when Lucy was born. It wasn't so much love that I felt when I first saw her, but an overwhelmingly physical drive—it was primitive and old and built into the cells of my body—to protect her at all costs. It was an evolutionary pull, designed to ensure I protected her and kept her alive. I remember it overwhelming me. Every time an auntie picked her up and cooed at her, I felt this otherworldly need to bite their face off. To rip the skin from the arms that held her with my claws. It was a shocking feeling to know that I would kill for this little human. And I would've.

I know I'm projecting. That maybe this is more about me than Destiny. Maybe she doesn't feel the way I feel at all.

But still, I want to know Joseph's mother. I have to make sure.

I'm a good stalker, so I use the foster care paperwork to track Destiny down in the Clark County Detention Center. I make an appointment.

We are going to see Mom.

* * *

The Clark County Detention Center, known as CCDC, is not as chilling as you might imagine.

It's the county jail right on Las Vegas Boulevard. From the outside, it's a blank-looking windowless office building, surrounded by palm trees and tourists carrying around yard-long margaritas. It's a holding place for those going into the greater carceral system. A last stop for small-time felons, drug addicts, the fully drunk-off-their-asses, folks with misdemeanors, and poor folks who can't pay their warrants and court charges.

It is also the biggest mental health facility in Nevada. Of the over 60,000 people arrested and jailed in CCDC yearly, according to KSNV, a local news outlet, it's estimated that at least 12,000 have a mental illness at any time throughout a given year. That doesn't count mental illnesses that can't be separated from addiction, such as mentally ill people who self-medicate with meth and opioids or people who become psychotic on drugs, like new meth.

There are cops everywhere, of course. Metal detectors. Tables to dump all your belongings and let people sort through them looking for weaponry.

Joseph leans out of my arms.

"I hate chu," Joseph says.

He is pointing at one of the officers behind the table.

The cop scoffs, but he looks away quickly.

Then, we are inside the big room. It's institutional, but not an uncomfortable room. It could be any DMV seating area in the country. And Joseph is delighted to see lots of kids there, families of all kinds.

There is hope in the room.

This is a room filled with people showing their love and support. Kids clamor into laps to get a look at Daddy. And boyfriends talk quietly to girlfriends inside. There is more happiness than I expected. More attempts to make some good out of a hard situation. And the room has a sense of order. Nothing happens without the officers, in a round, windowed booth, giving out numbers and information about the rules and how to proceed.

A lady in the booth calls us over when it's our turn. She gives us the number of what looks like a study carrel that you might find in a library. A desk with sides for privacy. I take a seat and pull a chair over for Joseph. He climbs up. There is a blank TV screen in front of us and a phone on the wall of the carrel.

Joseph reaches for it. He puts it to his ear and talks into it.

Then the light flickers on the TV. At first, I only see women walking around in jumpsuits in the background. Then a woman appears.

She is young, maybe late twenties. Beautiful. I see where Joseph gets his handsomeness. Her hair is braided in two straight, perfect rows, running along the sides of her head and down her back. She has high cheekbones and large doe eyes. She has no idea who I am.

"I'm Kim. I'm Joseph's foster mom. He is safe."

I can't get the "he's safe" part out fast enough. I want it to be the first thing I say. I want her to have known that yesterday.

Joseph pops his head into the TV frame. Big smile.

"Oh, my God!" she screams.

There are gobs of tears now. Mine. Hers.

"Hi, Mommy."

She takes a breath.

"Hi Butta-Man," she says.

She puts her hand against the screen of the TV on her side. He pushes himself up on his belly on the table so he can reach the screen and puts his hand on hers. She smiles.

"I know you are worried. But he is safe." I say it again.

"I figured he was in the system," she tells me, "but I haven't talked to a social worker yet, so I didn't know for sure."

I tell her about David and me, and Lucy and Edie. I tell her what Jada has told me about how he came to be at Child Haven.

"He eats everything and asks for seconds."

"That's my Butta-Man," she says, laughing.

I tell her about the great little school by our house. I tell her about the teachers, how they are giving him lots of extra love and attention. I know this because my friend Messeret is his teacher.

I show Destiny his drawings. I tell her about his nightmares, the ones where he wants to come into bed with us. But how it isn't allowed.

"Do it," she says. "If he needs to climb into your bed, let him."

I am struck by how easily she bypasses her own comfort to make sure he is okay. I give her my address so she can send Joseph letters. Another foster care no-no. But I trust my gut over rules.

She asks me if I might put some money into her commissary account.

"You can't get nothing unless you have money in your account," she tells me. It isn't easy for her to ask, and I am pissed at myself for not offering that earlier.

When I put an initial $40 in her account, it makes only a ripple in our bank account. But for Destiny, it means something more.

"It's the difference between being connected to the world and not," Destiny tells me, about her commissary account.

"Someone cares about you enough to put money in your account, and you are still a part of the outside world."

* * *

In jail, the commissary is everything.

For Destiny, and the women I speak to about their incarcerations, food and the commissary play an integral role in defining their experience.

Imagine a blank room. A blank room that is your life. There is time, a lot of it. It crawls like a starfish making tiny tracks across a vast, nearly endless ocean bottom. Going, but going nowhere. There is no freedom. No choices to make. People tell you where to go, what you can do, when you can do it. And this applies to eating, what food you can have and when.

It's also not a peaceful time. It's noisy. There are folks right next to you with mental illnesses. Talking to themselves. Rocking back and forth. They might be psychotic and off their meds. Prone to violence. Detoxing off hard drugs. People from hard lives who bring their hard lives with them, so that their hard lives become your hard life. There is no privacy. You can't even take a shit in private. Monotony is the punishment for crime.

Breakfast is around seven, lunch at eleven, and dinner at four. Meals on trays mark the passing of time, the moving forward of one part of the day to another.

Meals have to appeal to lots of people and their myriad dietary restrictions. The goal of prison food is to be mediocre. It has to hit the nutritional requirements while being as cheap as possible. Taste is not even in the top considerations. Salt is hardly used out of concern for heart disease and high blood pressure.

One dinner has to do it for the population.

There are exceptions, of course. Some prisons offer meals for people with different ethnicities, religious beliefs, allergies, and taste preferences. Some prisons offer vegan meals. But this doesn't always happen at the county jail level, where people are in and out much more quickly. The food, at the most foundational level, no matter how it is prepared and delivered, is bland as fuck.

Many prisons have food service programs that can include inmates prepping and cooking ingredients. They might even have inmate-run gardens that feed the prison and local food banks. But in county jails, where people come for shorter periods, where folks with misdemeanors and low-level felonies end up, there is far less in the way of culinary programs.

Kitchens are almost always an afterthought in jail planning.

Food service companies Aramark and Trinity—the two largest, both of which have had contracts, at different times, with CCDC—are brought in to feed inmates. These companies make food off-site, freeze it, and deliver it to the jails, where kitchen employees heat it up to serve inmates. That food will be refrigerated and reheated again at the end of the week, if there are leftovers.

Some of it will be taken back to cells secretly and repurposed.

Inmates are six times as likely to get food poisoning as the general public. It's easy to see why. By the time the food gets to an inmate, it has been processed and cooked multiple times.

Both Aramark and Trinity have spotty histories with the food they are making for inmates.

In 2017, Trinity Food Services was written up by the Southern Nevada Health District for the food they served at the jail. The list of grievances included rotten fruit, juice containers with mildew, lint and hair products in food, food not served at safe temperatures, sandwiches served to inmates after a week in storage, and an overall lack of nutritional value in the food being served.

Aramark, which no longer contracts with CCDC—but does contract with the Ely State Prison, about three hours outside of Nevada, where a hunger strike over portion size began in December 2022—was written up for a litany of infractions. This included dried food bits on dishes and pans, dirty fry baskets, brown slime in the soda machine, food left sitting at unsafe temps before serving, non-dated food, and excessive amounts of grease built up from lack of cleaning. Prisons in Michigan terminated their contract with Aramark after discovering two separate instances where maggots were found in food before going out to inmates.

Add to this the food that gets collected, hidden, and repurposed in the cells of the inmates, where it can collect bacteria and spoil. This happens when long-haul inmates make a wine called pruno from fermented fruit, candy, anything with high-fructose corn syrup, sugar, even ketchup.

Think of kombucha, where the ferment creates a mother, and then that is used over and over to generate the next batch. Fruit, like sugary cups of fruit cocktail, are heated and left to sit for a couple days. Pruno can be made with rudimentary heat sources, like radiators, and hidden in toilet tanks and trash cans. Then the brewer adds more sweetness, like ketchup. The bag is reheated every fifteen minutes or so for the next seventy-two hours. The brewer throws away the mash, and the wine is ready to drink.

Even two simple ingredients like sauerkraut and orange juice can make wine. Or a single ingredient, like leftover potato. A baked potato, taken from mealtime, stored for weeks in a cell and then made into pruno, was the culprit for an infamous botulism outbreak, the second largest in US history, in the Arizona prison system in 2006.

What is significant about pruno is that it is an act of pure resistance. It's dangerous. It pushes boundaries. It allows inmates to create something they want. A buzz. A high. An escape, outside the control of the prison guards and outside the day-to-day oppression they feel. It is a coping strategy and a way for people to beat the system a little.

But it comes at a cost.

Botulism is deadly and pruno making is one of the leading causes of outbreaks in the United States.

* * *

Nann Meador, a Las Vegas mom to several grown children, embezzled cash from the small business she worked for to support her gambling addiction. She spent time in CCDC and later was moved to the Florence McClure Women's Correctional Facility, the women's prison in Nevada, to finish out her sentence.

Nann now works tirelessly to advocate for gambling addicts in a city that enables and encourages an all-in, double-down, go-to-the-mattresses wagering mentality. And there are places to gamble nearly everywhere. My doctor's office is inside a casino. There are small "casino rooms" at the front of most supermarkets. In liquor stores. The airport. 7-Elevens. Even nursing homes can have slots.

"It was hard to tell what you were actually eating," Nann tells me about food in CCDC. "It's mixed together. Some sort of one-pot dish could have bologna mixed in with potatoes, and some sort of sauce."

I believe she is talking about nutraloaf—or "the loaf" for short—a controversial meatloaf-like slab of whatever foods happen to be left over that week. It usually consists of leftover cooked meat, vegetables, beans, cheese, breadcrumbs, eggs, and sauces. It gets broken down and blended into a mush with milk, and then re-baked to form a loaf. It can be drenched in gravy to make it palatable.

When inmates do not comply, the loaf, or a variation of it, is a common punishment.

"If it were not for the bread with the meal, you could go hungry," Nann tells me. "A lot of the girls aren't eating."

In many ways, the food that comes on trays represents the system. The man. The people who keep you down and in shackles.

But food takes on substantial meaning at the commissary.

That is where food belongs to the people.

Nann's family put money in her commissary account. She could buy tampons and other hygiene products, soap, cigarettes, and extra food items, like ramen, tuna, nuts, canned ravioli, cheese and crackers, Pop-Tarts, condiments, basic spices, sandwiches, chips, and cookies.

And this creates an opportunity for inmates to make food their own. To have choice. Autonomy.

Inmates use commissary offerings to put together a "spread" or a "bowl."

This is where we see the rise of a kind of individuality in jails. Where people express themselves and care for themselves at the same time.

The base is most always ramen noodles. Ramen is plentiful and provides the perfect blank canvas, either cooked to a wilted noodle or kept uncooked for its crunch and doused with the salty umami-flavored powder packets.

The idea is to transform foods into something else entirely—ramen noodles become nachos by adding hot Cheetos, squeeze cheese, a can of pinto beans, pickles, and Doritos. The book *Prison Ramen: Recipes and Stories from Behind Bars* includes orange porkies, a ramen-based meal where softened noodles are mixed with crunchy pork rinds, leftover rice, and orange-flavored Kool-Aid. Or ramen bean dip, combining softened noodles with the packet, topped with refried beans, chili beans, a chopped jalapeno, and shredded cheese.

Nann knows all about this.

"When the girls have microwaves in their pods, they make these beautiful concoctions," Nann tells me. The individual cells open out into small, clustered common areas known as pods.

"Coffee creamer and a little sugar, mixed with Sprite and chilled in the fridge, makes a pudding-like base," she tells me. "They use crumbled cookies to make a crust, microwave it, and use a melted Hershey bar as frosting. That's birthday cake."

Nann also tells me about the women in her pod making fried rice with a hot pot and microwave. Prison ID cards chop carrots and celery, and the rice cooks in the microwave with the vegetables and salt. Just add a little mayo and hot sauce.

"Voilà! Fried rice!" she says.

Mayo is a wonder ingredient, being both condiment and catalyst. Freeze it on a cold windowsill in the middle of winter, the oil separates and you have cooking oil. Oil is usually a no-no, since hot oil can be used as a weapon, but a little ingenuity gives you fat. Hot pots are designed not to boil (another potential weapon) but will still heat water. Chip bags are saved and used as makeshift bowls. Leftover pasta can be submerged for hours in water until it can be processed by hand into a dough. Sausage casings can be microwaved into a kind of crunchy pork rind.

Nann is animated and laughing while she explains all the dishes. There is a real creativity that comes through this food. People are able to express their personalities through what they make. And from there, a bonding and sisterhood is formed.

Cooking a spread is a group affair. This isn't about one person eating. A spread creates community. Because it brings together different kinds of food—from ramen to chips to beans—it is more food than one person can eat. It requires inmates chipping in food they pick up from the commissary. It is made together. It is eaten together. And its existence creates a social gathering that is powerful and "outside" the system.

I love how Nann sees the beauty of this food.

There is nothing local or homegrown or elevated about it. This is not food that comes from fantastic soil that enhances its deliciousness and nutrient value. This is the food humans make in the toughest of situations. In the place where they are most discarded by the rest of us.

And thus, this food creates what is lacking. It's community and connection when most of that has been ripped away. It's stretching the imagination. It's creating meaningful work.

It is wonderfully subversive.

Dr. Amy B. Smoyer, associate professor of social work at Southern Connecticut State University, conducted interviews with thirty formerly incarcerated women. She confirms that in jail women share what they know—recipes, knowledge about foods they grew up with. They try to re-create those flavors in their spread. Older women bring up younger women, long-haul inmates school newcomers.

"Participants spoke about poorly designed, sloppy food systems that left them feeling uncared for, ignored, frustrated, and humiliated," Smoyer writes. "Women articulate experiences of hunger that reflect both a deprivation of adequate food and a rationing of humane attentions."

This is truly the case for Destiny.

On one of our visits, Joseph plays with trucks while we talk.

Destiny tells me about her cellmate. A young, pregnant Mexican heroin addict who goes by the name Carmelita. She is going cold turkey off heroin.

"I'm in here for fighting," Destiny says. "But there are girls in here for much worse than me."

She tells me Carmelita gets no help or medical care while she detoxes.

"She has nobody," Destiny says.

"For the longest time she couldn't eat. She laid there and shook. But every night we got these hard little cookies as a snack. I kept them. I had four or five packages. So when she got her appetite back, I gave them to her. She was starving."

This makes her viscerally angry.

"They didn't care if she survived or starved," Destiny says. "No one cares about you in jail. That stays with you for a long time."

Perhaps this is the most inhumane part of incarceration: that it isn't enough to take someone's freedom, we are hell-bent on taking their dignity as well.

* * *

Destiny, Joseph, and I have visits every couple of weeks. This is what we are allowed.

I learn that Destiny braids hair for the other girls at the jail. And she schools me on how to keep Joseph's braids intact. It is somehow funny and stupid to have her give me braiding lessons while I have her kid on my lap. Phone in the crook of my neck. I'm fighting with stray hairs and trying to tighten everything up. Destiny laughs when Joseph has had enough of me fumbling through his hair.

But she never judges.

Doing his hair together helps us bond. It's like we are in this together, both of us working together for the best outcome. And I think being able to teach me helps make the relationship more balanced and connected. More equal. She doesn't just need me. I need her, too.

I listen to her story.

She tells me about the arrest. How it happened.

She meets someone who is renting out a little place. It's perfect for her and Joseph. She gives them all her cash and moves her few things and her son into the house. She is happy to be out of her sister's.

This way of renting—through the back door—might sound sketchy, but it's often what poor folks have to do when they have an arrest warrant appearing in their background check, or they have less than stellar credit.

Then there's the cost—the application fees, which can be as much as hundreds of dollars per listing.

"The management company can take nine, ten applications, totaling over $1,000 in fees, knowing they only have one apartment available," a well-known Vegas Realtor told me.

Part of the burden of being poor is having to work around the system, because the mechanics of the system are so biased against you.

A neighbor calls the police. The person she is renting from does not own the house. Destiny and Joseph are squatters.

The police burst in.

They come into the house with guns.

"Joseph was standing at the top of the stairs," she tells me. "He was so scared of the police, he was frozen. Pee was running down his leg."

I think back to the way Joseph tensed up around the officers.

A friend happened to be there and offered to take Joseph. But the friend didn't really want to take him for more than a few hours, so when the novelty wears off, he drops Joseph at Child Haven on the way out of town.

"The police called me a whore in front of my son," she tells me.

They give her a few months in jail.

Instead of helping her.

* * *

The misdemeanor system in the United States is a tracking device.

This system has always had a fraught history. Originally it was created to monitor and police Black people after Reconstruction.

Black people, after the end of their enslavement, began to work and create lives for themselves. They created wealth and communities, and that was powerfully threatening to white folks in power. The white people in charge couldn't force people to work or stay in line.

Misdemeanors were created.

Small infractions and made-up offenses, like loitering or vagrancy, allowed white people to police where Black people could be. How they lived. Where they walked. And it helped feed a system for free involuntary labor—if you arrest someone for a petty theft, for stealing a loaf of bread, you can impose lots of fines that you know they cannot pay. They will have to work off their debt, thereby creating free forced labor.

The documentary *Racially Charged: America's Misdemeanor Problem* tells the story of a man named John Owen, who took six ears of corn out of a corn field. He ended up arrested for theft and leased into convict labor, where he did two years for stealing and another year to pay back court costs.

This sounds like an antiquated system that no longer applies. But it is alive and well in nearly every state in the United States. And it isn't just Black people who get pulled into the misdemeanor system. That net is cast widely so that poor people of every race and ethnicity are also caught up in it.

* * *

Until 2023 in Nevada, traffic violations were criminal offenses punishable by jail and fines. It worked like this. Let's say I get pulled over for a traffic violation. There are no reminders mailed out. If I forget about the citation, which I did when we first moved here, or I can't pay the ticket price, usually around $200, that misdemeanor citation becomes a bench warrant. If I get stopped again, the officer will find my arrest warrant. And that means my Fourth Amendment rights to unlawful search and seizure will be mostly superseded by the warrant. They can search my car. My body. My phone, whatever is in the car. This warrant gives police cover to look deeper and uncover more charges to use against me.

I am joining the 70 percent of people in jail who are there because they committed a petty crime and cannot afford bail.

I will sit in jail for three days and wait for the judge to charge and sentence me. Or let me go.

If I'm an addict, I'm detoxing in a cell without medical assistance. In that time, my life is upended. I can lose my job. My kids can be taken into CPS custody. They will tow my car. If I have expired plates, I have to bring that up to date after the warrant has been cleared. That requires having money to pay for the warrant fees, jail fees, and the plates.

And this will take time, because I've lost my only form of transportation.

Maybe this will cost more than the price of the car, so maybe I ditch the car.

Now, I am paying for court costs, suspended license fees, jail fees, the crap-ass old-bologna-loaf they serve me in jail, drug testing, database fees, supervision fees, probation services, and electronic monitoring services. It piles on. I have to buy a new car because I need a car to work. The list of fees and debt grows, and impacts everyone in my family. I've got money going to lawyers. And papers need to be filed. I have to pay attention to this. I don't have a job anymore. My whole life is managing my traffic ticket.

All the cash that goes to my rent and food is now plugged up in the system. So I have to go pick up charity, hit the bread lines, work the food bank system. Also hard to do without a car. My life becomes about subsistence. My life is a hassle, one after the other.

Obstacles at every turn.

Because I rolled through a stop sign.

Nevada no longer sends people to jail and into debt over traffic violations, like speeding and having a broken taillight. There are, however, still more than sixty moving violations that are criminalized. These—like driving without a license, driving while having epilepsy, and following another car too closely—can trigger warrants, jail time, and a cycle of debt and repayment for people already struggling.

Nevada's new laws are a solid start. But there are still twelve states that criminalize minor traffic infractions. These laws might fill the coffers of municipalities, but they also keep real people and real families down.

Governments are meant to support their people. They should not be working to undermine our most vulnerable citizens.

* * *

I am parked on a dark side street, down a ways from the D Hotel in downtown Vegas.

Fremont Street.

Home to a zip line that hangs off an eleven-story slot machine (Slotzilla) and a burger shop that sells a nearly 10,000-calorie Quadruple Bypass Burger (Heart Attack Grill).

It is 2:30 a.m. I am sitting in our Jeep watching the back door of the CCDC because I know they will let Destiny out tonight. But they don't tell you when or exactly where, so you just kind of sit there, in an idling vehicle, waiting for someone you recognize to pop out of the unmarked door.

When she comes out, she has only a small bag of stuff and the clothes she is wearing. She has no ID, hardly any money. When she gets in the car, I see how thin and drawn she is. We hug for a good long time.

We walk in the house quietly so as not to wake my sleeping family. I hold her hand and guide her through the living room, dining room, down the hall, and into Joseph's room. There are bunk beds and dinosaur sheets and the angel she drew for him on lined paper, taped to the wall over his head.

She melts into the side of her sleeping boy. He wakes a little and stretches.

"Mama," he says, and smiles.

"Go to sleep, Butta-Man," she whispers. "I'm here."

Then she folds herself into the bed and he curls himself around her.

I make her a sandwich. I leave it in her room, with chips and pickles and a drink.

It's not exactly allowed, letting your foster kid's parent into your home in the dead of night, when you have custody of their kid. But David and I discussed this a lot. I've gotten to know Destiny through our visits and the letters we write each other. Her caseworker is supportive of a prompt reunification. This feels like the right thing to do.

Joseph's caseworker tells me Destiny can get her son back, even if she lives in a homeless shelter, but that seems like too rough a place for them both.

They deserve better.

* * *

Destiny stays with us the first night.

She sleeps in Joseph's room, next to him, so that when he wakes, she is there to comfort him.

I cook for her during the day. I make her salt and pepper crispy-fried pork chops, a Cantonese dish. Lamb sambusas for snacks. Spicy chicken drumsticks with sticky rice. Miso-glazed black cod with a leafy salad. Crab omelets for breakfast.

Joseph is true to his reputation and eats mostly everything, but he tries it all. He is used to Destiny cooking for him.

We get to know each other over dinners eaten on the patio, while Joseph blows bubbles through a straw in his drink while we eat. The table is a moving, thriving place. Candles burn down to nubs while the kids move around us. No one is pinned to their seats. There are no rules of engagement. Edie and Lucy practice singing "Popular" for a school theater audition and perform it for us as if we are in a dinner theater.

In the three months the kids have been together they have forged an uneasy but loving bond. The impermanent nature of his placement both helps them connect and creates tension. They are all falling in love with each other. For Lucy this means losing her new little brother. For Edie, it is a relief—Destiny's presence assures her that we won't be adopting Joseph or taking him in long term.

Destiny moves into my friend's house a few blocks away. Lauren, a special ed teacher, is the kind of activist who puts her money where her mouth is. She welcomes Destiny into her home as a rent-free roommate for a few months. In return, Destiny will bring her daughters to the bus stop every morning before school.

David gets Destiny a job as an usher at *Absinthe*, a long-running show at Caesars Palace.

David's assistant, Brandon, of his own volition, takes Destiny out to get her hipster clothes for work. He pays for them. And he treats Destiny to her first sushi dinner ever, which she tolerates and appreciates, but doesn't fully embrace.

Since she cannot take Joseph out on her own, she eats dinner with us.

Sometimes she cooks for me. Steaks on the grill, and baked potatoes overflowing with butter and sour cream and chives. She gives Joseph his baths at night. She comes with me to drop him at school in the mornings. She talks to his teachers. Kisses him goodbye. Sometimes when she has a couple hours, she just hangs out with us, even if Joseph is at school. She teaches Lucy to weave colorful cords into a complex pattern, something she learned as a girl in her group home. Destiny, Lucy, and Edie sit for hours and make bracelets and key chains. Or she and I talk about her life, filling in all the holes, while I wash the dishes and she dries.

It is this kind of mundaneness that brings us together. We exist together. Making dinner together. Cleaning up makes it normal. I chop the onions. She smashes the garlic. She starts calling Lucy and Edie Joseph's "godsisters," and they happily accept the title. I become his godmother in this scenario, a treasured auntie.

She fits into our family with the same ease that Joseph does. And it goes on this way for some time.

Until it changes.

* * *

CPS closes Destiny's case. Joseph no longer lives with us.

Destiny moves out of Lauren's into a modest apartment with an old boyfriend, Dre. He is a leftover from her life before jail. One night, they come over and cook us dinner.

A sweet thank-you.

They bring chuck steaks and make garlic mashed potatoes with parmesan, and string beans with almond slivers and little bursts of lemon and garlic salt and cayenne.

We eat on the back patio, which is now adorned with ferns and cactus. Old slab stones are now the floor of the patio. We are getting the house there a little at a time, even without Charlie. We have chickens pecking the ground and roaming around. Edie has named each one after an '80s sitcom, think *Golden Girls* and *Full House*. Dorothy, Blanche, Michelle Tanner. We sit on the DIY sectional David constructed out of the casita's old garage door. It has comfy cushions and throw pillows.

More and more the house feels like it is turning into our home.

I am happy Destiny has someone in her life. But I'm a little uneasy about Dre. He has moved her twenty minutes away from the community she has around her in downtown. He is pressuring her to take Joseph out of his school and go to a daycare near their apartment. I support her, but I worry, too.

I've heard from Brandon that, at *Absinthe*, Destiny is messing up. She comes in stoned. Falls asleep at the show. Comes in without her uniform or comes in late. There was that time she went out with the cast and crew of the show to a nightclub and got in a fight with another woman in the bathroom.

She had to be escorted out. Dre was with her.

I feel him moving her out of her support system. Contributing to her constant marijuana use. Controlling her in increments. When I am with them, it feels like he is competing with us for her. And that gives me pause. But it isn't my place. We have taken on a big sister–little sister role. I can be honest with her, but I am not in charge of her.

Her case is closed. This is her life to live.

We take Joseph whenever she needs a sitter.

On Easter, Lucy and Edie, who no longer believe in the Easter Bunny, fill 250 plastic pastel eggs with Hershey's Kisses and Smarties and Nerds. They help me make an Easter basket for Joseph. I make the girls' baskets in secret, in the bedroom.

In the early morning, the girls wake up and put the eggs all over the yard. In the most obvious and nonobvious places. On the grill. In the planters. Under the patio table. On the trampoline.

Dre drops off Joseph. Destiny is in the car. It's weird she doesn't come in, but I assume she's in a hurry.

The kids sit on the floor opening Easter baskets and shoving big wads of chocolate in their mouths. I make shakshouka, a well-known North African dish of eggs poached in cumin and paprika-scented tomatoes, onions, peppers, and tons of garlic. I add pillowy blobs of soft farm cheese and ground lamb to make it hearty and filling.

The kids have sugar for brekkie.

Dre picks Joseph up later in the afternoon.

Brandon texts me. Destiny is going to be fired from *Absinthe*.

Dre tells me Joseph is starting at a new school. It's next to their house, he says. He also lets me know I won't need to pick him up anymore. Or babysit him while Destiny works. Dre says he will be babysitting for Joseph.

I don't know it yet, but he is taking her to California. She thinks for fun. He wants her to care for his sick mom.

He will take her money. Her keys.

She will not be allowed to leave the house.

She will call me. We will make plans for her to get out.

After a few tries, she will get on a bus and come back to Vegas. With Joseph.

Dre will follow close behind.

I bring over groceries. Rice, pasta, jarred sauce. Broccoli. Chicken parts. Some hot sauce, garlic, and salt. Ice cream and cookies. Popsicles for Joseph.

Destiny and Joseph are back in the Vegas apartment. Dre is living with them.

The complex is safe enough. Lots of families. It's not a weekly. The apartment is clean and tidy. Simple dining room table. A chair. A small TV. A small bed for Joseph in his own room. A queen bed set and stripper pole in her room, something that made me laugh out loud the first time I saw it.

She has a tiny galley kitchen. It's functional and just right for them.

I set the bag down on the counter and start unpacking ice cream and putting it away. Joseph is out front, smacking a rock with the wooden handle of a broom. Hard. Over and over. Angry.

"Destiny! Where are ya?" I call out.

I put the cookies in an overhead cupboard. I call her name. When she comes in. I see the bruises and the swelling immediately.

Her cheek is deep purple. Her eye is sucked inside of swelling flesh. She tries to wear sunglasses inside. But I see it. He is beating her. At first, she doesn't want to talk about it. I keep putting the groceries away. I small talk her until she is ready to spill the details.

I sit at the table. She is across from me.

Dre took her money and ID. He controls where and when she can go. He has taken her away from most of her support. Slowly. Methodically. In the form of slippage. A cut here. A cut there. Until she is severed. Until he has complete control.

"Joseph put a hole in the wall. He's mad."

"He doesn't want to see his mama with bruises," I say.

She nods.

"He wasn't here when he beat you?"

"No," she says, "Joseph was at school."

"And he didn't just beat me, I beat him back," she makes sure to tell me. Because she doesn't want to be a victim. She is a fighter.

"He ain't looking so good."

"They could arrest you and put you back in jail."

"I'm not gonna let that fool beat me," she says, sitting up in her chair. "You know what he says to Joseph this morning?"

And this is what makes me stop. In my tracks. It makes the air escape my lungs.

"Joseph asked him what happened to my face and you know what he said?"

"What?"

I wait for it.

"That's what happens when your mother can't keep her mouth shut."

I look out the window and see Joseph in the front yard beating his rock with his stick. The beating is inside of him.

I talk to her about leaving him. Let's go now. Let's get your bags packed. Let's leave. Let's get Joseph out of this. I am ten steps ahead. They'll live with us. We'll help her find a place. We will start over. I think I can get him back into his school. We'll have to redo the paperwork, but that's fine . . .

I'm thinking. Thirty thoughts rushing at me. I'm moving. Hustling. I text David. I'm up from the chair.

"I ain't leaving him," she says. "He's just gonna have to do better."

* * *

"You have to report this," she says on the line.

It's Joseph's caseworker. The CPS case against Destiny is closed. But she has been a huge support to Destiny. I know I can have this conversation with her. I tell her what's happening with Dre. The fight. What he said to Joseph.

"You have no choice. You are a mandated reporter," she tells me.

I ask my licensing worker.

"You don't have a choice."

What if Dre kills her? Elaina, my licensing worker, asks. What if he kills her in front of Joseph? What if he hurts Joseph?

I pour myself several straight tequilas in a row. When this doesn't help, I pour myself more. I fall into bed, bleary-eyed and fucked up.

I know in the morning I will have to call the hotline and report the beating.

I will send the government into her house.

I will ruin our friendship.

I will put her family in jeopardy.

I will pull the only support system she has—us—out from under her.

I will penalize the one who has been beaten for being beaten.

David tucks in the children. Kisses their heads. He nestles them in warm blankets. He cleans the kitchen, does the last of the dishes. He turns the lights off when I am too drunk and sad to turn them off myself.

And yet no one has called this—the tequila binge, the sadness, the breakdown in my head and my heart, the total paralysis—parental neglect.

* * *

The mandated reporter system is—like the misdemeanor system—a way to keep eyes on poor folks.

Make no mistake. It exists to police their parenting.

The mandatory reporting system was created in the '70s by the federal government to report incidences of abuse and neglect in the community. The neglect piece of this is most important because it is amorphous. Neglect often coalesces around the comorbidities of poverty.

It is good to report cases of abuse. And it is good that we have teachers and caseworkers keeping an eye out for kids who really do need solid parenting and family support. No one argues with that.

But if you report a child who doesn't have enough food. Or running water. Or too many kids in a bedroom. Or a lack of dental care. Or that they have to spend the evenings alone because mom doesn't have childcare, you are reporting a family for being poor. Not being neglectful.

Neglect is fuzzy. And pervasive—it accounts for more than 70 percent of all CPS cases.

Neglect is completely at the discretion of the observer.

The kids might be removed and then go to a foster home, where foster parents receive a lot of financial and social support benefits that could've helped the biological family keep their kids home in the first place. This includes health insurance paid by the government. Clothes and toys at Christmas. Extra monthly money for raising the kids and sending them to dance classes and sporting events. Ample therapies and interventions that are difficult to access outside the system.

Perhaps, if the families had received these supports, they wouldn't be under stress and prone to neglecting their children.

This is especially meaningful for Black families, who are reported to CPS more often than white families. They are more likely to have their kids taken into foster care. In foster care, research indicates, Black children are in care, and out of their homes, for longer periods of time than white kids in comparable situations. And their parents lose their parental rights more often than white parents. Add to this that Black women are more likely to lose their kids by being sent to jail.

In deciding how to make sure Destiny and Joseph are safe, I don't think to consider any of this. I do not understand or see the enormous system of oppression of which I am a player.

I get up in the morning and call the hotline on someone I love and believe in.

* * *

My big mistake is not telling Destiny ahead of time.

It is perhaps the ugliest thing I have ever done in a friendship.

I will never do it again.

But I can't find the words to tell her. I am a coward. And perhaps I wouldn't have even thought about telling her. Warning her. Because in my head, I'm helping.

Instead, I call the hotline and report the beating. But with lots of caveats.

"She shouldn't have Joseph removed from the home," I say. "She is a good mom.

"I just want Dre to know we are watching, that we will not allow him to hurt them anymore.

"Maybe with a little pressure, she will leave him."

But what the social worker says when she shows up at Destiny's house is different. She tells her that they can remove Joseph. That they are watching. That she is not a good mom.

It is pressure. On top of pressure. On top of pressure. And now the government is back in her life again.

I pick up the phone on the second ring. All I can hear is screaming.

"You will never see Joseph. You will never see me. Fuck you."

I've treated Destiny like a CPS case.

"Fuck you, Kim. I cannot believe you did this to us."

I have punished a domestic abuse survivor by threatening to have her child removed.

"You were my friend."

I have taken our family away from her. We are a healthy, resource-rich support system for her. And now, she is alone again.

"God. God. God. Kim, how could you do this to me?"

I try to explain. She is having none of my reasons.

Destiny is a former foster child who trusts no one. But she trusted me. And now I have deepened the tender, sore well of trauma and mistrust.

She blocks me from all social media.

I cannot say I blame her.

HUNGER, HOARDING + HAVING ENOUGH

EDIE AND I first meet Johnnie in the Smith's checkout line.

Edie and I have this shopping safari we go on. The more stores the better for her; it's our time to connect away from the other kids. We hit International Marketplace for poi. And taro for attieke, an Ivorian dish their childhood friends Nakamae and Kissa's father taught me to make. To Jones Feed & Tack for dog, cat, and chicken and bunny food. Aladdin, a Middle Eastern mom-and-pop, for their excellent labneh and fresh flat breads. 99 Ranch for their milk toast, slabs of pork belly, sake, sushi-grade tuna and salmon, and fresh udon noodles.

We open the sunroof. Roll down the windows. We feel the dried, cracked air on our faces. The sun is popping at us through the palms, bleeding warm rays through our skin. We turn the volume up loud. We sing. Like drunk fools on karaoke night. AC/DC's "You Shook Me All Night Long." It gets us shrieking in the car.

We keep shopping.

To Costco for big quantities of beef cheek, ground lamb and goat cubes, cream, butter, and manchego. Rani's, an Indian mom-and-pop, for ajwain, saffron, and curry leaves. Ron's for Eastern European goods, Aleppo pepper, and mortadella. Cardenas for tortillas, avocado, lard, and candy for the kids. Melkham Market, where I buy Ethiopian injera, beef for kitfo, mitmita, and niter kibbeh. And Nakata Market, a small Japanese grocery, for sansho, real wasabi, and Ramune for the kids.

Last stop is the Smith's on Maryland, our neighborhood grocery.

We have cans of beans and tuna. Pastas. Frozen udon noodles. A parade of household supplies. A bag of broccoli. A package of nothing but the pope's noses from turkeys. This is the only supermarket I know that sells these plastic-wrapped packages of the fatty, protruding end bits of the turkey, known officially as uropygium, the fatty thing that holds the turkey's tail feathers upright. Turns out, it's the best for making thick ramen stocks, along with some gelatinous chicken feet, trotters, and bits of pork skin.

I throw it on the belt. Edie bags for me.

"I hate the feel of this in my mouth," Johnnie, our cashier, tells me, scanning the broccoli.

"I get it," I tell her. "My foster son is the same. He has the texture thing."

We haven't seen Joseph in months. Or heard from Destiny. Life keeps going. We have two new kids with us: Raffi, who is four, and his little sister, Desi, who is seven months.

"No boys, no babies," we had said.

But we have both now.

And an understanding that we do not choose children to live with us. They somehow choose us.

I blurt it out about our foster son without thinking. There is something about telling strangers you are a foster parent. Sometimes it is a signal to people who have been through hell. That you might be a safe landing pad for their truths, for the bad things they've been through.

Johnnie has dark, curly, short hair. Big weepy eyes. A pretty smile. She's also strong and rugged. She stands bent a little, as if she is trying to make herself smaller. Less noticeable.

"My mother kept me locked in the closet," she tells me nonchalantly, running paper towels across the belt. "Me and my dog."

Just like that, she says it. I'm not even sure I heard her correctly.

"She locked you in a closet . . . a lot?" I ask, trying to adjust my mind to such a deep revelation at the checkout.

"Yeah," she says. "Every day . . . when she and my stepdad weren't beating me to a pulp."

There is a moment of silence as she punches buttons on the cash register. I realize Edie has stopped bagging, and then, not knowing what else to do, she starts again.

"That's why I eat alone," she continues, not looking at me. "And I don't cook for myself.

"I wait until the last minute to eat anything."

These issues sound familiar to me. Our current foster son has been hoarding food in his bedroom, and in his school backpack. He tells the cafeteria workers at school he is hungry and they give him tons of fruit cups and granola bars and cartons of chocolate milk. They mostly go rancid before I find them.

But I learned. I go through his pack every day now and put everything in the fridge.

He needs that food "just in case."

"How old were you?" I ask.

I hold the Smith's card so it is right under the reader. Wait for the beep. I get the debit card in the slot, but I'm struggling with it. I fumble the PIN. I have to do the numbers twice. I can barely take my eyes off her.

"Six years old," she says.

There is another woman bagging my groceries now, and Edie is looking at her phone. There is a line behind me. It's like Johnnie and I are alone in a bubble, no one able to hear us. But of course, everyone is listening.

"My dog was in there with me," she tells me with a chuckle. Her face softens when she speaks about her.

"Sometimes we ate her dog food. Sometimes I shared my food with her."

She demonstrates, snapping an invisible Milk-Bone in two.

"I always fed her first and the most."

My brain stalls. She's so calm. She has pushed it so far back; she can share it with a stranger over a rolling belt.

"Did anyone ever come for you?"

As a foster parent, working inside the system, this matters to me.

"No," she says, handing me the receipt. "No one came.

"I was alone," she says. "And, with the Smith's card, you saved twenty-six dollars and thirty-four cents."

I am not the type of person to cry in the checkout line. But damned if I'm not crying.

I ask her to meet me for coffee.

* * *

Pretty much everyone in our neighborhood despises the Smith's on Maryland.

Except me.

I love it. Our local Smith's has hustle.

There are addicts looking for spare change, gathered in clumps, at the electronic door. Girl Scouts are selling cookies. Unhoused people ask to help carry your groceries to your car for cash. Basketball teams sell candy bars. Elderly folks work the slots. Teens with spray bottles and paper towels ask to clean your windshield for cash.

I have also never been in that parking lot without being pitched, hustled, or panhandled.

Something different happens every time I shop there.

There are long lines to cash checks. The booze is locked away. The baby and personal hygiene products, all the makeup, as well as over-the-counter meds are in a restricted area with a separate cashier. The lines are often long and winding through the aisles. There are never any carts in the store. You have to bring one in with you from the lot. It is simply the way of the store.

And forget the self-checkout. People come with their overstuffed carts, clogging the efficiency of it all. Shoplifting is rampant. And because of that, any real conveniences, or hopes of flying in and out to get something quickly, have been made impossible. Almost always someone will grab you in the meat aisle and ask to trade their food stamps for cash.

It's a hustle, for sure.

The neighborhood Facebook rants pop up every few months.

"I know it's not our Smith's," a commenter says, "but the Rancho/Oakey location has crab cakes that absolutely slap right now. At the seafood counter."

This—the mere mention of our Smith's, also known as "Murder Smith's"—triggers an avalanche of comments.

"Totally tangential, but was there not a serial floor shitter at the Maryland Smith's a couple years back?"

This jostles everyone's memories, and the comments come in, bullets in wartime. One after the other.

"Bwahhahahahahahaha I just remember going in the front door and, if I remember it right, this time Shitman had unleashed his superpowers in the self-checkout and they had it taped off."

Then, the punch line: "What a literal shit show. Sorry, the jokes write themselves."

"Mom! I got shit on my shoe!"

"It's okay, Jimmy! We're shopping at Smith's!"

And then, inevitably, someone says the thing that always gets said.

"We would love a Sprouts or a TJs or a Whole Foods."

Downtown Las Vegas is not getting an upscale grocery store. Not anytime soon.

Those stores avoid us like herpes. Not enough square footage to make it worth it for big supermarkets. Add to that a slew of dollar stores, gas station markets, and 7-Elevens that force competition with the big markets that need to push out a large volume of product to make their tight margins.

And I'm guessing, too many poor people in downtown Vegas.

Downtown is eclectic. Diverse racially, ethnically, and economically.

There are artists and writers living here. Teachers, hipsters, nurses, chefs, food truck owners, would-be gentrifiers, and UNLV professors. There are migrant workers, who come, put their kids in school, and then leave again, only to come back again to familiar faces. We have white people, Black people, Salvadorans, Cubans, Mexicans, Hawaiians, and Filipinos. There are old folks, disabled folks, foster families and kinship foster families, and families who have lost their kids to the system, and then gotten them back. And newly married people buying first houses. There are LGBTQ+ folks and people who are just coming back from the brink of poverty and starting over. So many of us are refugees from NYC, taken in by all the space, and what was once affordable housing and significantly better weather. There are a shitload of weekly hotels holding some of the most struggling people in our community. The kids who live there are in our kids' schools and in our houses afterward. There are unhoused folks, the mentally ill, and addicts living in our alleys, in tent cities, and near our shops, parks, and churches.

Poor old Smith's is the lightning rod for all of that. We are a large, wickedly dysfunctional family. And we have to constantly ask what progress means for everyone in our community.

There will be fights. And Facebook commiserations. And more pleas from the aspirational for fancier supermarkets, better services, more wine bars, and cooler coffee shops, set against the worry of pushing out people on the edges, of us turning ourselves into sanitized upper-class suburbia. This is the thing we moved here to avoid, and by moving here, we know we probably pushed it a little further toward that reality.

But still this neighborhood of artists, immigrants, gamblers, and pioneers looking for a better life out West is just the community to grapple with these complexities.

Smith's on Maryland is not perfect, by any stretch.

But it has salted duck eggs. And French baby carrots, and a whole organic section for folks who want that. You can get large, family-size portions of fresh fish and meats, along with the usual frozen and canned foods. They have duck fat and beef tallow, fermented black beans, patis, and Mexican cinnamon. You'll hear neighbors chatting away in the aisles in their native tongue: Spanish, Tagalog, and Chinese.

Management listens to customers' requests for particular ingredients. The staff are often long-haulers. They seem happy enough to work there. They are chatty and kind at the checkouts. Some of the cashiers are in transition from male to female, and this tells me something about what the company values. The workers are unionized. One of the baggers, Anita, offers me a graduate-level food anthropology lesson every time I shop there.

"A lot of formula and diapers going out today," she says. "That happens a lot around the first of the month," she tells me, an expert sensing the trends.

And then she'll tell me about something new to her, like fish sauce, and she'll ask me if I've tried it, and of course I use it a lot, and so I run to the shelves as the cashier slides food over the belt and buy her a bottle of Red Boat and tell her to dribble it into everything.

And really, that's why I like Smith's—besides the fact that they have those packages of turkey butts—I meet some of the coolest people there.

* * *

Johnnie and I sit down in the deli-café section.

I swear I have walked past the plastic tables and chairs a hundred times. The café is just off the vegetable aisles, next to the deli counter. I recognize its existence in some far-off place in my mind. It's there, but it exists as if looking through a veil.

It's never registered with me as a place I'd want to sit and hang out. No windows. No plastic vines or special cozy lighting to mark its presence. No acoustic Spotify playlists to lure you in to sit. It seems to exist without consideration.

It is, though, just fine for meeting Johnnie after her shift. Convenient. Blank. Not threatening.

It's safe.

I am a stranger, after all, who has asked her to meet and talk about the most personal and traumatizing aspects of her childhood.

"Have you tried the grapple?" she asks me.

Grapple is a fuji or gala apple soaked in a grape solution so that the skin picks up grape flavors. Some marketer somewhere is hoping this idea takes off.

"Everybody's buying them," she tells me. "I think moms are getting them for the kids."

I vow to try them next time I'm in. Which is always soon.

Johnnie starts talking. I put down my phone with the voice memo on.

She wants her story out there.

Johnnie's mom, Estrella, is a pretty good mom for the first few years of her life, she tells me.

They live in Santa Barbara, California. Estrella makes her meals. Johnnie remembers them well. Arroz con gandules. Pollo guisado. Sopas: Sopa de res con fideo. Sopa de pollo con mofongo. Warm, filling sancochos with chunks of beef, carrots, yautia, potato, green plantains, and cassava.

It is all very normal and loving. Johnnie, her mom, and her two older sisters, Camila and Angeline, eat together around a small kitchen table. They talk. They joke. They go to school. They play in the neighborhood. Everything is fine.

Until it's not.

Estrella begins drinking when Johnnie is five. Probably to combat the oncoming symptoms of schizophrenia. They move to Vegas. Her biological dad, Hugo, is a chef at Caesars Palace.

Hugo is gay. He lives and works away from the family. Johnnie does not know him during her childhood. She will meet him years later through Ancestry.com.

"Your dad was a chef a few miles away from you." I mention this with a little irony in my voice.

"Did the guy who fed other people for a living know you were starving?"

"No," she says.

"He would never have let us go hungry."

And yet he did. Simply by not being there.

Still, she has absolved him of responsibility. She talks about him only with kindness. And a certain pride that she might have inherited his gayness. A connection. A common thread across the vast terrain of his absence.

The drinking intensifies alongside Estrella's schizophrenia. Johnnie says it's subtle in the beginning.

"Like she is cutting corners a little."

But the drinking and her symptoms get worse.

Estrella stops sleeping. She and her new husband, a man who remains nameless and faceless in Johnnie's story, become more and more angry with the children. Johnnie feels a kind of detachment unfolding in the family as the grown-ups move away from day-to-day life with the kids. Johnnie senses the shift, but at the time she has no words to explain it or make it make sense.

The house devolves into chaos.

Estrella stops grocery shopping. She stops taking the kids to the doctor. She stops making them food or having food in the house. It's slow but devastating. Slippage.

Estrella is quick to flare. She and her husband beat Johnnie as her delusions slide into intense paranoia.

"I had no preparation for this," she tells me. "Everything was always okay."

Her sisters, Camila and Angeline (Angie for short), are older. They stay out of the house more. If anyone notices the onset of Estrella's symptoms, they don't think to check on the kids.

"There might've been beer and eggs in the fridge," Johnnie tells me. "But it was mostly bare, mostly dirty," she says, sipping a cup of coffee.

"And I couldn't use the stove anyway. If it wasn't in a package," she tells me, "it was useless to me."

Packaged food becomes the food she trusts. It's safe. Predictable. You can eat it quickly before your mom notices you have food. It can easily be hidden.

And packaged food comes to symbolize how she can save herself.

* * *

Schizophrenia is considered to be one of the most debilitating and life-altering of the psychiatric illnesses.

It's a stealthy and terrifying onslaught of hallucinations and visions and voices that can be merciless, dark, and violent. It can upend the whole world of the person who has it and anyone around them. Making it a landscape of false beliefs, filled with malevolent voices that chide, insult, push, punish, and demand.

Schizophrenia usually starts in the teenage and young adult years. The disease is marked by delusions and ideas and visions that aren't true. Sometimes catatonia. And hallucinations, mostly auditory, hearing voices that aren't there. It is progressive, meaning it gets worse over time. And it is so debilitating that it frequently ends in chronic and profound isolation away from other people. No less than 10 percent of people with it will eventually kill themselves.

It is also a disease that people without schizophrenia have a hard time handling.

"When an illness is viewed as inexplicable and impenetrable, people tend to react to it with one of two extremes," says Michael Foster Green, PhD, a professor in the UCLA Department of Psychiatry, in Andrew Solomon's book *Far from the Tree: Parents, Children and the Search for Identity.*

"They stigmatize it or they romanticize it. It's hard to know which is worse."

There is no way to know if Estrella is taking her meds for her schizophrenia, or if she even goes to a doctor, but all indications from Johnnie's story suggest not. Estrella's behavior becomes more volatile and erratic. It is a total downward spiral. She loses touch with reality. And as is often the case with schizophrenia, the disease drives the family into greater isolation.

Which proves perilous for Johnnie and her sisters.

In *Night Falls Fast: Understanding Suicide,* by Dr. Kay Redfield Jamison, a professor of psychiatry at the Johns Hopkins School of Medicine, Robert Bayley, a patient with schizophrenia, describes what he goes through.

It might help to understand what Estrella's life might have been like:

The reality for myself is almost constant pain and torment. The voices and visions, which are so commonly experienced, intrude and so disturb my everyday life. The voices are predominantly destructive, either rambling in alien tongues or screaming orders to carry out violent acts. They also persecute me by way of unwavering commentary and ridicule to deceive, derange, and force me into a world of crippling paranoia. Their commands are abrasive and all-encompassing and have resulted in periods of suicidal behavior and self-mutilation. I have run in front of speeding cars and severed arteries while feeling this compulsion to destroy my own life. . . . During periods of acute bombardment, paving stones transform into demonic faces, shattering in front of my petrified eyes. When I am in contact with people, they can be grossly deformed, their skin peeling away to reveal decomposing inner muscles and organs.

"I was pulled from my bed, often . . . torn really," Johnnie says. "In the middle of the night."

Estrella raged.

"She stopped making sense."

There is no reasoning. No bargaining. No meaningful argument. Johnnie's life is constant, unpredictable change. There is no flooring or foundation to get herself stable. It's bad surprise after worse surprise.

Camila and Angie suffer, too. Camila takes a lot of the beatings for Johnnie. But when they are old enough, the sisters leave.

"Camila always cared for me," Johnnie tells me.

"She made sure I ate and was bathed. She took beatings for me. Covered me when my mother was crazy."

But then she left.

To this day, Johnnie will not speak to her sisters. She feels they abandoned her. She cannot forgive them for saving themselves and leaving her behind.

"Angie never cared," she says.

"She tried to kill herself later.

"But she still left."

A lot of the anger Johnnie has is directed toward her sisters, the other victims of the abuse, and not her absent father or her spiraling mother. I am struck by how complex our brains are in comforting and protecting us.

But I also see her logic. This must be the most potent form of being alone, I think. To have had cover, and then to lose it. And to still be under the age of ten.

In fact, loneliness is a huge and devastating pattern of schizophrenia. The symptoms can be so severe as to confound and push people away. But also people with schizophrenia have impaired empathy as part of the disease. Dr. Green says his patients have certain kinds of empathy, for example, like the kind we feel when we see someone hurt. We want to help. We feel compassion.

But schizophrenia can steal the kind of empathy that allows us to put ourselves in someone's shoes, empathy in which you actually can imagine yourself feeling that pain, being in those circumstances. And relate to it intimately. It's a more profound sense of empathy. And that can hamper a person like Estrella from being able to connect with other humans outside of her disease.

And it might mean missing the signs she is abusing her child.

As Estrella plunges further into the disease, she gets further and further away from being able to see her children's needs, to feel a connection to their pain, or even recognize that she is abusing them.

Estrella stops caring about herself. She stops being invested in the house and in her remaining daughter at home. She sleeps all the time. The house falls into bedlam, chaos, and filth. Dishes pile up in the sink. Clothes lie dirty on the floor. Old food plates litter the floor. The tabletops. There are mice. Roaches. There are cigarette butts in heaping ashtrays, and the yellow of nicotine on the walls.

Johnnie has a single set of clothes for school. She rarely takes baths. The kids in school make fun of her for wearing the same clothes every day. Dirty clothes. They laugh at her because she smells bad. She becomes more and more disconnected from her peers. And so, the loneliness and isolation that happen for people with schizophrenia can also happen to the people in their lives, like their children or their parents.

What Johnnie learns from all this? She is not good enough.

She is not worthy of good things.

She is not worthy of food.

Of attention.

Of love.

It is all intertwined. This sets the tone for her entire life.

"I tiptoe around the house because I don't want to wake her up and get beaten.

"I still do it," she tells me. "Today, this morning, I still do it.

"I'm always quiet in my house. I don't slam doors or make a racket."

She keeps herself small.

I ask her about friends in the neighborhood. Or if anyone notices. Does anyone think to ask about the girl they rarely see anymore? But even as I ask, I know how easy it is for a neighborhood not to notice.

As I am interviewing Johnnie, I have questions about the house kitty-corner to us.

Gray stucco. Overgrown front lawn. A thin husky in the side yard that is outside every day and every night, regardless of the weather. There is a girl who lives there. Lucy and Edie's age. She never comes out.

I knock a couple times.

I introduce Lucy and Edie to the girl, Maya. She is younger than Lucy, older than Edie, with deep-set, liquid brown eyes. Quiet. Beautiful.

So quiet.

But there is no connection or spark between the girls. Maya is disengaged. Her eyes don't meet Lucy's and Edie's. I invite Maya over. Mom is not open to letting her leave the house. Mom is polite but doesn't make conversation easily. There are enough awkward pauses and stilted conversations that I get the message and give up.

Our other neighbors notice the the dog, a young Husky out in the monsoon without cover. They form a Facebook posse to save the dog. Neighbors knock on the door. They slide water and food under the fence. They try to find cover for the dog. A makeshift plastic tarp so the dog isn't subjected to the torrential beatdown of desert rains and heaving winds.

But they don't notice the girl. And I have no proof of anything. I mind my own.

Just like Johnnie. No one forms a posse for the girl.

And then someone does.

One night the family moves out. All their things get thrown into the hatch of their car. In the middle of darkness. A teacher at the local school reported them to CPS. Signs of sexual abuse.

And they are in the wind.

We didn't give that girl cover.

It's hard to blame Johnnie's neighbors for not looking harder. But it makes me sad that no one ever saves her.

Then Estrella starts locking Johnnie in the closet.

* * *

Food is not love.

Folks often use the expression "Food is love." Or pizza is love. Or pasta is love. But that's not exactly accurate.

In Katja Rowell's *Love Me, Feed Me: The Adoptive Parent's Guide to Ending the Worry About Weight, Picky Eating, Power Struggles and More*, the bible for feeding adopted and traumatized kids, she writes in depth about the act of feeding someone and what it means.

Turns out that feeding people is love. Not the food itself.

Love is *the act* of feeding someone.

"The attachment cycle is fulfilled by meeting physical and emotional needs over and over again," she writes in her book. "Food is simply one of the most reliable and obvious opportunities to help a child feel safe and cared for—and to build trust."

For babies, all experiences are personal. Babies cannot protect themselves. They are completely vulnerable and dependent on their caregivers. They have to let the world know they are tired. Or hungry. Or uncomfortable.

They scream.

They cry.

They get loud until they get what they need.

When a baby screams and a parent comes rushing to them with a bottle or a nipple, or a comforting snuggle, an attachment bond is formed. Every time this happens, their bond gets stronger. The baby becomes more and more secure in the world. They know, with every ounce of their being, that the same person (or persons) is going to come for them every time.

This builds trust and security.

The baby with a secure attachment, according to John Bowlby's well-referenced attachment theory, is the baby who gets consistent reactions to their crying. Their reaching out. Their bubble blowing. Their cooing and screaming. Every time Dad comes rushing in to give a warm bottle to fill a hungry belly, a lattice of confidence and safety sets like mortar in the child's brain.

This kid grows up knowing the world is secure. And development happens in that framework, as does attachment to other humans.

Attachment is a sticky thing. No caregiver can be there at all times for a baby. Some studies have suggested that even in healthy, attached families, this kind of asking–receiving success happens only about 50 percent of the time. This is because parents are working, stressed, making dinner, managing siblings. But the attachment also comes from the rupture and the repair.

"I might not be able to get to you right now, kiddo," a mom will say. "But I will get you those raspberries after I fry the last of this chicken."

When she gets her raspberries, finally, the rupture is healed. The baby gets that it may not happen when and how she wants it, but it will happen.

Life goes on.

Safety is reinforced.

All is well.

Because humans need food, consistently, multiple times a day, food is one of the first ways children gauge how safe they are. Food, how much they get, when they get it, and how their caregiver provides for them when they cry out, sends a foundational message about their worth in the world.

That message is hardwired into their brain's pathways. It stays with them, always.

Being fed consistently is safety.

So, the meatloaf you make from scratch might not be a physical incarnation of love. But making it lovingly, warming it to just the right temperature. Talking softly and sweetly to your toddler while you hand-feed her the food. Making the choo-choo-train song that makes her smile as you put the meatloaf in her mouth. Doing it every day at roughly the same time when she is hungry, filling her need for sustenance, is most definitely love.

Compare that with kids who are in abusive homes or homes with severe neglect. This could also apply to families where there is a lot of love but also scarcity and extreme poverty. Same for families with severe mental health and addiction issues. Kids in these families learn on some primal level that the world might not be safe for them. That their needs might not get met. That they will want, and no one will come for them or help them.

And these schisms, these unanswered calls for comfort and nurturance, create cracks in the foundation that affect every development that comes after. In fact, all development from then on is fruit from the poison tree.

Kids from hard places want this safety and security so much because they crave it on a cellular level. Because it is an ache that never leaves them, they bring that schism into their relationships with other people. They cannot trust other humans the same way that a securely attached child trusts.

They see themselves as inherently unworthy.

And that feeling sticks with them. It is hardwired into the system.

"It's the fight of 'I don't deserve to eat,' and it will be with me for life," Johnnie comments on an Instagram post I wrote about hunger.

"It's a horrible inner fight . . . and I'm sixty years old."

Hunger is lifelong.

* * *

"I was a fucking dog no one wanted."

This time, Johnnie and I are talking at Denny's. It takes a couple rounds of planning. Some last-minute cancellations on Johnnie's end. Johnnie has a hard time making the dates we set. She is gung-ho to get together, but when it actually is in front of us, about to happen, there are excuses and last-minute decisions to pull out.

It's a schism. She wants to make the attachment. It's hard to get there.

I have a western omelet and a Diet Coke. Johnnie is eating pancakes and sipping iced tea. Her therapist told her to always leave a little food on the plate, instead of stuffing it all down out of fear that it might go away. She leaves a little wedge of pancake in a puddle of syrup on the plate. Her knife and fork are crossed over each other.

She explains how she kept the closet door unlocked by jamming in the corner so it didn't close properly. Those rare times she gets the door open, she waits for the house to empty. She makes her move.

"We used to have C&H Sugar," she says. She is specific about the brand.

"I ran straight to the kitchen, to the sugar bowl or the box of C&H, whatever was closest."

She pours the sugar directly into her mouth. She tips the box. Lets it rush into her mouth. Or she shovels it by the tablespoon.

This is backed up by research: kids often experience less pain when consuming sweet foods.

She tells me the Milk-Bone story again. This time with precious details. The careful sharing of the dry biscuit. The cracking into two parts. Giving the biggest to Ginger, the German shepherd–Lab mix. The taste of the dry biscuit on her lips, the way the little jagged bits cling to her tongue, the taste of it, bland, gross, crumbling, dry. Filling.

She tells me about the family kittens that starve to death.

When her mother leaves, she secretly buries the limp bodies in her backyard. She cries over their hidden graves. Her knees in the dirt. She feels responsible. Like it is her fault they starved to death. Like she had choices or power. She is stuck with this feeling, as kids often are, that they can control things they can't. That feeling never leaves.

Now Johnnie has three cats, Dave, Milk, and Reggie. Reggie is her favorite.

"I would starve myself for them."

Starving for Johnnie is a measure of her love and its depths.

She posts photos of the cats, her family, on Facebook. Reggie is a gorgeous honey-colored sweetheart. They are her world. The companions who never hurt her. Whom she protects.

"I yelled at the cats this morning," she tells me tearfully on a day when I see her in Smith's. She works the separate toiletries section now. It has its own cash register.

"God, I'm just like my mother."

"You aren't your mom," I say. "You're just struggling."

There is no one behind me checking out, so we can be indulgent with time.

"I don't like to yell at them, but I haven't been able to keep it together," she says. "I lost control."

She wipes the tears away. I put my arms around her. She leans in. We are hugging in the shampoo section. As you do.

"I hate myself."

There is no consoling her on this day. She is broken. Her meds aren't working, she tells me.

"I want to die every day," she says, moving out of our hug. She tries to compose herself.

"Sometimes it's hard to stay alive."

"How often do you feel this way?" I ask.

"Every day. Every day I fight not to kill myself."

* * *

The closet, of course, is a terrifying place for a child. Folklorically, it is darkness, where unseen bad things lurk.

Monsters live in closets. Bugs crawl in closets. Things that hide in the walls come in and out of the closet. Things pop out of the closet, at you, in ways you can't see coming. And there is no way out when it's locked. It can be pitch black. All-confining. Merciful cracks bring the only light. It is seclusion. Loneliness. Isolation from family. From the whole world. The mark of a child who is aberrant and different. A bad child. A child deserving of such horrors.

It is a casket. A kind of death while alive.

In C. S. Lewis's *The Lion, The Witch and the Wardrobe*, the closet is a portal to another world. But that's fantasy. The scary thing transforms into the way out, toward something else, an even better, more fantastical life. The reality of the closet is that it's more about a child being worthy of darkness, who, like Harry Potter, can be saved only by some kind of extreme, magic, or otherworldly intervention that is mammoth and nearly impossible to conjure.

The Lauren Kavanaugh case is one of the most pronounced and horrific examples of how the closet and food can be used as tools of abuse with catastrophic consequences. Lauren Kavanaugh was left in the closet at the hands of her biological mother and stepfather, Barbie and Ken Atkinson.

Barbie and Ken sat at the kitchen table of their mobile home, according to an eight-part series in *The Dallas Morning News* in 2013. They ate potato salad and brisket. Down the short hall of their double-wide was their little girl, curled up in the darkness, starving.

Lauren was rescued in 2001, at the age of eight. She had spent nearly a lifetime inside her family's closet. She was found covered in cigarette burns. Puncture wounds. Lice. And her esophagus was filled with carpet fibers and her own feces.

She weighed a little over twenty-five pounds at age eight. The weight of a typical two-year-old.

Lauren's adoptive mom, Sabrina Kavanaugh, expected physical signs of being isolated. She expected severe signs of starvation, the body eating itself, cannibalizing the fats and muscles, glucose and tissue, until there is nothing left. And the way in which food has to be introduced slowly to keep the body from heaving into cardiac arrest.

But the ongoing issues of starvation stayed with Lauren and her adoptive family for years.

Even with food ever-present and available at the Kavanaughs' home, Lauren continued to wake in the middle of the night and gorge until she threw up. Doctors suggested locking up the food. But the Kavanaughs did the opposite—they made food ever-present and available for her. They reassured her that she would always be able to eat.

The Kavanaughs left her cookies and lemonade in the middle of the night.

Lauren often went through the trash for food. She tried to eat objects like crayons and toothpaste, a condition called pica, in which people eat inedible things like mattress stuffing and sand. Pica has its origins in hunger. The Kavanaughs found her sleeping in her closet. In response, they took the doors off every closet in the house.

When there was a problem or Lauren needed redirection, Lauren went right to her fears about not having food.

"Now you're not going to feed me anymore," she'd say.

There was never a moment when scarcity and hunger had not rewired her brain, where the closet had not done its damage.

There's this one thing in Lauren's story that always reminds me so much of Johnnie. It's when Sabrina Kavanaugh talks about how her daughter never asked for candy or a toy.

This resonates for Johnnie.

"I don't deserve to feel hungry," she tells me in one of our talks.

"I don't deserve to want things."

Johnnie is afraid to want things, because she knows from experience that she won't get them, and this reinforces what she knows about herself—that she is not worthy of having even the most basic of her needs met.

* * *

Barbie Atkinson, Lauren's biological mom, who locked her in the closet, has her own sad story. She is both a victim and Lauren's perpetrator. Just like Estrella.

As a child, Barbie was sexually abused by strange men her mother brought into the house. Her mother suffered from schizophrenia, as well. She had intense delusions, paranoia, and self-medicated with street drugs. Barbie's early life was filled with chaos, violence, fear, and repeated rape.

Then someone came for Barbie. CPS took her out of the home.

She was adopted by a family. But like so many kids in foster care, taken from everything they know, she spent her life pining for the approval of her elusive biological mom. Barbie gave birth to five kids, whom she seemed to treat well. But then she had Lauren.

Barbie felt something was off with the baby. She tried to put her up for adoption at birth. She got pregnant again and suffered a miscarriage; this drove Barbie deeper into postpartum blackness and psychosis.

"Lauren was not mine. Lauren was never mine," Barbie told *The Dallas Morning News*. "There was no bonding. She didn't like to just come up to me and give me a hug like my other kids. She did to other people. But she didn't to me."

The depression triggered dissociative episodes. In interviews, Barbie often refers to Lauren as "it."

"It [Lauren] was the problem. It was what was causing everything," Atkinson, then thirty-one, said in the same piece. "Out of sight, out of mind. I shut it away and don't think of it. . . . I couldn't stop her being in the closet."

Barbie is in jail now serving a life sentence. She is more stable. There is a strict routine and medications, counseling, and a clarity she didn't have in her life before.

When you dig into dysfunctional families, you often find blurred lines between the oppressor and oppressed, victim and perpetrator. I'm thinking about Charlie, who sexually assaulted his sister, acting out violence that he had learned as his father's victim.

How are we to think of people who are both hurt and hurt others? When we know the first hurt helped cause the second? I think about this a lot.

"Sometimes you almost feel like you're in the presence of evil, and other times you feel like you're with someone who just doesn't get it, and you feel pity for them," Dr. Barbara Rila said in *The Dallas Morning News*, talking about Barbie. Rila is a psychologist who worked with Barbie's kids. "I think there is something basically human missing."

But isn't this wrong? Isn't this all human?

These are the ways in which manufactured social media fury, sound bites on TV, and drumbeats of cancellation don't work in nuanced real lives. Tweets and memes aren't generally able to handle the granular complexity of generational trauma, pain passed from one grandmother to mother to granddaughter, with dysfunctions so deeply set into the composition of families that it's impossible to lay blame in any one place.

It is easy to dismiss Barbie as Lauren's perpetrator. Estrella as Johnnie's. Charlie as his sister's, and his father as his. But we get into dangerous territory when we start talking about mental illness as lacking humanity.

Disability is humanity.

The truth is that people who come from traumatic family situations, including mental illness, extreme trauma, and addiction, are sometimes incredibly difficult to love. Or like. Or even sometimes see as human. But being human is intrinsically a part of mental illness. It's important not to lose sight of that.

In *Imagining Robert: My Brother, Madness and Survival*, author Jay Neugeboren writes about his brother who suffered from schizophrenia:

> For paid professionals to act as if Robert was merely a vessel of flesh in which (bad) chemicals somehow rose up once upon a time and made him ill, and in which other (good) chemicals must now be poured, deprives Robert of what he still possesses in abundance: his humanity. How not to cry out against any and all attempts, when it comes to being human beings with lives like Robert, to reduce their humanity to their biology?

It is nearly impossible to think of Barbie as a person who deserves empathy after what she did to Lauren. It is the same with Estrella. In the first drafts of writing this, I paint her as a villain and abuser. It was the way I thought of her. But it's Johnnie who changes my thoughts on this.

In a lucid moment, Estrella wrote Johnnie a letter before she died. In it, she apologized.

Johnnie often posts photos of her mom on Facebook.

"I love you, Mami," she writes.

Or, "I miss you, Mami."

I ask Johnnie how she can pine for her mother after all the pain she brought to her life.

"If I don't forgive her," she tells me, "I won't be able to move on."

We almost always love our parents. No matter what they do to us. Raffi, the boy who is settling into our lives with his baby sister, Desi, loves his mother, too. No matter what she does or doesn't do. He will always love her.

But because Estrella was severely mentally ill, Johnnie can't blame her. It wasn't her fault. She didn't do it on purpose. So, the only place for the pain is to turn it all inward. Onto herself.

She tells me about being expelled from school. About teachers failing her and letting her drift away without finding out why she was falling off the edges of the earth. She couldn't focus in school. She took pills to feel numb. She drank until she felt nothing. She drank until she had to go to rehab.

She is sober now. But she tells me about the deep sadness that is simply a part of her life.

She has crippling bouts of anxiety daily. Sometimes by the minute and the hour. Sometimes she stays in bed. She sleeps a lot. It is an escape hatch from the constant struggling to stay afloat.

But she also comes to me with hope.

When we talk about the long hours in the closet again, I ask her what she thought about. What she told herself about being inside. In the dark.

And what she tells me is really a child's eternal hope.

"I kept telling myself tomorrow Mami would let me out of the closet. Tomorrow, Mami will give me clean clothes for school. Tomorrow she will feed me," she says, pushing the last saved bit of pancake around her plate with the edge of the fork, but not eating it.

"Tomorrow she will love me."

* * *

There are starvation habits that linger for Johnnie.

The starvation she encountered as a girl permeates every moment of her life now. Right down to the fact that the girl who was starved has always worked in supermarkets, surrounded by food. No matter where she goes, there is always food available to her. If there is food around her, there is less panic and pain and worry. Less obsessing and ruminating.

And, yet, she doesn't love food. Or the taste of it.

She needs it. But she doesn't love eating.

"I eat too fast," she tells me. "I'm always afraid it will go away, so I have to get it down before it disappears."

She eats to stave off the feelings of hunger. That's all food means to her now.

"I have to live," she says.

It is an uneasy relationship she must manage multiple times a day.

She doesn't care about taste. Food is not about enjoyment. She does not savor any of it. She is the opposite of foodies who post pics of their dinners and cooks who obsess about the provenance of ingredients. She doesn't care if it is fresh or frozen. Or if it came from a farmers market with hefty price tags. She is not going to wax poetic over a homegrown tomato. The idea of posting a dish of food on social media is ludicrous to her, and when I talk about it, she pushes it away as if it's utter nonsense.

"I don't have favorite foods because food goes away, so why bother."

This is how food and attachment mirror each other. In these conversations, you can substitute any food with love and attachment.

She could just as easily have said, "I don't have favorite people because they go away, so why bother."

* * *

Johnnie also talks about her sister making meatloaf and mashed potatoes for her, before things got bad in the house. And how she loved it. She recognizes that cooking for other people is important. She tells me she does cook when she is in a relationship.

Because feeding people is love. She gets that.

But she would never cook for herself or nurture herself in that way. There is still a large part of her that will always feel unworthy of having food.

Johnnie swears her last girlfriend left because she couldn't handle the depths of her sadness.

She talks about eating together.

"When she makes food, I taught her to leave some in the pan," she tells me. "That way I know I have more if I need it."

It is not lost on me that Raffi is the same. I hand him a bowl of mac and cheese.

"Is there more?" he asks.

"Can I get more after this?"

He looks inside the pan to make sure. His body loosens when he sees there is more there and that it has been earmarked for him. In the short time he is with us, he trains me to keep some in the pan for him just in case. He hoards food under his bed. It rots and I find it by smell, but I know that he has to have it there. I replace with fresh after he falls asleep.

We embrace Katja Rowell's trust-based plan for feeding kids who come from hunger. We stock the fridge's snack drawer with healthy stuff—ham, cheeses, yogurts, hummus, veg, pita bread, nuts. We control what kind of food, but he chooses when and how much he eats.

He eats the way Johnnie eats—as if it will vanish, with great anxiety attached to it, and as if it is not supposed to taste good or be pleasurable.

Johnnie lives alone, but still hides her cookies.

"Knowing my cookies are there gives me something to look forward to."

I am reminded of the cookies when I find twenty cups of fruit in syrup Raffi has taken from school, smooshed at the bottom of his backpack. He needs to look forward to them even if he never eats them.

"I like Cap'n Crunch cereal," Johnnie tells me. "I have a pattern. I eat the same things over and over and over again. I live on cereal. Things in bags and boxes. Ready to swallow. Sugar is very important," she tells me.

She buys the same brand of sugar as Estrella had in her kitchen: C&H.

There are so many similarities between Johnnie and Raffi. When she talks about the anxiety around mealtimes, it helps explain his behaviors to me.

"You better make something I like for dinner," he barks at me like a chauvinistic husband, demanding to be served. But I can read the real messages he wants me to hear because of Johnnie: Did you make something I like? Can I eat this? Will there be enough? Are you taking care of me? Do you love me? Am I safe?

"Can I give you a hug while we wait for dinner to be ready?" I ask Raffi, with my arms open. I am moving away from the stove to him.

He struggles with this momentarily. He wants his food the minute he wants it. But then his body softens, and he buries himself into me for a hug. I wrap him up in my arms, hold him tight.

He forgets about being hungry. For a minute. Because feeding him and giving him love are the same thing.

They are the same.

Intertwined, and substitutions for each other.

* * *

I haven't seen Johnnie in a while.

I try to see her multiple times at Smith's. We miss each other.

I text her. We set dates. But something always comes up. She doesn't answer. Or she'll come up with an excuse at the last minute. I invite her to dinner. To small dinner parties. To large dinner parties where she can lose herself. Meals with just the family. Meals with just me.

I invite her to brunch over Easter. Thanksgiving dinner. New Year's Eve. I offer to pick her up. Drive her home. Whatever makes her feel comfortable. But nothing ever really does.

She wants to see me. I want to see her. We are friends now. We are people who hug in the middle of Smith's when we see each other. But the intimacy is hard for her. The closer we get, the scarier our friendship gets. She always cancels.

I worry I might be triggering some of her issues. I don't want to be a nag, or give her anxiety, so I back off. I stop asking her to meet me. But when I back off, I hurt her. She sees David at Smith's. She asks him why I haven't called her.

It's as if I've stopped liking her. She gets mad and refuses to speak to me even when she sees me in Smith's. She is working self-checkout. We have a come-to-Jesus right there. Edie is with me, as usual. She is running a heap of groceries through the machine. We have too many for self-checkout, but it's the only way I can connect with Johnnie.

"I'm sorry," I say, fast, so it's the first thing Johnnie hears. So she can't stop me.

It's the first time I see how vulnerable and wounded she is. It takes a minute, but she tells me how I've hurt her. We talk it through right there in self-checkout. And hug.

Edie tries to ignore our PDA.

I am learning. If I come at Johnnie too fast, she will flinch. She wants to run. If I give her space, she feels abandoned. This is an important dance that will come to dominate our lives as friends.

This is the byproduct of abuse and neglect. Of having a schism in how you attach to people around you. It is the very definition of an insecure attachment. You want them to love you. You need and ache hard for love and attention. But when it comes, it is overwhelming, too intense. Even painful.

She lives in this in-between of wanting love but pushing it away.

Because of her hunger.

It's Johnnie to whom I go for counsel when Raffi struggles hard with food.

And giving and getting love.

4

FOOD THAT IS FAST + FULL OF MEANING

W ARE AT a McDonald's on Boulder Highway. It's 4 p.m. I'm antsy.

David and I are waiting for Chrissy and Jay, Raffi and Desi's mom and dad. The kids are now five and one. They have been with us, as their foster parents, for roughly a year.

This is the most dismal McDonald's I've been in for a while. But this McDonald's serves its community. It exists for everyone, democratically— junkies sliding through their heroin highs and lows over coffee, the Boulder Highway prostitutes taking a bathroom break, neighborhood moms from the nearby weeklies taking their kids there for dinner.

It's depressing, but maybe it's just me and it isn't this McDonald's. Maybe it's because of what we are doing here. We are stuffed into a tiny booth. David and me on one side. Jammed up together. The seat across from us, dead empty. The booth is scattered with French fry bits. The table is sticky.

School kids jubilantly explode through the door. They are laughing. Gossiping. Yelling at each other. Scanning their phones. Suddenly it's the busiest friggin' McDonald's I've ever seen. A bunch of kids hang out by the soda machine, drinking and refilling their small cups.

It's not the sober environment you imagine for a negotiation.

And Chrissy is late.

Chrissy is always late. And not by a little. Not like five minutes or something. She is forty-five minutes late to everything. But I get why she is late this time.

This is not going to be fun.

This is the moment she has been running from, for years. The thing she escapes with heroin. Morphine. Oxy. Fentanyl. Meth. Pot. Benzos. Hard booze. Whatever she can get, although opioids and vodka are her drugs of choice.

We are a half hour into the wait. David is sipping a coffee. I have a Diet Coke, which I got by parting the Red Sea of teenagers around the beverage station.

Jay has been waiting for her outside. He smokes. Crushes his cigarette under his toe and finally lumbers in. He is white. His skin is a deep, deep brown. He is tall, broad-shouldered. He has dopey, blue eyes, the kind like Desi's that slant downward at the edges.

Raffi is not biologically related to Jay. Jay and Chrissy met when she was pregnant with him. But Jay embraced Raffi as his son. Raffi has always seen him as his father.

We wait for Chrissy. Jay makes some excuses, but we all know why she isn't here.

We can't blame her.

We buy coffees for Jay, and for Chrissy when she comes. We chitchat.

How are you?

How is work?

Jay tells us about playing Captain America on the Strip, busking on the sidewalk for tourists. The characters of Hulk, Hello Kitty, Mario Brothers, even young skinny girls dressed as Las Vegas showgirls. These characters on the Strip and on Fremont Street are street performers. They are all managed by companies who lease out the costumes to day workers. The workers make cash from tourists posing for photos. Jay often plays the superheroes because he is tall.

He adds a few packets of sugar to his coffee.

He tells us about the weekly he moved into. The weekly motel is one of those things I've been slowly learning about in Vegas. They sometimes function as low-income housing, even though they cost more than most apartments. Charlie and Tessie live in them. Chrissy and Jay live in them when they have enough money. Jay is not able to make the kind of money Charlie can make because he doesn't have the same carpentry and building skills.

I look up weekly motels on the internet and read that the one Jay is staying at has been called "Roachland" on TripAdvisor. It apparently has legendary populations of roaches and bedbugs. And the occasional scorpion.

"Run! Before the roaches get you!" a reviewer writes.

The name sticks. Weeklies are now "Roachlands" to me.

Jay is squeezed into a one-bedroom with a bunch of people, a sort of commune for panhandlers. When someone disappears—and they always do—he wants Chrissy to move in. She is staying someplace else, he tells me, but offers few details, which means it probably is unstable and unpleasant.

Moving into Roachland will be a step up for Chrissy.

* * *

Chrissy appears outside.

She stays there, despite the relentless heat. She stalks the sidewalk. She smokes and stalks. She avoids our eyes.

One of the teens drops chicken nuggets in the doorway. Kids run by, in and out of the door. There is rattling and banging. Lots of commotion. The nuggets get kicked to the side. They skitter this way and that.

I can't take my eyes off them.

This food is both important—it is still food after all—and disposable.

A necessary dysfunction.

Chrissy's fingers tremble as she holds the cigarette to her lips. The dread is palpable. Jay goes out to her. Brings her the coffee. They stay outside, talking, stalking, drinking from their cups, circling each other.

She drops her butt on the ground and comes in.

We are here to negotiate the open adoption of their children, Raffi and Desi.

* * *

Like Chrissy and Jay, all Raffi wants is to be with his family again. But this McDonald's negotiation means they will never be that same family unit again.

Raffi came to us from Child Haven. Jasmine, his social worker, introduced us to Raffi on a playground inside Child Haven.

He went through hell, she tells me. And it seemed obvious. He couldn't look at me. He was boisterous and angry. Jasmine had been his caseworker through multiple placements and a disruption from his last adoptive home.

She wanted to get his next placement right. A placement that would also accept his baby sister, Desi.

Jasmine has watched Raffi become angrier and angrier. More disconnected from home to home. She wanted this placement to stick.

Jasmine let us know she wouldn't be putting him in our home the traditional way. We will have to visit him a couple times first, Jasmine told us. Maybe a couple day outings together. Maybe an overnight after that.

This wasn't the first time we'd seen this kid. We met him once, briefly, at Child Haven with Jasmine. David and I walked through the campus, with little kids running up to us, asking us if we are coming to take them home.

It's sad to hear a child beg you to take them home. But it's also indicative of living in an institution. No one wants to live in a ward, no matter how nice the living, no matter how kind the staff.

Raffi was found at the intersection of 15th and Fremont Streets, a sketchy block of abandoned, ramshackle motels from Vegas's midcentury heyday and shitty weekly apartments. He was alone, three years old, walking the family dog at 3 a.m. in one of the most dangerous sections of the city. His mom, Chrissy, was passed out. Jay was working the Strip for cash.

Raffi was picked up by CPS and taken into foster care. He never went back home.

When Jay tells the story, he puts the blame on their son.

"He could figure out any lock and get out of the room," he tells me.

"He was always pulling things out of the fridge, always wild and getting into things."

Raffi unlocked the door and left.

For Jay, it speaks to Raffi's superior abilities and curiosity, his ability to pick locks and feed himself. But there is a schism there. Because it's more about being unsupervised, neglected, underfed. It's more about what this child is left to do because no one is paying attention.

Neither Chrissy nor Jay can see that. It is their biggest error.

There are numerous reports in his file of Raffi walking the parking lot of the weekly in nothing but a T-shirt and saggy diaper.

During the time that Raffi was moving from Child Haven to foster home to foster home to Child Haven again, Chrissy gave birth to another child, Desi. She was birthed on a scorching sidewalk in August on Bonanza

Avenue, another bleak and aching part of town. Chrissy was too hopped up on black tar heroin to notice the contractions.

Desi, in the first days of her life, did a step-down methadone program to ween her off opioids. And when heavy drugs are involved, our pediatrician told us, alcohol is usually an issue as well.

"She tried to not drink during Raffi's pregnancy," a friend of Chrissy's tells me over Facebook Messenger. "But by the time she was pregnant with Desi, she couldn't stop."

Raffi could speak only seven words when he was taken into foster care at age three. Seven. He could barely understand simple directions. By the time we met him, he had cycled through five foster homes. He did two lengthy stints at Child Haven. He came to view every adult he met as a potential caregiver. We worried that he would get into a car or enter anyone's house, go anywhere with anyone, as long as they seemed kind enough.

He had been ripped from families that loved him but couldn't handle him. Families that loved him but couldn't take his baby sister. And families who never loved or understood him. Every time his placement was disrupted, it wounded him more and more.

Even now at this writing, I am unable to say whether most of his trauma came from the neglect that comes from addiction and poverty or from being removed from his family and sent through a cascade of strangers' houses. Probably all of it.

Raffi was sickly looking. His muscles flabby from too much sitting around and eating junk food. And he was so constipated, and hadn't pooped in so long, that he was in constant discomfort. He was afraid to go to the bathroom for fear of the pain.

Raffi hadn't come across many of the basics of family life. He didn't know what a vacation was—he thought we were moving when we went to the beach for the weekend. He had never been to a birthday party, so he didn't understand the order of events—play, pizza, singing, cake, presents, et cetera. Or why one kid gets gifts and the others don't. He was wild and angry. He couldn't make eye contact. His paperwork said he has reactive attachment disorder (RAD), the rare but controversial diagnosis afflicting babies in orphanages who aren't held and spoken to, oppositional defiance disorder (ODD), and severe ADHD.

It's like the alphabet soup of diagnoses. We simply refer to it all as complex trauma.

Jasmine was dead honest about his issues. She was not sure he would ever really connect with people. And even watching him play with other kids, it was obvious he couldn't have a meaningful friendship with anyone. Disagreements devolved immediately into punching, kicking, and hair pulling. And there were always disagreements. He had to have complete control and compliance or the relationship couldn't last. He was unaware of the other person in the relationship. He saw only himself. His wants. His needs. There was no empathy. No sharing. No friendship. He was hard on everyone: people, animals. Himself.

If we took this kid, we knew we were looking at a high-needs placement. And that we would be expected to step up for his significant needs. It was on us to figure out if we had what it takes to be foster parents to this kid.

Could we be the parents who deserved to parent this kid?

The main thing we have to decide is how to parent a child who might never get better. We just weren't sure he'd ever be able to bridge the gap of attachment. Lucy and Edie pad out into the dark and sit in our laps. We tell them what we are thinking.

These kids need a home, we tell them.

Lucy is not keen on the brother part, but the baby part is exciting. Edie is not happy about any of it. But I know her; she will soften like butter in a summer kitchen.

Later, I get a message from Darcy, a foster parent who had both Raffi and Desi.

"He needs to be in a high-level therapeutic home," she told me.

She said he was angry, impulsive, physically aggressive. He wreaked hell in their house. She told me her daughter hid in her room for a lot of the placement.

We understand how that happens. I remember Lucy and Edie hiding in their rooms from Jaden and Tyson.

And the baby has her own issues, Darcy shared.

She never sleeps because she is on methadone, weaning off black tar heroin. She might have some early facial feature signs of fetal alcohol spectrum disorder. It was a lot for their family—an angry impulsive mad boy and his equally unhappy sister.

They dropped Raffi and Desi off at Child Haven a week before Christmas. It was too much.

Darcy told me how she had him in therapy four times a week. And OT. And all kinds of doctor appointments. They tried everything to make it work.

"What if she's right? What if we can't handle this kid and his trauma?" I asked David.

We settled in on the patio, slumped into one another. The girls were in their room. I put out some macadamia nuts. I grab a couple cold bottles.

We kept talking into the thick of night, as if talking was actually going to answer all the unknowns.

* * *

In the morning, Joseph's caseworker came over with some paperwork.

It's all perfunctory and quick. Just business.

But I trust her. So I ask.

I tell her about Raffi and the conversation with Darcy, who did her best and wanted so much for the placement to work. But it didn't.

I tell her about all his therapy appointments and doctor visits. All the things she tried.

"What makes us think we will be any different for this kid?"

And she says the thing that maybe is the most life-changing thing that anyone has ever said to me:

"Maybe he doesn't need four therapy sessions a week?" she asked no one in particular. "What if he needs a family where he can just be a kid?"

This stops me cold.

What if he plays ball? And builds Legos? And goes on vacations, and rides his bike everywhere?

Of course, this is bullshit.

Love and bike riding can't save a kid's life or wrangle them into a family. Or heal them from the trauma of a shitty early life, when all those key brain development things are happening. The part of the adoption narrative that has never worked is the one that says love will get these kids through.

It's not true. Loving them is not enough.

But still. It sits with me.

I remember back to when we were preparing to become foster parents.

"No boys. No babies," we said. Just girls, older girls.

But the universe has its plans.

* * *

We picked up Raffi at Child Haven for a try-out visit.

We went to Gravady, an indoor trampoline park. Everyone piled into the car.

Raffi had long hair like David. They weirdly look like father and son, with their auburn curls piled on top of their heads in man buns.

Everyone loved the trampoline park. We ate hot dogs and chips and cans of cold soda. The kids jumped until they were sweaty and exhausted and happy. But we had Raffi for only a few hours. In the parking lot, we told him we had to take him back to Child Haven.

He crumpled into a small ball on the ground. And sobbed. He begged us not to take him back. He cried so hard his body spasmed.

"Hey you," I said as David and I bent down to talk to him. "We are going to come get you next weekend for an overnight visit."

"Would you like that?" David added.

"I don't want to go back." He sniffled and nodded his head.

He cried. But he wasn't sad. He didn't feel sadness exactly. He went right to anger. Everything was anger with this kid. His crying is mad crying, screaming, beating himself with fists. It was a total fight, freeze, or flight situation. He couldn't breathe. He couldn't be convinced that we would come back for him.

And really why should he?

"Please let me stay," he begged. "Please!!" he screamed at us.

We hugged this kid who didn't fit perfectly in our arms yet, because we hadn't had time to connect, to get to know each other. But who was already truly our son, even though we didn't know if he would stay with us forever, or go back to his folks, or to a family member.

Even today, Raffi remembers the very spot where he stood and cried about leaving us. We point it out and relive it every time we go to this trampoline park.

"I was so sad," he tells me.

But he doesn't really remember. Like a lot of adopted kids, me included, the story of his beginning and his family are puzzle pieces he keeps reliving. And piecing together.

And going over and over and over in his mind, so he can create a sense of himself.

* * *

We met Desi in her second foster home.

The family was large and Mormon, with lots of handsome, clean-cut kids, mostly boys. It's the kind of home that is very child-centric. There is a small trampoline in the living room. Lots of sensory toys. An indoor jungle gym and sensory swing set off a living room with a big leather sectional around a large-screen TV.

Always a giveaway.

They put her in our arms. She was beautiful and alert.

"A terrible sleeper," the foster mom, Bettie, says. But we knew this. It's common with drug-addicted babies.

When we got her home, Desi was sweet and sleepless and calm.

"She looks like a sloth," Edie said when she first saw her.

It's sweet. But I also know it is a little bit of a hit. Edie is dubious about the baby. Lucy had been walking around, making her arms into a cradle, letting us know we needed to foster babies, even though the idea of diapers and car seats felt like going backward. But never Edie. Kids had been in and out of our home for a while now. Some they love, some not so much. But all have exhausted and challenged them. We knew that taking Raffi and Desi would be a longer placement, while Mom and Dad worked their reunification plan.

I reminded Edie: We are rooting for the kids to be with their family again.

Edie rooted for them, too.

It takes three months to settle a kid into a home.

That's not scientific. It's what we've figured out for ourselves after some experience. Everything is just figuring it out, trying things, getting to know each other until around that mark.

On the first day he came to live with us, I found Edie sitting in the top bunk. Raffi was next to her. She was explaining a game that he wanted to play on the iPad but didn't know how. She saw me and gave me a little grimace to let me know she was put out by having to be nice to him.

I sent a kiss through the air. She smiled back at me even though she didn't want to.

She doesn't know it yet, but she will be the best big and little sister in the family. The one they all depend on and look up to. The one David and I will depend on and look to. To fill in gaps.

She will struggle. But she will also rise to all of this.

* * *

Raffi is all about the rage.

He hurled objects at animals. He was a destroyer. He hit me. Daily. Kicked. Slammed doors. Punched walls. He destroyed things, dismantled appliances. He was rough with everyone. With himself. If he didn't want one of us to pass, he would stand in front of us, so we couldn't move. He threatened to pummel us if we tried to walk past. He had this face he made, where he lifts up his eyebrows and moves them around, as if he were an evil villain. He thought it scared people away.

This child did everything to scare everyone away.

He refused to be loved. He had one emotion—anger.

"Would you like to ride the scooter?" we asked.

"No," he barked.

"Would you like to have ice cream?"

"No."

"Would you like this Matchbox car?"

"No. Why didn't you buy me two cars?

"I wanted the red one, not the blue one."

One of the biggest surprises about parenting kids from trauma is the appearance of a kind of unexpected entitlement. We think kids who come from hard places will be grateful to have abundance. That they might fall back into a soft pillow of relief because there is abundance. But this is not how the brain works. It's not at all like Oliver Twist and his empty bowl and sad, pitiful face saying, "Please sir, may I have some more?"

Kids with serious issues with attachment, because of neglect or abuse, like Raffi, have no connection to the meaning of gifts. Or where they come from. Or how much they cost. Or why gifts are given. This is a hard lesson for new foster parents. As it was for us with Jaden and Tyson and the garbage bags filled with the corporate Christmas presents they flung carelessly around our house.

"I think the sense of entitlement is partially a foster care/welfare mentality," an adoptive mom (who has given back one of her adopted kids because of their violent behaviors) writes in a chat group: "My kid's bio parents have never worked a day in their lives, yet according to the kids got them whatever they wanted."

But what feels a lot like entitlement—"Why didn't you get me the big one? I want the big one!"—is really a survival strategy that has been woven into the plasticity of the brain during hard times.

Excess is unmanageable for these kids. Too much is painful. Chaotic. It reminds me of the parched Mojave dirt that cries out for rain, and then when the monsoons come, the ground can't take it. Everything floods. The water never seeps in.

A caseworker in the chat group responds to the adoptive mom with wise words:

"An attachment disordered child has no concept of give and take. They just assume that their needs come first. It isn't a result of media, advertising or overindulgence. In their case, it's the wiring of their brains. It's survival," she goes on to say. "Children with attachment disorder don't know how to get satisfaction from inside. They crave the superficial happiness from things. As the child heals, they will learn."

Raffi could be the poster child of this message.

Sometimes David had to pick him up and put him in his room for our safety and for his. David sat with him there so he wasn't alone. There is no "time-out" with our foster (and bio) kids. Leaving them in time-out can feel like being abandoned all over again.

Raffi thrashed. Broke his toys. And punched holes in the walls. Screamed at David, who read a book and talked softly to Raffi, until he had enough. And then David would read to him, and soon Raffi snuggled in closer and closer.

We will have to routinely buy new dining room chairs, as one by one they get smashed and destroyed.

This will go on for years.

He did everything he could to derail being attached to us, and us to him, while experiencing chronic terror that we would send him back to Child Haven.

It is the schism that defines attachment disorder.

And makes it challenging to parent these kids. But mostly, it is hardest for the kids who have to live their lives with this brain.

* * *

Raffi had it out for me.

Because I'm the mom that's there. And not the mom he misses.

I reminded him every day of what he lost.

And he hated me for it.

"I don't think he will ever be able to have relationships with other people," I said to David.

I meant it.

"We will prepare him to be alone and be okay," David said.

And that's what we set about to do.

But we seriously underestimated this boy.

* * *

Back at McDonald's, Jay tells me that Chrissy has bipolar.

That she is unmedicated.

I never find out if this is true. But it makes sense. Chrissy is the youngest of the kids in her family, by a big gap. Her mother remarried late. Her new husband wanted kids, but she was in her forties. And done.

She got pregnant anyway. The age difference disconnected Chrissy from her older siblings. And the air seemed to have gone out of Mom and Dad's energy for parenting as she got older.

Chrissy is oppositional right from the womb.

She pummels her family with anger, mood swings. She starts with drugs as a young teen and dates much older men. She may have been sexually abused by a relative, the family lore goes, but none of her half-siblings are home—they have their own young families. They do not know what is happening with her.

She drops out of school in the eighth grade. Her parents aren't sure what to do with her.

She marries. She cheats and ends the marriage. She gets pregnant with Raffi. CPS chases them from Oakland to Arizona to Pahrump, Nevada, to Las Vegas.

The desert welcomes all the parched people.

They come to Vegas to hustle the streets.

To blend in.

To disappear.

* * *

The courts will most likely terminate Chrissy's parental rights in the coming months.

We know it.

She knows it, too, in theory.

She is still deeply in denial. She does whatever she can to push it all away. Or numb it. Because it is the worst-case scenario. The nightmare. Nothing is harder than this.

And everything is hard.

Chrissy has not worked her program with CPS. She screams racist slurs at caseworkers. She hangs up when CPS calls her. She lets drug-addled friends yell into the phone at her social worker. She refuses to tell them where she lives or let them come out for a home visit. She puts them off. Drags things out. She wastes people's time.

Mostly, she does this because her life is a mess, and she has no help. She flails emotionally because she barely has a support system.

She wants her kids back.

She wants to mother them, but she has no ladder to climb out of this hole. And no one is extending one to her.

She screams at people because she is untethered by her powerlessness.

And when that happens, she scares people with her anger. She feeds the fear middle-class people often feel for people who are poor, addicted, and mentally ill. Different.

They see her unruly, impolite behaviors and label her "dangerous." They avoid her. Stay away. They do not help her. They leave her twisting in the tornado of her life and are not at all shocked when she cannot right herself.

The solution, of course, is to abandon Chrissy as collateral damage and adopt out her kids. Increase the domestic supply of infants at the cost to people who are the most vulnerable.

Chrissy's situation is not Destiny's.

Chrissy is not a mom who needs a hand or a break. Chrissy's problems are entrenched. So complex and rooted in the drugs she uses to self-medicate, and whatever untreated mental illnesses she has, the sum of her traumas, that it would take a team, a concerted effort, a program with intense and consistent follow-up and outreach to support her, over years, into a better life.

It would be complex.

It would take years to unravel her.

It would be fraught with multiple failures: two steps forward, one step back.

There wouldn't even be a guarantee it all would work.

But we, as a country, don't have the bandwidth or the stamina for this kind of open-ended commitment to humans in our cities. It's easier to see people like Chrissy as collateral damage. And go in and save the kids by adopting them out to healthy people with easier lives and more privilege.

But what if our goal is different: What if the goal isn't to save the children but to save the family?

* * *

Chrissy cries as soon as she slides across the booth, and Jay drops in after her.

Jay grabs her leg. I grab her hand across the table. David offers encouraging words. I don't have any words. We are taking her children.

We chitchat about the kids at the table. I show her a video of Desi trying to say "pumpkin," which comes out "pom-pom." We all laugh.

A moment of relief and camaraderie. Then to business.

Chrissy wants every holiday with the kids. She wants overnight visits. They want us to drop the kids for Christmas dinners and birthdays. She envisions co-parenting, making decisions together, sharing the children. She might not be able to sidestep the strict boundaries of CPS, but maybe through the open adoption she feels like she can slide into their lives. In through the back door.

I get it. I would do the same. She is fighting for them the way she can.

A pause. She is gasping for air. Crying again.

Jay squeezes her knee. He is wiping his eyes. I hold her hands, as if that will catch her, stop her sliding off the cliff of her own despair.

The teenagers are leaving. Noisy laughter grows and echoes around the door. They do not notice the life-changing revelation unfolding in the front booth. They walk over the dirty nuggets. They don't notice someone's world caving in, her world rocking, back and forth, in an ocean of roiling sadness.

And it is invisible. To McDonald's. To the kids.

"I just want Raffi and Desi to be happy," Jay says, all of a sudden.

We all turn to him. It is part selflessness, part love, part experience. He has lost a child before. He has barely been a father to his sixteen-year-old daughter, Fiona.

Chrissy hyperventilates.

My mother-heart hurts for her. But my mother-heart also hurts for Raffi and Desi. Because they will carry all the damage she has caused. It will be a lifetime getting out from under this trauma. I'm juggling anger and empathy as we negotiate. I love her, as she brought these children into the world. Into our world. They and she are inextricably connected.

To love them is to love her.

But I also have rage. Pure. Unadulterated. Fucking in-your-face rage. At her, for the neglect of the children's spirits and bodies. For all the things she did and didn't do to them. And for them. For all the baggage they have to carry. All that crazy brokenness that is so hard to fix, because of what Chrissy and Jay did and didn't do, at the most critical stages of their kids' development as humans.

It's complicated. I love her. I feel her loss, the gravity of what she is losing at this table in this shitty McDonald's.

And I want to punch her in the face.

I hold all of that in me.

Love and rage.

I'm sure she has both love and rage for me, too.

This is how we stay in this together. Chrissy and I are connected, irretrievably, by the most severe extremes of our emotions.

I muster all of my directness. I carefully outline what we are prepared to give and not give. Yes, they can visit the kids, whenever the kids want to visit. And this could be often enough, as Raffi loves them and wants to see them. We will send videos and pictures. I already do that. Several times a week. As is my nature, I will stay obsessively in contact with her. She will not lose track of the kids.

Jay technically has no biological claim to Raffi, but he will have a claim with us because Jay matters to him. They can FaceTime the kids anytime. We will invite them to plays and recitals and games and school events. And birthday parties and holidays.

Chrissy and Jay listen and absorb. They stop crying.

There is banter now. Another reprieve. A joke about Desi being the spitting image of Jay. We smile. All together, just thinking of her. We have this one enormous thing together—we all love the hell out of the kids.

This makes us family.

We agree to proceed . . . despite their nagging fear that we will take their kids and run. Understandable. And for us, our own worries about the hard truths of addiction and mental illness, and how that will be a big part of family life going forward. Also understandable. We know, from Charlie and Tessie, not to expect too much.

We hug. I tell Chrissy to text if she needs to talk.

She will call me later. She doesn't have a lot of support outside of Jay.

David and I slide awkwardly, wearily, from the booth. I refill my Diet Coke on the way out.

There is no one around the soda machine now. Without the raucous kid energy, the place feels like an empty cave. We step over the seemingly indestructible nuggets. Chrissy and Jay are standing outside, smoking, silent. Her face is still wet. Sad.

It takes me days to shake off their sadness.

I cannot pass a McDonald's without feeling it. There are McDonald's everywhere in Vegas.

I feel the sadness many times a day.

* * *

The best visits with their parents, for Raffi and Desi, happen at McDonald's.

With Chrissy and Jay always thirty or so minutes late, there is extra time for Happy Meals and fun in the Play Place. When Chrissy and Jay arrive, I slide out to the other room.

I keep one eye on things through the window that surrounds the Play Place. Write in my book. Scroll through my phone and sip Diet Coke.

McDonald's may be criticized, and rightly so, for its large-scale impact on greenhouse gas emissions, and for making food that is chemicalized, nutritionally lacking, and served in large portions at cheap prices, but for many, it's a refuge. Like other privileged New Yorkers, we made big parental pushes to keep Lucy and Edie out of fast-food joints. Raffi, however, already grew up on fast food. It was what Chrissy and Jay fed him—McDonald's, 7-Eleven, gas station food—because it was affordable and filling.

And he loves it.

It evokes the same sense memories in Raffi as Grandma's chicken and biscuits. But McDonald's itself is not pure evil.

McDonald's offers something substantial to the communities it inhabits.

For my son and many kids in the system, fast-food restaurants offer comfort. They provide consistency and permanence in their unpredictable lives.

The burger always tastes the same. The nuggets. The fries. They never change. And wherever you go, whatever family takes you in this time, no matter how many times you move, the Play Place rocks the same colors. The same netting. The same slides and tunnels. The same smell. The same place to take off your shoes and push them into the little shoe holder that is the same in every franchise.

As foster parents, our first move after picking up new kids is to hang out at McDonald's. Just as we did after picking up Joseph from Child Haven. It's a familiar, neutral place to take a breath, size us up, and meet the other kids in the home. They get to run around, laugh for a bit. And break the ice.

Starbucks calls itself "the third place," the space we inhabit outside of home, work, school. But McDonald's is America's third place for a much larger, if less privileged, population. This is where the complexity of McDonald's as a company comes in, because in many ways it is a restaurant that offers a safe space to people not usually allowed to have safety in public spaces.

For the unhoused, addicted, and the hardest-struggling people in our communities, McDonald's offers luxuries, like Wi-Fi. Cheap food. Bathrooms. Outlets for phone charging. And a lenient staff who often allow people to hang out in booths, sipping coffee. It's a place to connect with other people, where no one will shoo you away.

This helps folks flex the social muscle that keeps them from being and feeling isolated.

". . . McDonald's provide[s] . . . the chance to make real and valuable connections," writes Chris Arnade in *The Guardian*, in a piece called "McDonald's: You Can Sneer, but It's the Glue That Holds Communities Together." He goes on: "When faced with the greatest challenges, with a personal loss, wealthier Americans turn to expensive therapists, others without the resources or the availability, turn to each other."

For many months, Raffi and Desi have visits with Chrissy and Jay at whatever McDonald's is closest to where they are living. It changes often to accommodate them.

Then one day something pivotal happens at a particular visit.

Chrissy and Jay bring an extra guy along to the visit.

His name is James.

I met James before. His face is cut up by meth. Most of his teeth are gone. He wears a biker patch on his leather jacket, but he no longer has a bike. The first time I met him, he opened with the statement that all his kids are in foster care.

I think he tells me this to make a connection with me as a foster mom.

It backfires.

James is supposed to be Chrissy's fiancé. I suspect she and Jay are still together and scamming him for his disability checks. This is dangerous business—James is erratic and unpredictable.

One night, in a meth-fueled stupor, James threw Chrissy across the room. He slammed her into the nightstand by her bed. Chrissy sent me the photos. The lamp and table were busted up, and so was Chrissy. Her back and legs were covered in bright, flaring purple and yellow bruises. Her face was puffy and swollen. There were welts around one eye.

She called the police. But she was fucked up herself. She went ballistic on the cops as they pulled up. She screamed and raged. They threw her, not James, into the Clark County Detention Center.

I do not like James at all. I don't trust him. So much so that when he walks in, a part of me shivers a little, electricity flaring along my skin. He is worrisome.

James stays outside. He is smoking, pacing. A wild animal.

But then he comes in. Chrissy is holding Desi. She is standing in the Play Place. Raffi is playing in the tubes. I watch the three of them, Chrissy, Jay, and James, talk. Then point fingers at each other. Chrissy gets mad, spitting mad. She is in James's face. With Desi in her arms. She is screaming at him about rent money. He is screaming at her about rent money. Desi looks toward me through the window that separates us. She is terrified.

I am off the chair and running.

Being in Nevada—a state that often runs blue at election time but has a thriving and entrenched pro-gun, Wild West, don't-tell-me-how-to-live, libertarian bent—I'm completely terrified that someone will pull a weapon.

Desi sees me. She reaches out for me. James pulls his arm back, his hand balling into a fist. His face is a grimace of anger.

I push my way in. I pull the baby out of Chrissy's arms. Then I grab her arm and pull her out of the fight.

I am the disapproving, scolding adult. They are the grumbling children.

"James needs to leave the property if you want the visit to continue," I say to her, loud enough for James and Jay to hear.

I want the visit to be over. It should be.

But Raffi still needs to see her. He shouldn't have to pay the price for her bad judgment. I let him have her for a little longer. But I settle myself at a table inside the Play Place. Desi sits on my lap for a bit, before she pushes herself off me and runs to Raffi.

I have to report the incident.

Mandatory reporting again. But unlike with Destiny, this one is clear-cut. There is imminent danger to the kids during a visit in the community. This is a no-brainer.

As a result, the kids' social worker calls off all visits at McDonald's.

This is a huge bummer for Raffi.

Having visits at Child Haven is a constant stressor for him. Every time we go, he thinks I am taking him back there forever. His body tenses. He starts kicking the back of my seat. He asks me over and over: "You aren't leaving me here, Mama?

"Don't go far away, I want to make sure I go home with you?"

I promise him over and over again.

"Who is my favorite boy?"

"Me."

"Who is the boy I love most in the world?"

"Me."

"Who is the fastest boy in BMX?"

"Me."

"Who is never going to live at Child Haven again?"

"Me."

We repeat this every night and right before visits.

Still, he doesn't trust us yet.

Trust will take years.

* * *

Court dates are looming. Every day Chrissy is closer to losing the kids for good. It wears at her. When she comes for visits, she is weepy and depressed.

In fact, Chrissy is a becoming a ghost.

She is gaunt and frail. She has mystery illnesses. Her face is pulling in on itself. She tells me she is clean, but it feels like whatever she is doing, she is doing more, not less.

Her eczema flares. Her skin is dotted with scars and abrasions. She skin-picks obsessively. She colors her hair all kinds of extreme shades. Bright pinks. Neon blues. A mad red as she begins to deteriorate physically, as if she's trying to distract the world from what is happening to her.

In one of Raffi's favorite photos of her, Chrissy's hair is a brilliant deep red, nearly the color of prickly pear blossoms and rambutans. She is smiling from behind her fingers. Neglect, poverty, and a whole lotta meth have taken most of her teeth.

She doesn't like to smile.

If we show up for a visit, and she doesn't come, Raffi is a mess. This happens so often, CPS workers require her to call in. I start not telling Raffi when we have visits scheduled with Chrissy until I get a text from her that she is truly coming.

The visits with Raffi and Desi, when they do come, are nightmares for all of them.

Chrissy is sad. She cries a lot. The kids are a reminder of what she has lost.

At the visits, the baby is unsettled and unbonded to Chrissy. She gets no satisfaction from this baby who barely knows her. They have no history.

And Chrissy favors Raffi anyway.

Chrissy focuses her attention on Raffi, showing him her deep, deep sadness at losing him. He tries to comfort her. But he's only five. He quickly tires of caregiving for his weepy mother. He runs off to play. He roughhouses with Jay. She gets morose. Then angry.

She demands he hug her. Love her. Take care of her.

He devolves into anger. He pushes her away. He says things he doesn't mean. He tells her she is no longer his mom, that I am his mom.

He wants to hurt her.

And when he does, she hurts him right back.

This is so complicated and unexplainable to a five-year-old. It is so above his pay grade, he needs to hit things after every visit.

"Raffi hurt my feelings today," Chrissy yells to me when I come to grab the kids after the visit.

She is across the room. But she is talking to me, loudly.

Raffi escapes under her arm. He throws himself on my leg.

"He is a bad boy," Chrissy shouts at Raffi. I come out of the foster parent room to meet them. She hands me the baby, who has her arms out.

"Chrissy was so hurt," Jay chimes in from behind. He is always on her side.

"She was crying in there today," he tells me, tattling on Raffi.

He wants me to punish Raffi for hurting her.

"Raffi said I'm not his mom," Chrissy whines to me, like I'm her parent.

I hug her.

"I'm sorry. I know that hurts you," I say.

I look right into her eyes.

"You are his mom," I say. "He's going through a lot. But that never changes."

She looks back at me. Smiles. And covers her mouth with her hand.

A caseworker arrives to check on the commotion. Chrissy pulls herself together and holds her hand out to Raffi. She makes the American Sign Language sign for "I love you."

Their special goodbye.

He does it back at her. They touch hands. And he sprints toward the door.

In the parking lot, he explodes. Screams. He kicks the seat of the car. Not a little. Hard. He rattles the car with his anger. He punches himself in the head. Over. And over.

I suggest McDonald's.

His body pauses. He listens.

I make a deal. Drive-thru only. Because the other kids are home and probably super-hungry.

He reluctantly agrees, whining about missing the Play Place. He needs to run the tunnels and tubes. He needs to shake out some of his anger. But we have other kids who have needs, too, and they are waiting for me to make fish tacos. Little grilled parcels of cod in warm corn tortillas with pickled red cabbage, slices of jalapenos, squirts of lime, and thick gobs of crema.

Raffi isn't there yet, with fish. But he is getting more adventurous. He tries more foods. But today he needs the comfort. He needs to know some things are always the same.

Our love. And those cheeseburgers. Plain, just cheese, meat, and bun.

He gets a Happy Meal and a small, bubbly 7-Up.

He chows down the last of his cheeseburger.

"Bad visit," I text David.

When we get home, I grill the cod outside and put out all the things for the tacos on the butcher block in the kitchen. Lucy and Edie eat. Desi stuffs fish in her mouth. Most of it goes on the floor. David grabs a taco to-go. He and Raffi head off on their bikes.

David takes him riding through the tiny back streets of downtown Vegas. They ride out the rage. The confusion. Until the desert sky is on fire, with the orange of chrysanthemums, the purple of lavender, and the pink of camellias.

They ride and ride, until Raffi comes home exhausted and sweaty. He is calm now, bonded to David.

He is so wiped out, he sleeps.

* * *

The court date for TPR arrives.

TPR is short for termination of parental rights. It means that this court date could give Chrissy and Jay more time to work toward getting their kids back. Or it could end all their rights as parents.

But she hasn't been compliant—and compliance is everything—and this will weigh against her.

Chrissy and Jay do not show up to court.

This is a fairly common thing for parents losing their rights. A foster parent in an online chat wrote: "They didn't care enough to even show up to court for their kids."

But this is a misreading of their absence, I think.

Many folks in the system have poor emotional supports, which have contributed to losing their kids. The very idea of being present while the courts remove their children permanently makes it unbearable.

To have it happen is terrible. Unrecoverable. But to be present and watch it happen is a brutality most of these folks can't manage. I mean imagine it for a moment: the court is taking your kids away and you get to watch that happen and hear how you have failed them and created this pain for yourself. It is forcing people to sit in their powerlessness and inequity and be mindful of it.

Chrissy cannot face losing her kids. I can't blame her.

But because she doesn't come, the courts have no choice anyway. She seals her own fate. They terminate their parental rights.

I am there. I go early to look for her. To hold her up. To remind her this is not the end. But they are not in the chairs outside the courtroom.

I look in their usual smoking places. Nothing.

I call her. I leave a message offering to come get her. She must be falling into a long, black hole. There is no response for hours.

I can't let it go.

I drop Edie off at the gym for her contortion training. I pull into a nearby McDonald's parking lot. It is familiar. And empty. I order a Diet Coke at the drive-thru, and park under trees and pretend the spot is beautiful. I roll down the windows. The cool evening floods the Jeep. Not knowing what to say, I text:

"Hi. How are you?"

She responds from her newest number.

"Hey Kim, this is my state phone. I can only cry and call. I can't get video/picture mail on here."

Another text pings.

"Can you talk?" she writes.

I take a drag of the McDonald's Diet Coke, letting it course through my body. I slump into the seat and call.

The first notes of her "hello" feel like a deep, animal howl. A mother who has lost her babies. It cracks me apart.

I cry. She cries. We are silent and sniffling for a few minutes.

She coughs, hard. I listen and wait for her.

"I'm sorry," I say. "I'm sorry."

And I am. I know that any time I'm happy that we get to have these kids in our family, and I'm happy a lot, I am trampling on her. I am winning because she is losing.

One mother takes another mother's children, which feels like the exact opposite of mothering.

She tells me she loves me.

"I love you too," I say.

"I know you love them, and you and David will take care of them," she adds.

"You are going to be in their lives," I say. "This doesn't change our relationship."

But I know it does. There is no hope that she can get the kids back legally and she is in no shape to parent them. In a way, I used to work for her. I was standing in until she could catch up. But now, she works for me. I am the acting-mother now, and she is in the background pining for glimpses.

This is uncomfortable.

There is silence.

"I could use this time to get myself together," she says, tentative. It's almost in the form of a question, as if looking for permission.

"Yes," I say. "And the healthier you are, Chrissy, the more your kids will have you in their lives."

I mean it. If she gets well, she can be in their lives as much as they want. The things she wished for across the McDonald's table—unsupervised overnights and holidays, co-parenting together—could conceivably happen.

And yet a question nags down deep.

Do I mean it?

Do I think she can do this? Have I actually given up on her? The way I gave up on Charlie and Tessie?

As soon as the phone clicks off, the world gets lighter and breezier again. I realize I've been holding my breath.

I breathe. Inhale. Exhale. And drive out of McDonald's. I pick up Edie.

I feel the warm air sliding through the open windows. I love a Nevada night. I know my way around now. It's been long enough to figure out the shortcuts and take the back streets like the locals do. And then, like locals would rarely do, I turn left at the Cosmopolitan to take the long way home along the Strip.

Las Vegas Boulevard is throbbing tonight.

I see crowds of people crushed together at stoplights, and it's the balm I need. People hold yard-long alcoholic slushy drinks, and sip on them through straws. Boys hang on to girls. Girls hang on to girls, and people pash on each other. Friends from other places laugh and take pics of themselves.

It makes me feel like there is more than loss.

I drive slow. I take in the people, the celebrations, the revelers. I see you, fuck boys and girls in skimpy latex dresses, those heels that make you walk like a newborn fawn after a few drinks. The gamblers, the moneymakers, and the people who lose it all. Scraps of music come from cars and casinos. I smell cocoa butter and cigarettes. A couple ladies are dressed as show girls, in costumes too flimsy and cheap and crudely spangled to be the real thing. But the crowd loves them anyway. There is the smell of pot. Pungent and familiar.

It all feels so wild and unruly and fun.

Edie puts on Lady Gaga's "Born This Way." Loud. It's what we play every time we drive the Strip.

Edie rolls down the windows.

It's perfect.

I turn it up even louder.

I've got light on my face from the neon bouncing off the rearview.

Did you know neon is one of the things that stars are made of?

Did you know that even though my son will be adopted by people who love him and whom he loves, he will always pine for his first mother?

Did you know neon is the fifth most common element in the galaxy, but on Earth it is beyond rare?

We are all born superstars.
Did you know that this loss will define his life?
Did you know neon isn't even used in signs anymore, it's all LED now?
Did you know that this loss will define Chrissy's whole life, too?
I'm on the right track, baby, I was born to survive.
Did you know neon is invisible?
Did you know she is invisible?
She is. And so is her pain.

* * *

I've learned some big lessons about adoption. One of them is that it brings great joy and great loss.

Now, with Raffi and Desi, half my kids are adopted.

I'm adopted.

The first loss of adoption belongs to the birth mother. Sometimes, her loss begins before the baby is even born.

"The promise that birth mothers would surrender their babies and 'move on' turned out to be a lie."

Kelly O'Connor writes in a 2021 *Time* magazine article, "They did not go back to normal; they did not forget. Far from a youthful mistake they could leave in the rearview mirror, the experience became a pivotal life event."

Then there's the loss the children face.

Adopted kids suffer a trauma the minute they are born. This happens at the separation of them from the person who birthed them. Adopted kids manage all kinds of attachment trauma, lack of self-identity, fear of abandonment, anxiety, depression, a sense of not belonging to either our birth or adoptive families, feeling like outsiders in our own families.

Sometimes the first people we know who share our biology are our kids.

It is a truly glorious feeling to see your own person reflected back to you for the first time. For me it was like finally my feet finding the ground. Adopted kids often feel they have to do more, and be better, just to breathe the same air as other people. We learn easily to be grateful for our new life, for what we have been given. The fear of being given away can be chronic and terrifying.

I mean, if our moms gave us away . . . then who the hell is gonna keep us?

Many adoptees, not surprisingly, are devout people pleasers.

My own experience is common enough. I was born in the Baby Scoop Era. I was one of two million white babies adopted out during the 1960s in the United States. This was a few years after loosened sexual rules and the invention of the pill, but before the 1972 ruling allowing unmarried people the right to use the pill. *Roe v. Wade*, which provided for legal abortions, would happen a year later.

The Baby Scoop Era shows us the long-term effects of children being separated from families of origin. It's where we hear stories of moms who didn't want to give up their babies. Or were coerced. Even forced.

In the '70s, attitudes shifted.

White moms began keeping their babies, getting abortions, and using birth control to prevent pregnancy. This lowered the number of available domestic babies for adoption and pushed white hopeful adoptive parents into foreign countries to adopt their infants.

This spawned an evangelical movement that called people to go out and adopt "orphans" as a benevolent Christian act. It was grounded in Bible verses, missionary work, and pulpit sermons. Much of this was well intended and there were, of course, many kids in genuine need. But as demand for adoptable babies exploded, so, too, did corruption.

Take the example of a boy named Subash, whose mother Sivagama was profiled in a *Mother Jones* article written in 2009 by Scott Carney.

Subash was kidnapped in Chennai, India. Thrown into a rickshaw. Taken to an orphanage where the kidnapper was paid in cash for him. He was adopted by a family in the Midwest.

Sadly, such stories are not rare.

In Subash's case, Sivagama and her husband spent years searching for her son. They hired private detectives and reduced their whole family to poverty trying to find him. When they found him, they hoped to have contact with him.

They didn't even want a claim to him.

Just to speak to him. To have him in their lives.

The adoptive parents refused all contact, saying to Carney: "We have to consider our son's best interest. What would it do to him if he found out?"

But really the question is: What will Subash think of his adoptive parents when he finds out they knew his origin story all along and lied to him?

How will Subash be okay in the world when he learns his entire childhood is a lie?

How can he be whole when so much has been taken from him?

When Subash's adoptive mom said to Carney, "To him, India does not exist," the adoptive parents lost me.

Adoption—and in this case transracial adoption—didn't just remove the child from his home. It removed him from his people. His devoted family. His customs. Who he intrinsically is as a human being. His parents who love him and wanted him and moved the earth to get him back.

Subash will spend his life trying to put together all the puzzle pieces of who he is.

* * *

Corruption can also extend to CPS, which can be overzealous in taking kids who do not need to be separated from their families of origin.

It's not that social workers aren't hardworking or compassionate. In fact, it's the opposite. They are overworked, underpaid humans who love children, and they are the first ones to be looked at when a kid is hurt or killed in their family. In Vegas, I have never met a caseworker who didn't absolutely love children and try to do their best by them.

It's not the workers; it's how the system is built. And the culprit is neglect.

Neglect is nebulous. It can be lack of food, inadequate housing, lack of clothes, leaving the child by themselves without proper supervision. Of course, there are parents, like Estrella, who are withholding these needs on purpose. But most parents in neglect situations are poor. They are struggling to provide for their families.

They are having trouble keeping the lights on.

They are running from food panty to food pantry trying to cobble together dinner.

They are working full-time without childcare because it's unaffordable.

They are cutting corners and making poor decisions because they are stressed and desperate.

But instead of helping these families with money, childcare, and support, CPS often takes their kids. Much like mandated reporting, the system doesn't offer a lot of other options.

What happens next tacks on more work to get your kids back. Hoops to jump through. Classes to take and therapies they must engage in. We set up court date after court date and make them run complicated gauntlets of services to prove their worthiness to keep their kids in their lives.

"After 5 months of going to rehab, going to therapy, going to parenting class, seeking domestic violence counseling, and a negative hair follicle test, I'm getting my daughter back!!" writes a woman in a Facebook support group for biological parents with kids in the system.

Meanwhile, foster parents are given a subsidy to pay for the things that same child needs.

Here in Nevada that is roughly $20 to $50 a day based on the ages of the kids and whether the foster parents are taking in kids with higher levels of need.

It's not a ton of money, but it helps with extracurriculars, clothes, and necessities.

Foster parents are given full Medicaid (my youngest kids have much better insurance than the rest of the family). And access to all kinds of therapies and treatments. Here in Nevada, we have a program that pays for all or most of daycare for kids in the system, newborn to school age. And if we don't know how to navigate the system, there is a group of veteran foster parents, called Foster Parent Champions, that can help guide us.

But what if the biological families got that extra $20 to $50 a day?

What if, when CPS rolled up to someone's door, they breathed a sigh of relief because help is here?

What if free daycare was available for every family, particularly struggling ones?

In 1997, the Clinton administration enacted the Adoption and Safe Families Act (ASFA). This government grant focuses on permanency for kids. It supports all kinds of foster placements, and the federal government reimburses the states for their expenses.

The system is incentivized for adoption by the foster parents, not the families of origin. There is less incentive for agencies to pursue reunification. In fact, part of ASFA is often called an "adoption bounty."

In a 2019 examination of the foster care system for *Talk Poverty*, Richard Wexler, executive director of the National Coalition for Child Protection Reform, speaks to the incentives to get foster parents to adopt. "Adoption bounties range from $4,000 to $12,000 per child," Wexler says, "the harder the system deems the child to place, the higher the bounty."

He goes on to explain that for states to get the money reimbursed, they must have more adoptions this year than last. This incentivizes agencies to adopt out kids to foster parents to secure that money. And they have to keep up the pace to finalize more adoptions every year.

Add this to the murkiness of neglect. The racial and cultural bias, which lands a higher proportion of Black children in care almost across the board. And how observers identify neglect differently—what is the difference between "free-range" kids and neglected kids, for example?—and it's no surprise that CPS can often be viewed as predatory and overreaching.

Even among veteran caseworkers, according to Wexler's research, there is as much as a 50 percent disagreement rate about whether a child should be removed or stay in the home.

And this is because neglect is stubbornly fuzzy and defies clarity. And is mostly in the eye of the beholder.

The system also pits foster parents against biological parents. And this is, perhaps, the saddest part of the story for me.

Birth moms occupy two divergent spaces in American life. One says they are heroes, selfless. These women are seen as making a choice to put their babies up for adoption. This is seen as the highest form of love—the woman who gives away a child for their own good is the most selfless. The worthiest of our respect.

The other is the woman who loses her child because she is flawed, poor, incapable. Irresponsible. In the same way we can see people with schizophrenia only as either brave overcomers or derelicts. Or women as Madonnas or whores. We see birth moms as either cartoonishly brave or low-rent abusers. And if they fight for their kids, we often view them as selfish.

Foster parents often don't know why kids are in their care. So many of us try to fill in the blanks, with bits and pieces from social workers, anything we can find online, and the kids themselves. The idea that "the kids must have been taken for a reason" is something that feels pervasive.

Bio families see us as part of the system, which we are. And foster families see bio families as categorically neglectful before we even know the facts. Instead of foster families working with families of origin to get children as quickly back into their homes as possible, foster parents are given all kinds of messages that the kids in their care are better off with them.

This is backed up by a 2002 Purdue University study, helmed by Kathryn A. Sweeney. The study looks at how white adoptive parents feel about the mothers and fathers of their adopted children of any race. What she found was that 40 percent of people blamed "individuals for their financial position and thought that those experiencing poverty could/should work harder or 'do something' to bring themselves out of poverty."

I often hear foster parents in group chats talking about how their adopted kids' biological parents are "dangerous." Obviously, a small minority of those parents might be actually murderous, but mostly they are simply in more difficult circumstances, and these circumstances might be completely unfamiliar to someone living in a bubble of affluence.

"Adoptive parents perceived their child's birth mother as being irresponsible and making 'bad' choices that lead to pregnancy," Sweeney writes in her study. "Parents in this sample often relied on ideas that stemmed from a culture of poverty framework, rather than considering individual circumstances or larger systemic factors that contribute to pregnancy . . . or ability to keep or care for a child . . ."

This view, that hustle alone creates financial stability, and that poor people lack hustle, perpetuates the idea that taking babies away from poor people is a solution to the problems of poverty, addiction, generational family trauma, and mental illness.

I know this to be true.

In writing the first drafts of this chapter, I am prone to casting Chrissy as the neglectful mom and me as the savior of her children. Every message I get tells me this. It requires an act of will to not think of our family in such high regard.

The established narrative goes: David and I saved those kids. Where would they be without us?

But did we?

What if more resources were put into placing Raffi and Desi with Chrissy's family in California? They had no idea the kids were even in care, and we knew nothing of them.

What if Chrissy had been able to go into a program for addicted mothers? A residential treatment house like the one Tessie went to in Texas?

What if she could receive help and support for her addictions and mental health issues while parenting her kids in a supported environment of professionals who help her make good decisions?

What if social workers had more solutions to offer people that included ways to keep the family together?

What if Chrissy and Destiny got all the resources and support we get for being foster parents before they lost their kids?

We think we can fight these huge societal problems by punishing families at their lowest, when really the only thing that helps mental illness and addiction is treatment. Family separation weakens the fabric of our communities and adds trauma. And the only thing that fights poverty is a living wage, either through decently paid work or government programs.

* * *

"Chrissy is dead."

It's Jay. He is hysterical. Crying. Blubbering out the words.

"What?" I'm not sure what he said.

"We were watching movies," he tells me.

I'm pacing in the street. Barefoot. I am scared to be in the house in case the kids see my face and demand to know what's happening.

"We, um . . . James and I . . . thought she fell asleep . . ." He can barely get the words out.

"I tried to wake her up . . ."

James. Of course he is there.

"But blood came out of her mouth."

He is sobbing now.

"I gave her CPR, but at the hospital, they said she was brain dead. They let her go . . ."

I let this sink in.

Chrissy is twenty-six.

She's dead. Jesus.

"Tell me the truth," I say in my most serious mom-of-a-drug-addict voice. Because that's what I feel like.

"Was she doing drugs? Drugs she wasn't supposed to be doing?"

I know the answer.

"Yes."

What kind?

"Morphine . . . I told her not to take it anymore. I told her."

He is crying again. Hard.

"The end for her was losing the kids," he says.

"Are you saying she did this on purpose?" I ask.

I'm defensive.

"No. No. I don't think it was on purp . . ." he says, but his voice is tentative.

"I told her she can have a relationship with the kids, Jay!"

I'm screaming at him now.

In the street. Pacing. I do not care if the neighbors hear.

"I told her that," I say again. Because I think if I keep saying it, he and I will believe it.

"I told her she could see the kids. She would be in their lives. Didn't she know that?"

"Yes," he whispers. "I don't know . . ."

He cries some more. He vows to call me tomorrow.

But he digs himself a hole so deep and dark, I don't hear from him again for months.

* * *

I look in the window and see the kids in the house with David.

He is at the stove, spooning salmon rice from a donabe into bowls for the kids and their friends. They are clamoring around the butcher block, talking over one another. Laughing. Arguing. Chatting. Taking turns holding the baby. Like I'm watching a TV commercial. Other people's people. Not mine.

God, how will we tell Raffi?

I walk in. Slide close to them. Whisper in David's ear. I go to the bedroom, and he follows a few minutes later. I fill him in. I cry into his shoulder.

And then we make a plan.

We decide to let it sit for today. We will tell him in the morning.

This is a relief. I need the evening to get myself together. We do the day and get everyone to bed. Which is when I let it all go.

I have a habit of moving into the fridge when things get hard. Not like standing in front of it, and grabbing a pork and cabbage roll, or something. But living in the fridge, taking up metaphorical residence there.

I eat the egg roll. Some flecks of salmon, left over from the rice. I move on to a stone bowl of phat thai, noodles with shrimp, tofu, and peanuts, an Andy Ricker recipe from his book *Pok Pok*, that I had forgotten was there. I use my fingers on the oily, salty noodles. Then I realize a fork will get me more bang for the buck. I go at it that way.

I'm hurting.

And powering down noodles.

Twining them into balls on my fork. Shoving them in my mouth.

I put ice in a tumbler and pour straight tequila. It's not a double. It's a triple or quintuple or whatever. I don't care. I want to be numb.

I am going for black-out drunk. Or falling asleep drunk. Or feel nothing. Ever. Drunk.

I know full well this is not healthy. This is not what functional people do. I am more like Chrissy than I like to admit.

David finds me there, living in the fridge.

I am refilling my glass over and over.

Drinking to meet oblivion.

He puts his arms around my waist and leads me to the quiet, dark living room. I sob endlessly with his arms around me. And when I am finished, he puts a movie on. A dumb comedy. It's the thing I need, and the only thing I can handle. I fall onto his chest and watch. And forget.

It helps.

* * *

I don't remember the night. It is blurry.

But the next day, I remember David and me clearly breaking apart my son's world with the loss of his first mom. And as soon as we do, we are reminded how grief is for children. How it is long and serpentine and unpredictable, popping up and dissolving away, over and over.

Raffi goes from talking about his dead mother to whoever he meets in public, to making up stories about things they did together that clearly never happened, as if he is desperately trying to build back narratives to hold her here. Then his teacher tells me he is sobbing uncontrollably in the schoolyard. The next day, he rolls his fist back and punches an unsuspecting kid in the face. Then another day he is sobbing. Then he is hitting me, pummeling me with his hands and feet, as if he is pissed off that I am here and she is not. And then other days he forgets she is gone and asks me when we can visit her again at McDonald's.

And over and over as his brain processes it all.

He sleeps with the blanket Chrissy and Jay gave him. He sleeps with "Puppy," a soft, floppy-eared dog they gave him during one of their visits at Child Haven. It's technically a dog toy—it has a squeaker in one ear—but he doesn't care. I make him a memory box with photos of him, Desi, Chrissy, and Jay, and things I kept from her, like the roses she made for me from palm fronds, items that she made and sold on Fremont Street. He doesn't talk about it much the first few weeks, even though I check in often, but then the big questions surface.

Why?

"Mommy was very sick, and she took medicine to help her pain," I say, "but she took too much. She was watching a movie and went to sleep. Her body stopped working."

Someday we will tell him everything. We will keep nothing from him.

But not now.

He wants to know about her heart. And her brain, and how they both slowed down and stopped working. He wants to know about the movie.

"People can die while watching movies," he says with extreme confidence.

It is now a fact. He knows these things to be true.

Was I too specific?

Why did I link movies with death? Jeez.

*　*　*

I call Jay multiple times.

I think it would be good for Raffi to work through some of this loss with Jay. But Jay is bereft and unreachable and enveloped in his own rigid darkness. He has little in the way of support, or his own coping strategies or resources, and so he has nothing left for Raffi. He gets high and melts into the abyss. While James receives the support and outpourings on Facebook for losing his "fiancée," Jay will carry the real grief for her, and it will pull him under into the gloom for years.

Then something unexpected happens to help Raffi heal.

Chrissy's death brings one of Chrissy's sisters to Vegas to pick up her body. It's the thing that helps put him back together. And maybe me too.

We meet Chrissy's sister, Jane, who had no idea the kids were even in foster care. Or that her sister was addicted to drugs. Or that she lived in squalor in someone's trailer off Boulder Highway.

Aunt Jane is lovely. She is stylish. She has this youthful, devilish spirit. She refurbishes and sells antiques. In her mid-fifties, she has three grown, beautiful, college-bound kids. A house with a pool in California. No one called her about the kids being in foster care.

Unlike Chrissy, it is easy to love Jane.

In no time, our families are intertwined. Raffi meets his cousin Tommy, who is his age and lives in Vegas. Raffi helps Jane. And Jane helps Raffi. It's not Jay who shares this loss with him. It's Raffi's aunt who is there.

And this is important.

Adopted kids need to have strong relationships with their biological families so they can see themselves. You are your genes. You need them reflected back to you, in the form of biological family, as you navigate your life. If not, then many adoptees will struggle to know themselves at all.

Shortly after, we meet Fiona, sixteen, who lives in Arkansas. Jay's daughter. She and her girlfriend, Mia, start coming to visit Desi two times a year, and they come as much for the rest of us as for Desi, I suspect. And Nacio, Raffi's biological dad, and his daughter, Gabby, who celebrate Raffi's birthdays with piñatas and tamales to connect him to his Indigenous Mexican heritage.

These new people and new information crack him open and give him other people to cling to.

Adding people into our lives changes the game. It's just what he needs.

It's also what we need. Even if we didn't know it.

On Chrissy's birthday, Aunt Jane brings green and yellow helium balloons. She and Raffi launch them into the air and watch them fly away. Desi stretches her hands to the sky after them.

Jane cries when Raffi cries.

There is no substitute for biology.

* * *

"Desi and I will have to get a new family if you and Mommy and Lucy and Edie die," Raffi says to David.

It's been a few months since Chrissy died. David is packing to go on a business trip and I'm packing a cooler for a trip to the park. Raffi is worried David might not come back.

"We won't die for a long, long time," David tells him.

I make a joke about how I'm going to drive him bat-shit crazy well into his adulthood.

"You will always be with us. We will always love you," says David, hugging him hard.

We say this a lot.

But Raffi knows that people die.

He knows caseworkers come in the night and take you.

He knows you can live your young life in Child Haven with shift workers as guardians.

He knows you can be dropped off at Child Haven when you are too much, and you don't even know why and how you're too much.

You can be given back. He knows love has limits.

We repeat. And repeat. "Who is my favorite boy?"

"Me."

"Who is the boy I love most in the world?"

"Me."

"Who is the fastest boy in BMX?"

"Me."

"Who is never going to live at Child Haven again?"

"Me."

We added a last line:

"Who is going to be in this family no matter what forever?"

"Me."

We send David off. Lucy and Edie are out with friends.

It's just Raffi, Desi, and me.

I've got berries, pear slices, little rolls of pink ham, slices of cheese, thick slabs of naan, hummus, and cashews for munching.

But Raffi wants to go to McDonald's.

"I used to see Mommy Chrissy there," he reminds me.

* * *

We haven't been to a fast-food place for a while.

Raffi eats cheese and meats now. And nuts and berries. He tries new foods. Salmon, the gateway fish, is a new favorite, although I cheat and make Vietnamese-style caramel salmon, because he loves how sweet it is.

He is proud when he tries something and finds out he loves it.

Like cacio e pepe. Or a very rare and crunchy on the outside, lightly salted and peppered steak. Once he ate a bite of steak with arugula and we all started high-fiving him like he'd won the Super Bowl.

He loves baked potatoes with butter and chives. He loves roast chicken, especially when he can dip it in the pan fats and sloppily stuff it into his mouth, juice running down his chin.

He ate asparagus once, and even though he made a crazy-ugly face, I picked him up and twirled him around.

Once, when my friends Sonja and Kristy were recording their food podcast for NPR about grasshoppers invading Vegas, we got Raffi to try grasshoppers. They are the very definition of "local."

I make them two ways. The first is a play on Oaxaca-style chapulín tacos with the grasshoppers. I stir-fry them in oil with chili, salt, and lime and serve them in warm tortillas with fresh tomatoes and creamy queso fresco. And a Southeast Asian–inspired salad: crunchy little deep-fried hoppers in chili and lemongrass and seasoned with soy sauce, sugar, and MSG. I serve them on a bed of pea tendrils with a little oil, salt, and lime.

Raffi is more weirded out by the pea tendrils than grasshoppers.

I pay him a buck. He eats them. And happily pockets his cash.

Still years later, he tells the story of how he ate grasshoppers. It is a point of pride.

* * *

I drive to McDonald's, the one by our house with the Play Place.

I order him a Happy Meal with a cheeseburger plain. He is thrilled.

I order Desi a large fry. And a juice.

He asks for a Fanta. Then he runs off and disappears into the big tunnel, so that I only hear the distorted yelling and squealing of kids behind plastic tubing.

I bring the food to the play area and let Desi toddle around. Raffi comes over and slides into the seat near me. Desi climbs into the booster seat. He lays the food out in front of him and makes sure everything is neat and arranged just so. And that his cheeseburger is indeed plain.

He checks each side of the burger and looks relieved. He takes a long slurp of Fanta.

"Mama," he says.

"Yes, baby."

"We used to come here and visit Mommy," he tells me.

He wants to talk about her. This is his memorial service.

"Yes, we did," I say, looking around at the kids playing and the bright, sun-kissed colors. From where I sit, with my soon-to-be-official youngest son and daughter.

"It was fun to be with her, wasn't it?"

"Yes," he says, mouth full.

"What do you remember?" I ask.

He tells me a long story, and I see he is making up details from the room. He is filling in all his blanks.

"It's okay if you don't remember everything about her," I say, reaching out and touching his hand.

"You have so much of your mom in you. She is a part of you."

McDonald's. Where they, and we, remember the dead.

It is more than a third place to us now. McDonald's is a memorial.

A grave. A mausoleum.

A church. A temple.

A monastery.

A holder of my children's memories. It is the physical manifestation of their dead mother. I don't know it yet, but McDonald's will become one of the most significant places in the world to them.

Desi sees another toddler playing with a toy. She climbs out of the booster and runs off.

"I didn't grow in her tummy," he tells me.

"Yes, you did," I say.

"No, I didn't." He takes another big bite of cheeseburger, plain.

"I'm from foster care."

"No, baby," I say, and I reach across the table to stroke his long, wild, surfer curls.

"You don't remember, but when you were very little you came from Mommy Chrissy's tummy."

"No, Mommy."

He is so sure.

"I grew in foster care." He is urgent now. "I come from Child Haven."

And then he takes another bite. And cracks open the toy.

It's cheap and plastic and satisfying as fuck.

He makes the ASL sign for "I love you." I make it, too. We touch fingers. Chrissy is with us.

And then he's gone. Running toward the play structure, laughing.

I let him go. I take a long drag on my Diet Coke.

He has the last word on his own life.

5

CHARITY, THE GIVING + TAKING OF FOOD

THREE TIMES A night.

Refilling the fridge and the pantry pretty much never ends.

Gallons of milk. Lettuce from the homeless veterans' garden. Oranges. Bags of apples. Potatoes. Onions. Zucchini. Tubs of yogurt and cottage cheese. Some chips, crackers. And a few cakes that are sitting right at their expiration dates, but still look magically fancy. One with pink fondant roses. The other with thick shaved chocolate ribbons piled on top.

Then the dry goods. Pasta. Rice. Cans of soup. Chili. And ready-to-eat foods, like Rice-A-Roni for the elderly and people who can't stand at the stove for long. Or who don't have the equipment.

For fun, small containers of nikujaga, a Japanese beef and potato stew I made. Which is just like American-style beef stew except for all the mirin, sake, and soy sauce, and the beef is in thin papery slices, not big chunks. I put it in containers labeled with the date, contents, and potential allergens.

Someone who doesn't have a kitchen will eat that. Probably before they hit the end of the street. So I throw in plastic forks and spoons. Then one last check to make sure some of the soups and ready-to-eat canned goods have pop-tops.

I put out some cat and dog food.

They have to eat, too, but mostly I want to distract Marina, a neighbor, from taking packs of tuna for her cat. I love her and her cats, but I'd prefer the tuna goes to humans. And the cat food goes to the cats.

Although once it's in her hands, it's up to her. I've learned—it's not my business.

* * *

We start the pantry to share a few items with neighbors, just as the pandemic gets rolling.

It's a small gesture. We have a Little Free Library on our curb, housing children's books for the local elementary school kids. But when the pandemic starts and we all go into lockdown, David suggests I put out some toilet paper, pasta, toothpaste, things people might not have been able to buy.

Neighbors take what they need and leave their excess items. It's simple. It requires no work. It's out on the street, having its own life. And because we are all staying inside for the most part, going out to talk to a neighbor from a six-foot distance is the balm we all need.

The pantry connects us to the outside world.

In the first few days, I'm simply putting out extras from my pre-lockdown shopping panic. Like everyone, I'd madly stocked up on rice, pasta, vegetables, frozen foods, beans, meat, and fish. We tossed the suitcases from the hallway closet and stocked it like an underground bunker.

We are set.

The privilege of low-key prepping is not lost on me. Our neighbors on tight budgets can't race around town scooping up heaps of just-in-case groceries.

Preparing for scarcity requires a lack of scarcity.

As the lockdown lingers, our neighbors living paycheck to paycheck start living breakfast to lunch. And lunch to supper. More people come by the pantry. Things are changing.

It's slippage again, a little every day.

Everything is sliding into a new sense of urgency.

It's not just neighbors now. Strangers drive up. They ask if they can take a roll of paper towels and some wipes. Another car idles out front. Six people inside. They ask if we have any food.

I make up plastic to-go containers of our dinner leftovers. Slabs of Ottolenghi's lamb meatloaf with a labneh-garlic sauce, hasselback potatoes drenched in butter, soft roasted garlic, chives, and salt, and green beans with almonds, garlic, and squirts of lemon. I hand it to them through the cracked window.

David makes a lame Marie Antoinette joke. And Desi, now five, is carrying containers out to the pantry, shouting, "Let them eat Ottolenghi!"

I add groceries from my pantry. The folks waiting in the car are so grateful and desperate that it shocks me. It's at that minute, that second in time, that I realize how badly they need this food.

Not want but need.

This moment, this idling car, is the beginning of a change.

My tectonic plates shift.

This is a new world.

* * *

The next day, a local bar owner offers us a beer fridge.

David sets it up curbside. Before I can name it or tell people or decide it's something we are doing, we have a community pantry. This includes a fridge for fresh perishable foods.

It's in our front yard.

Everything snowballs. Word gets round, and neighbors donate often. The fridge fills with fresh vegetables. Shannon, a neighbor and teacher, buys extra leafy greens and fresh cold cuts and cheeses whenever she buys for herself. Others join her. My friends Elizabeth and Larry in San Diego want to do good from their house, and they start sending money to worthy causes. One of them is us. Our pantry Venmo is getting money from more and more folks.

I head to Smith's, and to Costco, and buy what the pantry needs.

The items are gone nearly as soon as they arrive.

People are hungry.

* * *

Bettina lets her car idle with her baby boy, Isaac, inside.

We have to shout over the heinous muffler of her shitty-ass, rusted-out Suburban as we load it.

I only have size 3 diapers. Bettina, who needs size 5 diapers, is disappointed. I offer up baby formula as a sort of peace offering. It's her brand and luckily what she uses. It's something.

Bettina is in her early thirties. Her boyfriend, the baby's father, left her during the first weeks of the pandemic. He felt trapped. He used the pandemic to break out. She is carrying it all. Isolated. She manages depression. She is on leave from the local Amazon warehouse. She is still in the throes of wondering why he left. She reels.

What will become of them?

She isn't sure. She is minute-to-minute now.

We stand in the cool February night. Masks on. Far enough apart not to breathe on each other. Is there a hack? Can we MacGyver a size 5 baby into a size 3 diaper?

We can't. But it's not for lack of trying.

But she takes a frozen chicken and a dozen eggs from my chickens. A box of tampons. The formula. And a large pack of wipes to make up for failing her.

I go back inside our warm, paid-for house. I obsess about diapers. I think about how many folks are swaddling the bums of their babies in dishcloths and paper towels tonight.

* * *

The next morning, a man lingers on the curb. He is looking at the pantry. He is wary.

"Hi," I blurt out. "Everything there is free. Take whatever you want."

His name is Ben. He is here in Vegas to work. From Oregon. He is tall, thin, pale. His beard is scruffy. Ben is wearing working jeans that hang low on his hips. And a T-shirt. He's here on foot.

"I was sleeping in my truck," he says. "I came here to do handiwork, plumbing, carpentry," he says. "Make a little money."

He had a job at $16 an hour. It's hard work. But he loves it. He is good at it. But he doesn't have money for a motel right away, so he sleeps in his car. The police find him. They arrest him on misdemeanor vagrancy. The police throw him in jail for sleeping. They impound his car and his tools.

He loses his job. Because handymen need their tools.

Today is Ben's first official day as an unhoused person. All his security is gone. His plans are faint, fading ghosts. He has two school-size chocolate milks in his hand, an apple, and a small bag of chips in his pocket.

I watch him walk away, down our little street. I yell after him. I ask for his phone number. A way to connect to him. I'm yelling after him in the street, but he raises his hand in a wave and doesn't turn around.

* * *

My phone dings.

"¿Tienes leche?" Cindy texts. "Mi hermana estará aquí en una hora para recogerla."

My Spanish is broken. Cindy forces me to practice Spanish and I help her practice English.

Cindy lives across the street. She helps her extended family with food from the pantry. She hooks people up at her church, too. She donates often. Anything extra she has. Sometimes she comes over with a spray bottle of soap, a roll of paper towels, and wipes down the fridge, an angel organizing my chaos.

We're running low again.

But Cindy knows I have a fridge and chest freezer on the side porch, also from donors. Her sister gets a box of vegetables and fresh meat. Oil and butter. Eggs and cheese. Salt and adobo. Chives. Cilantro and parsley. A bottle of canola oil. Tortillas. And a bag of nixtamal, because I remember her sister makes the tortillas from scratch.

I know what she likes now.

You get to know people.

I'll fill the pantry one more time tonight before bed. It'll be gutted by morning.

There is shame in needing help.

The givers donate by day.

The receivers come in the dark, when no one can judge them.

* * *

"Every time we open the door," Gilda says, "magically, there is food."

Roy + Gilda, unhoused partners from a nearby homeless encampment, have a name for the fridge + pantry.

They call it "The Magic Pantry."

I want to paint the words "The Magic Pantry" on a big board and place it over the fridge and the library, now a dry goods pantry. I refer to them both, in combo, as "The Pantry." I want to paint the fridge all kinds of bright colors and have welcoming words, in lots of languages, written on it that invite people to come and take. I want it to feel welcoming. But everything happens so fast.

There's no time to make things pretty.

The needs are immediate. It's a permanent hustle to keep the fridge full.

A new wave of neighbors drives by. They stop, roll down their windows. I invite them to take and give. The pantry is becoming a hub of socially distanced, six-feet-apart conversation.

Cindy and Sylvia, who lives next door to Cindy, are adding packages of shredded cheddar and Monterey Jack. Both families are from El Salvador. Cindy is a young mom of a baby and a daughter, Sherlynn, one of Desi's best friends.

Sylvia is a young grandma. Her teen grandkids come over on the weekends. The kids help make the street lively and busy. Riding bikes. Kicking balls. Playing basketball on a hoop set up in the street. Sherlynn and Desi ride on scooters. They have matching *Frozen* dresses that make cornflower trails in the wind behind them.

One day, I am making melty, spicy chicken tinga on oily, crisp tortillas. They are from *Tacopedia*, a cookbook Christmas gift from David, a hint to up my taco game. Desi and Raffi take Cindy some tinga.

The tingas are mounded with cold iceberg and slices of avocado. A generous spritz of homemade hot sauce from my garden peppers. A little crema. Some farm cheese I made that reads like queso fresco. Cindy's husband gives a thumbs-up, so I give her a tub of leftover chicken in sauce for lunch the next day.

In a return volley, Cindy makes pupusas stuffed with chicharron, peppers, and onions. A pile of curtido on the side, a vinegary slaw that cuts across the deep savoriness of the masa shell and the pork inside.

I feel so lucky to taste this. And also, to share, back and forth, with Cindy.

Raffi eats his first pupusa. He resists. But I offer him the dollar. He takes the money and a bite. Snatches the dollar. Of course, he loves it.

I text her a thank-you.

It takes a pantry and a pandemic to forge this community.

* * *

"You cooked this fresh?" Danny is asking me. He is holding the bowl.

I'm by his rattly, old black truck on the curb. His window is rolled down.

Danny is better today.

Last time he was here, sometime last week, he was a mess. Sobbing in his truck, full body shaking. The deep, ugly kind of crying where you just can't right yourself.

Danny is in his early thirties. Handy. Has tools in the back of his truck. He is olive-skinned. Loose unruly curls. Scruffy beard.

He is on his way to the Day Laborers Office, the same place we met Charlie. But lockdown work there has been scattered and inconsistent. He's tired. Worried about getting roused by the cops while sleeping. He's been waiting at the Day Laborers Office for days and days.

Nothing yet.

He keeps showing up to the pantry for food.

We let him park in front of the house so he can get some sleep.

"No one will call the police here," I say.

I don't think anyone will call the police. We have cool neighbors.

I warm up leftover pork tingas. Fatty butt meat, and chilies, and sausage meat all mixed together in a stewed tomato sauce. Cold rice that I add drops of water to and reheat. Two eggs over easy, hot sauce, little flecks of cilantro to green up the dish. And ten dollars in gas money.

He needs the heat right now. Vegas is cold as fuck.

* * *

We rarely get snow downtown, but some places, out by the mountains, have it today.

It's dank. The kind of cold we rarely get, that settles into the joints and stiffens them up. We might be able to withstand 117 degrees in the summer. But our bodies balk at 55. We feel drafts like they are polar winds. Our East

Coast bodies have become desert bodies. The threat of precipitation settles into deep tissue so thoroughly you need a scalding shower. Or a seat right at the fireplace to burn it all off.

Danny has neither bath nor fireplace.

I consider letting him come inside to shower and eat, but I made a pact with David about boundaries.

People. Strangers. They come inside of our house all the time now. The doorbell rings all day, long into the evening. We are open to the community. But we can only do this if there are boundaries. Mine are elastic and pliable and negotiable. But David's are clean. Clearly drawn and solid.

I defer to him.

I do not offer Danny a hot shower, or a good night's sleep in a soft, warm bed. Because there are too many Dannys.

He gulps down the food. And sleeps for a while in the cab.

Later, I look out the window.

He is gone.

I'm pretty sure I'll see him again.

But I never do.

* * *

Neighbors start dropping off their extra groceries. The local news makes several visits.

A full-on street pantry in a front yard is a good "feel good" story during Covid. I'm getting used to people seeing me on the local morning shows, but I don't particularly like this.

I don't like being on TV.

I never know what to say. Or I say too much. I drone on about something not important at all. I am unpolished and filled with anxiety. I want to interject "fuck" and other swear words into whatever I'm saying, so I am eternally censoring myself. I freeze up at other times, not sure how to answer. Data disappears from my head as if my brain is a sieve. My hands are everywhere. And my turkey neck is no longer TV ready.

But it's the only way to make sure people know the pantry exists.

I never get better at it. But it becomes less painful.

People ask what I need.

"Bread. Milk. Cheeses. Meats. Greek yogurt. Eggs. Fish. Condiments. Canned Meats. Vegetables. All the damned vegetables. Salady things. Oil. Butter. Salt," I say, rattling off the most popular things.

"Healthy," I say.

For a while, I control what goes inside the pantry. But this changes quickly.

* * *

Clark County School District, in remote-learning mode, distributes school lunches at pick-up spots around town. One is half a block away at Raffi's elementary school.

Each day, the distribution folks drop their remnants and leftovers in the pantry. Suddenly, and unexpectedly, institutionalized food is battling it out fisticuffs style with my feel-good community food.

Clark County School District has a monumental task—they feed some 300,000 kids in the country's fifth-largest school district. The meals they serve have to provide the requisite nutrients and calories set out by the USDA. They have to avoid common allergens and respect cultural preferences in a very diverse city. And they have to somehow stay afloat financially, manage waste, and tend to the special needs of kids living in cars, shelters, apartments with no running water, or Roachlands with broken ovens, no pots and pans, and pests running in and out of the cracks in the kitchen wall.

I understand that this food is a stand-in for families who need to eat. But seeing bag after bag of Doritos stuffed into the pantry, boxes of single-serve Corn Pops and Frosted Flakes, little cartons of chocolate milk, as well as countless chocolate Pop-Tarts and doughnuts, startles me.

It feels so dysfunctional and off to me.

I'm not a food snob—I've just written about our devotion to McDonald's. But I have this vision that the pantry will be a place to find real, whole, nutrient-dense foods. A comforting balm during a rough time. I'm happy offering occasional cookies and cakes, but I want them to be sitting next to vegetables and meats, dairy and grains.

When I think about why this feels important, it reminds me of British food writer and author Bee Wilson's 2022 *Guardian* piece, "When My Husband Left Me, I Headed for the Kitchen—Here's How Comfort Food Can Save the Soul." In it she writes:

> People talk about "comfort food" as if it were a kind of trivial indulgence. But this is missing the point. True comfort food isn't sticky toffee pudding on a cosy night in, or sausages and mash on a crisp cold night. It's the deeply personal flavours and textures you turn to when life has punched you in the gut. Comfort food should really be called trauma food. It's what you cook and eat to remind you you're alive when you are not entirely sure this is true. At least, this is how it has been for me.

Trauma food.

Trauma food is what I'm trying to provide, even though I won't have the words for it until I read Wilson's piece. I want the pantry to provide foods that will help people feel well when maybe they aren't well at all.

Raffi, however, is beyond thrilled about this new packaged food development. He is ravenous for branded food.

There are tacos and burritos wrapped in cellophane amid the prepackaged school options. Chicken sandwiches with lettuce. Quesadillas. And a host of tiny individual packs of baby carrots slung into the back of the fridge, like the nuggets on the floor in McDonald's.

Those little bags of carrots mock me. So forgotten. Functional and yet not.

I grab them, along with little bags of shelled edamame. When I have enough, I open them all up, dice the carrots, and dump them all into cold rice with celery bits, a couple of cracked eggs, scallions, fish, and soy sauce. I add bits of fatty pork belly and make belly fried rice with carrots and edamame.

The fried rice dish gives the scattered bags of vegetables some context. A functionality, instead of just eating them raw or shuffling them around the back of the fridge.

At about 3:45 p.m. each day, the house grows eerily quiet. Raffi and Desi are AWOL. They're out front, little faces pushed up against the door glass of the fridge, like Gollum craving the ring.

My Precious.

For our traumatized kids, the pantry is now a Hieronymus Bosch–level reboot. With an orgy of dyes, synthetic flavorings, chemicals that create texture and satisfying smells, sugar, aspartame, and shitty oils. Substances that disrupt metabolism at a cellular level.

But Raffi doesn't care. He wants to slurp down every syrupy fruit cup. Every toaster pastry frosted with icing. Every juice box. For the longest time, David and I controlled the type of foods he ate at home, while he controlled when he ate and how much. But now, he is delirious over the availability of twenty-four-hour-a-day junk food. It opens up all kinds of questions for me:

Is the pantry just another conduit for giving out junk food?

Should we police the kind of foods we offer?

What is our role in supporting the community?

Why do I not want my own kids to eat this food, but it's okay for other kids to eat it?

These are now questions I'm asking myself daily.

* * *

Clark County operates a 300,000-square-foot central kitchen out by the motor speedway that employs several hundred people to prep, test, cook, and taste a million lunches a week just for Vegas and the surrounding areas. They take feeding kids seriously. They are good people trying to do what they can with what they have.

The origins of corporate school food started decades ago with Reagan-era politics.

The administration slashed federal school lunch funds, which opened the gates for for-profit frozen food manufacturers and food service management companies to get inside school districts. (Remember Aramark? They not only serve prison food, they also serve some children school lunch.) These kitchens are cost-cutting machines. Without government support, schools need to bring in low-cost processed food to help them stay afloat.

Cue huge food companies like Tyson, General Mills, and Kraft Heinz, all jumping into the game.

For them, this is worth billions of dollars in profit. This is paid-for marketing—they are getting into schools early. They are actively setting up our kids' taste preferences for their products. This will bring in untold billions as these kids grow into adulthood and purchase these products again and again, establishing brand loyalty for their kids and over generations.

The government has tried to stay on top of brands and packaged foods and their relationship to kids. The Healthy, Hunger-Free Kids Act that passed Congress in 2010 under Obama tries to get healthier foods into vending machines, alongside branded foods that attract kids. But the companies have deep-pocket funds to find loopholes, and the foods they sell are often built on cheap ingredients, like corn and wheat, which are highly subsidized by the government.

They simply create "healthy" brands of their junk food. They rejigger the fat, salt, and sugar contents. They slap on a picture of a tranquil farm. A cow in a pasture. And the word "healthy."

Families are being sold a lie—that these foods are healthy and good for them.

All of a sudden, Fruit by the Foot is a nutritious snack.

A few years ago, parents in one Colorado school district were surprised to learn their elementary kids were eating Raisels for breakfast.

Raisels are raisins, already naturally sweet, covered in sour-tasting sugar dust, with flavors like Watermelon Shock and Fiesta Pineapple. The school served artificially flavored fruit juice, Raisels, and graham crackers for in-school breakfast, using the Raisels as a fruit stand-in, to meet nutrient requirements.

One orange has about 9 grams of naturally occurring sugar, about 2 teaspoons. A small pack of Raisels has 27 grams of added refined sugar per box—7 teaspoons.

Day in and day out, this makes a difference in the actual bodies of our children.

The Raisels show up daily in the pantry now.

Raffi obsesses over them. He walks around talking about them and how many boxes he hopes to get. He stands by the window, mournfully waiting for the school food people to drop off their food. Or makes silent intrepid trips to the pantry to see if the Raisels have arrived.

I am not against the presence of junk and fast food entirely. Or even corporations making money. I pretty much keep the Coca-Cola Company flush single-handedly, buying flats of Diet Coke at Costco. Which I hide in the back of my Jeep so the kids can't find it.

Also, David can't Coke-shame me nearly as often this way.

But Raisels cross some line for me.

Raffi and Desi wrestle over them in the street in front of the pantry, like they are little pieces of sour-dusted gold. They wash the Raisels back with cardboard cartons of TruMoo chocolate milk, also a school lunch staple.

I try to get them to eat my hoshigaki, the hachiya persimmons I have drying on the side porch by the kitchen. It's a small but satisfying annual task for me. Little orange globes hang from kitchen string from the lattice overhead, drying and caving in on themselves as their sugars bleed onto the surface of the fruit. Desi says they are like little hot air balloons floating and bobbing outside our kitchen window.

Maybe someday she will eat them with me. But not right now.

When I offer her a slice of the sweet, chewy persimmon, Desi refuses. She turns on her toes and walks away.

"I like Raisels," she says as she goes.

"Blech," Raffi says. "That's not even good."

He spits the hoshigaki into the trash.

He goes back to his box of Raisels.

Of course, little persimmons can't compete with the rip-your-face-off chemical sourness of industrial candy. And this is precisely the point.

Later, I'm picking up dirty clothes from the floor in Raffi's room. He has maybe ten boxes (over a cup and a half of sugar right there) stashed behind his dresser.

I leave two boxes of Raisels tucked away.

"Moderation," I think.

I add some packages of beef jerky, peanut butter and crackers, rice rolls, his favorite Korean seaweed, and a small tin of Vienna sausages to his stash.

I pitch the Raisels into the garbage can, the big one outside so he won't catch me throwing away the gold dust.

I do not feel guilty about wasting this food at all.

It is a dysfunction.

* * *

I go back to the kitchen to make us dinner. Something in the face of doing nothing.

Home cooking today feels like a revolutionary act. It is resistance against the swell of crap food in the pantry, and in the stomachs of all our kids.

I make karaage, Japanese-style fried chicken thighs. Little nuggets that have been dusted in potato starch and deep fried. I make a salad with creamy carrot dressing and reheat some cold rice in the microwave. I chop cucumbers to go with it and put out some spicy Szechuan pickles I've made for David and the teens.

Lucy is sixteen now, and a vegan, so I make her some fiery tofu chunks also rolled in potato starch and fried. Anything to lure her out of the black, time-sucking hole of her pandemic bedroom.

Fried chicken is not exactly health food. But it's explosively crunchy and tastes of sesame and soy. And I make it with my own hands while my children and my dogs bounce around under my feet. The kids eat the little chunks as soon as they come out of the oil and are loaded onto thick piles of paper towels on the butcher block. I sprinkle them with salt.

I make extra and load them into plastic containers with rice, salad, and pickled cucumbers and share them with our friends who come to the pantry. But not before I fill Raffi's bowl with chicken and put some to the side, just in case he wants more or just wants to know it's there. I pay him $1 to eat a bite of salad.

He does. Wrinkles his nose. But swallows anyway.

And demands his payment.

* * *

I meet Katinka through a friend. Tink, for short.

She is a Hungarian fireball.

She is one of those people who moves constantly. She is molecules in motion. She has things brewing in her head. She makes things happen. Tink sparks ideas and plans and has the mettle to carry them out. In regular times, Tink runs a sought-after event staffing business. I am convinced she can organize anything.

Next to Tink, I am a mess.

I am an ADHD-fueled ball of chaos. I have good intentions, but nothing in the way of actually getting shit done. David calls me an absentminded professor.

He is not wrong.

Our house is strewn with cardboard boxes. Bags of rice, like sandbags in foxholes, slung into the corner. There are cases of marinara, on top of cases of marinara, on top of more that have been donated. There are cans of beans and vegetables in towers, toppling over. The dining room table is littered with government cheese and bottles of salad dressing.

Tink's house is organized. Seven fridges are lined up in a spare bedroom, deep freezers line the garage. She has a proper team delivering for her. She manages them with lists and calendars that are not just efficient, but gorgeous, drawn in multicolored cartoonish bubble letters.

She can make art while ordering everything around her.

Her kids, Hudson, three, and Caleb, eleven, play in between boxes of potatoes, onions, artichokes, and beans, while Tink sorts through them. She pulls food out for the people on her master list who need meals.

Tink is inspired to feed people during the pandemic when she finds out many grocery chains are still throwing away nearly expired meat and still viable vegetables. Often, meat, veg, and dairy sitting close to expiration are still good to eat for a few more days, possibly a week or two. If the label says "Best if used by" or "Best if used before," that isn't about the safety of the product; it's more the freshness and peak taste.

It drives Tink bonkers.

"They throw food away that is still good," she tells me, exasperated. "Then they lock the dumpsters, so no one can go in and get the food."

She finds this so ridiculous that she says it with full-body exasperation.

"There's no reason we can't take this food that is being thrown away," she says, "and give it to people who need groceries right now."

It is a testament to Tink's tenacity and charm that she forms a functioning organization seemingly overnight and gets several supermarket chains in Vegas, including Albertsons and Vons, to give her the runoff.

And she shares her excess with our pantry.

That means several times a week, Desi and I go out to her house in the burbs of Henderson.

We pick up whatever she has left over for the fridge: boxes of celery, onions, potatoes, kale, eggplants, green beans, fresh herbs. Greens of all kinds. Baked goods, like birthday cakes, muffins, breads. And meat, whole chickens, chicken parts, top rounds of beef, pork ribs, single serve steaks with little pads of compound butter, sausages, pot roasts, hamburger meat, and ground pork.

This transforms the pantry.

We go from sporadic food donations and cobbling funds together through Venmo to a steady stream of food. It is no longer haphazard. We aren't dependent on the kindness of people who buy things here and there. Or on the Raisels and the packaged tacos.

I lay everything out at the pantry so it looks like a green market. The fridge is stocked with yogurt, cheese, lunch meat, and perishables. I put the veg out in boxes, tipped just so, so it feels like a farmers market. I add chuck roast, pork chops, baby back ribs, and packages of ground turkey and beef. And those containers of single portion meat—a sirloin steak with a pad of herb butter, chicken rolled up around spinach and parmesan.

I make a short, no-frills video that goes on our pantry Facebook group page.

"This is what we have today," I say, making the camera loop over every box. "Come on down!"

Sometimes I get Edie to do the video for me. Or Raffi and Desi hop into the frame and start rattling off the names of vegetables, occasionally looking up to learn the words "broccoli rabe" or "red cabbage."

Within minutes, cars pull up. Bikes, and people in motorized wheelchairs. Like a real shop, I put out bags for people to put their food in. I am filling the pantry six times a day.

The need in the community is pulsing now. There is no stimulus money from the government yet for regular folks. People are stressed, fearful, and worried.

The desperation and fear are coalescing in our front yard.

I get a note from a server who worked at David Chang's Momofuku restaurant at the Cosmopolitan Hotel.

"I haven't been able to buy vegetables for weeks," the note says in black pen.

"I stood outside in the street and cried over boxes of your vegetables."

* * *

Sasha is at the fridge.

I'm returning from Tink's. She is bent down on the balls of her feet, shoving two packs of short ribs into her backpack.

"Hey, how are you?"

"Fine," she says, quick and abrupt. She has a cigarette bobbing up and down on her lips.

"Do you have a bag? . . . I need a bag."

I check the nail where I hang bags.

"Sorry, we're out."

Folks have been dropping off their insulated food delivery bags for others to use. I'm shocked we don't have any left. I feel like I live in a house of bags.

"How can you have a store here and not have any bags?" she asks, disgusted.

I mumble something in my head about how it's not really a store. Sasha and I already know each other. The first time I met Sasha was the morning she knocked on the door at 6 a.m.

"Why haven't you filled the fridge?" she asked.

I was barefoot in panties and a T-shirt. I just got out of bed.

"Um what?" I asked. I was still asleep.

"You haven't filled the fridge," she said impatiently. "People are hungry."

She is demanding. Difficult. And apparently unaware that I am a volunteer.

I do not like Sasha.

Does she even have a kitchen to cook the raw meat she takes?

She is either a drug addict or a recovering one. Her face is fucked up by meth. I'm guessing it's her drug of choice. She is very thin, a walking skeleton. Thin, papery layers cover her jutting bones. Her hair is a rainbow, tangled. A few strands have mashed themselves into twinelike dreadlocks.

She reminds me of Chrissy. She doesn't make it easy to help her. Perhaps mentally ill, or in withdrawal, or just fucked up from living in the streets. Or all of it. She might be all of these things mixed up into one pink, wiry, jittering package.

Something is up with Sasha. Something is wrong about her taking all this meat. But I can't put my finger on it.

I want her to be just the tiniest bit appreciative.

I want her to understand how much work has gone into this.

How my kids are now pantry workers.

How my husband is carting boxes around and doing maintenance on the fridge to keep it running.

How the neighbors are cleaning it, stocking shelves, wiping everything down with rags and Fabuloso. How we are paying for some of these groceries with our own money. How those short ribs should go to someone who will cook them up for their family.

How I wonder if she deserves those fucking short ribs.

* * *

That's it. There it is.

I want that meat to go to someone who deserves to have it.

What does this even mean—to deserve food?

And I know this makes me the asshole.

Fuck.

But I want someone who will cook them up and eat them to have them.

Someone who has lots of kids and will make a filling stew, flavoring the meat with cumin, turmeric, allspice, Scotch bonnets, curry powder, paprika, and maybe, if one is super lucky, a glug or two of warm wine left from the night before. They will dump the wine into the braise, almost as an afterthought, and everything in the pot will change with time and heat, until it's a comforting pile of supple velvet-meat lying on top of rice. Or potatoes. The last of the hot juices will get soaked up hungrily into slices of bread.

That's my fantasy for this food.

But even as I think it, I know this is saviorism. And stupidity.

It's the desire to be appreciated and to have the transaction of giving to someone else be positive and full of meaning. To have the giving shine back on me so I can feel good about being a giver is the hallmark of saviorism. It's my ego. The vainest part of me, that wants to control how Sasha cooks it. Eats it. And enjoys it.

And then I get to feel good about that.

But I'm too in the moment to process it right there in my front yard.

"Do you have a kitchen?" I ask Sasha.

I've learned a few standard questions so I can direct folks to the right food. A person without a kitchen doesn't need raw meat.

"I have a house," Sasha says.

She is weary of me. Her body is thrumming fight or flight.

"That's a lot of meat," I say, trying to keep my voice chill.

She is now pushing a big chuck roast into the backpack.

"Do you have kids to feed?"

She is working fast now. She doesn't like me asking questions.

"I'm fine," she says. "I'll be gone in a second."

And true to her word, she is.

Taking every bit of meat I've put into the pantry.

* * *

I calm myself after this exchange by ranging around the kitchen, seeing what I have. I settle on making a confit byaldi. Better known as the rata-touille Remy makes in the movie *Ratatouille*.

Best movie ever.

I make a piperade, a Basque-style stew of onions, green peppers, tomatoes, and garlic. The stew is flecked with piment d'Espelette, a fruity, briny, low-heat chili pepper that is subtle and round in this sauce. I sauté it all in beef tallow. Slice the zucchini into thin, skinny-legend slices. I have trained myself to cut them all by hand, because I am an absolute blood-gushing lunatic with a mandolin.

I arrange the slices of zucchini and eggplant so that they form tight circles around my paella pan. Purple. Red. Light and dark green. And yellow. With slices of the Romas in there, too. I douse it all with good olive oil, salt and pepper, handfuls of torn herbs, and garlic confit. A hit or three of black vinegar gives it some tang. Then it's in the oven for a couple hours on low.

I make one for the family. A small one without beef tallow for Lucy. And another that I will cut into slabs and put into microwavable containers with a label naming the dish and its information.

All of these will be gone in an hour. Both inside our home and from the pantry.

I have the privilege of picking what I want to make every night. I choose my own groceries.

It's only fair Sasha has that privilege, too.

* * *

Choosing your own food—which you will put inside your body, which will fire you up, power you through, run you down, make you well, make you sick—should be a basic right.

At food banks, food is often chosen for people based on what the organization has and how much the food bank can give. This makes practical sense for these organizations. It helps them run more efficiently and help more people.

But it also robs people of something inherent and fundamental to our humanness, in the form of freedom of choice. So many people are not able to do this basic, basic thing—go to a place and choose what they want to make for the next meal. The quality, the quantity, the brand. Even special snacks and treats they know will please their children and get them extra parenting points.

Imagine it for a moment.

You are going to get food for your family. You have to wait in a long line. Maybe you have a couple toddlers with you. They are bored and your phone is running out of battery.

The entire time you are waiting in line, you watch everyone ahead of you. You monitor how much food is left compared with how many people are in the line. You worry if there will be food left. It kills you to think of the time in this line—what if you walk away with nothing? You feel the stress crackle and twist in your spine. Your head feels light and fuzzy. You want to sit. But there is nowhere to sit but the ground. You pick up a whiny child. You can't blame her. You make a promise that it will be soon. You know it won't be.

The line is a reminder of your social status. It reminds you of the ways in which you are beholden to and dependent on others.

Then, after waiting and waiting, you get to the front of the line where people hand you a box of goods to feed your family. They tell you it's one box per family. Or if you are driving, one box per car.

You do not have any choices to make. This is what you waited for.

Invariably you will not get enough of what you need. Maybe nothing of what you need. You'll get a bunch of things you don't want and will never use. Or maybe you get lucky and it's great. You can work with the contents.

Fucking relief.

That box has to feed your family whether you are two people or eight. It doesn't matter whether you are Mexican or Indian or Native or white. Or cook particular cuisines. Or don't cook much. Or have a broken stove. Or you are living in your car or have food allergies and dietary preferences. It doesn't matter if you are vegan or vegetarian.

That box is your box.

Over and over again.

This doesn't mean the people feeding you aren't well-intentioned. Or that they want you to feel like utter shit for being in this position. But with no money, you are at everyone's whim. You control very little. You are at the mercy of everybody.

You are poor. And you feel it.

The food bank system is designed to do one thing very well—get food to people who need it. They excel at this.

Our food bank, Three Square, powered by Feeding America, is a literal lifesaver for the Vegas community. They supply pantries, churches, and non-profits with food for anyone who needs it, including backpack programs, after-school kids' meals, and meal delivery for the elderly.

They are quite literally filling in gaps for people who are struggling with hunger.

Food banks and their subsidiary pantries, originally conceived to be stopgap, temporary setups to get people through disasters and economic downturns, are generally not focused on dismantling the systems of poverty and hunger.

They are, inadvertently, engaged in maintaining it.

What does that mean?

Well, food banks are one of the things both Republicans and Democrats can get behind together. Republicans like providing money to corporations that will provide food for low-income people, bolstering businesses that provide that food. Democrats love helping poor people. Everyone benefits, except the struggling families who will continue to struggle.

They will be dependent on the system of saviors feeding them.

Many pantries only give out food, but they can be so much more for people, according to Katie S. Martin, who wrote *Reinventing Food Banks and Pantries: New Tools to End Hunger*.

Pantries and food banks can be a hub for folks to get information. Benefits. Interview training, nutrition advocacy. Tutoring for school. Cooking demos. Locate where the jobs are and meet people who have been where they are now and who can be assets in their lives.

"We lack justice and equity within our food system, we lack the courage or patience to tackle the root causes of poverty, and we lack the political will to ensure living wages and a strong social safety net," Martin writes. She goes on to say that in an effort to respond to this problem, "we have designed systems that are largely transactional, with a focus on serving as many people as possible, as quickly as possible."

A pantry that can be a community hub will be better at navigating inclusion.

They won't be monitoring how much you can take. Or when are you allowed to visit again. It will be designed with the input and voices of the people being served. I am firm in this belief that everyone at our little pantry should have choice over their food.

We are small. We can move and change.

I even feel righteous. I'm pretty opinionated about it.

My pantry is for the people. I have this all nailed down.

It's only later that I find out Sasha is a using addict. She is selling the meat from the pantry.

To buy meth.

* * *

I do not want to take Marina's Salvadoran quesadillas when she first offers them to us.

I'm going to politely decline. But Raffi takes them from her before I can stop him. I am embarrassed. We have so much and she has so little.

How can I take a gift from her?

Marina is about seventy. She lives two streets over. Her neighbors call the police on her fairly often because she has several non-running cars in her yard. She lives benefit check to benefit check. She hoards a bit. She leads a chaotic and dramatic life. Her house is a mess. She is almost always in the middle of a crisis.

I listen as she throws her hands in the air.

"I need to get my cars fixed," she says from an open car window. The car is idling out in front of the pantry.

Raffi has already escaped with the quesadilla. Salvadoran quesadillas are not like Mexican quesadillas. They are more of a corn cake with cheese. It's light and a really beautiful cake to eat with coffee or tea.

Raffi is probably ripping it apart and stuffing it into his mouth, even before he reaches the kitchen.

"They want to take my cars," she says, looking away. "Those cars can be fixed. They can run . . ."

She stops midsentence.

"Can you give me some of your chicken eggs?" she asks, frustrated.

I get a dozen. They are a deep dark brown. Some olive. A couple are a dusty, powdery blue. A light tan or two. A spotted turkey egg from Marge, which will be nearly the contents of two hen eggs. And two small eggs from Cheese, Desi's favorite chicken. Cheese is a very small bantam who free ranges the backyard. Unlike the other girls, she gets loved on by Desi and comes in to watch TV with her.

Cheese rarely lays anymore. But when she does, the egg is the tiniest little pearly thing.

"Cheese eggs are for luck," Desi tells people.

"Do you have a mechanic?" Marina asks.

She lays the eggs I've handed her on the front seat. On top of a mess of bags and clothes, hairbrushes, and empty plastic drink cups.

"You know they are threatening to call the police again," she reminds me.

Marina is struggling financially. But her poverty is not simply about the numbers. Or money in, money out. Marina is poor in other ways.

Robert Sapolsky, author and professor of biology, neurology, and neurological sciences at Stanford University, maintains that what poverty is really about is how much you have compared with everyone else.

"Once basic needs are met, it is an inevitable fact that if everyone is poor, and I mean everyone, then no one is," Sapolsky writes in his book, *Why Zebras Don't Get Ulcers: The Acclaimed Guide to Stress, Stress-Related Diseases, and Coping*. "It's not about being poor. It's about feeling poor, which is to say, it's about feeling poorer than others around you."

Marina's neighbors are generally lower-middle and middle class. They take pride in their houses. They care about curb appeal and property values. Marina's cars make the street look messy. The constant war, the way they look down on her, makes Marina *feel* poor.

"They hate me," she tells me through the open window.

I don't know if it's true. But Marina certainly believes it. That is all that is required to make her feel isolated and stressed out.

There is a lot of scarcity in Marina's life.

She rents. Has just enough money to get by. She lives on government benefits. She doesn't have family to look in on her. She is mobile and drives, but she is no longer light on her feet. She is slow. Her life is, from what I can tell, rather small.

I suspect the car hoarding gives her some sense of security. She owns something. They might be able to run someday. She can sell them. Make some cash. It probably feels like having money in the bank when you don't have much money in the bank.

Then there's social capital—the value of Marina's social networks, the people around her who can be valuable resources to her—how they raise her up, buoy her in times of hardship.

Marina has very little social capital.

* * *

The United States tends to have low social capital.

A community with a high degree of social capital has social features like neighborhood poker nights and street festivals, community gardens, Little League, available housing, tenant rights groups, and strong levels of volunteerism. That community might have affordable and available child-care, strong health care for everyone, low crime because there would be little unrest and frustration. There would be low suicide rates because of proper care for the mentally ill, lots of family planning options, and across-the-board income equality with less sexism, racism, homophobia, and, in general, bigotry.

"It incorporates elements of trust, reciprocity, lack of hostility, heavy participation in organizations for a common good," Sapolsky writes.

Sapolsky invites you to think about how you feel in your community, your state, your country: Do you believe most people will take advantage of you or treat you with fairness and dignity? Do you believe that people around you will fail to understand you, see you, hear you, or treat you with respect?

Having a high degree of social capital is an actual type of "culture."

It starts in the home with how we are raised and extends through everyone to companies, governments, and institutions. If someone passes out in your front yard, are you calling the police or checking on them to make sure they are okay? If a family is going through a tough time, are you bringing over dinner or calling CPS on them?

The United States has low social capital because we have "enormous wealth, enormous income inequality, high crime," Sapolsky writes. Add to that: the rich in our country prefer "private affluence" and living separately while tolerating "public squalor" for everyone else.

Here in Nevada, according to the Joint Economic Committee of the US Congress, in a study commissioned in 2018, Nevada was ranked 50th— dead last in social capital. New York was 43rd, and California was 40th.

In places with high social capital (albeit with more homogeneous populations)—think Iceland, Norway, Sweden, and Finland—people feel like they can trust that their needs will be taken care of. That they can turn to others for help. There would be low or manageable levels of inequality and injustice. They would feel confident that the government, their employers, their politicians, and their neighbors would take care of them. They are not going it alone.

This doesn't make these countries perfect. It means they have systems in place to meet challenges.

The pandemic is a perfect example of this. Countries with high social capital created systems that withstood the challenges. They did better during the pandemic.

According to Robert Putnam, author of *Bowling Alone: The Collapse and Revival of American Community* and the guy who coined the term, social capital is "a fundamental building block of democracy."

If Marina had good social capital, someone might come and fix a car for her. Or call a garage mechanic who can do a little favor for some quick cash. Or a social worker would be assigned to her to assist with the problem. Or someone might call someone who buys junk cars. She might not have dead cars littering her lawn like roaches after a fumigation. Or she might see someone at a party or social gathering in the neighborhood and that connection helps her solve her problem. Her neighbors might offer help, not the police.

And in this culture, Marina would contribute. Just as she does with me.

The reciprocity is integral. It mitigates shame and feeling like you are poor.

It also is universal. Almost everyone who comes to the pantry picks up food for a family member, a friend, or a neighbor. No one is in it just for themselves. They want to give. They want to be givers, not receivers. Because it knits them into the community.

"Can I make a box for the elderly couple on my street?" people ask me.

"I'd like to take some meat to my sister-in-law; they have four kids."

"I'm a college student, picking up for my grandma."

"I'm working now. Please take this $20 to feed someone else."

Everyone wants to be able to give.

* * *

I start using some of the donated foods for my own cooking.

Before, my lines were clearly drawn: There's our family's food, which we purchase. And the rest of the food, which is food for the pantry. They exist separately. For the longest time, I mark the donated food as food for people who need it, as if I might be stealing from them if I use it.

Then the shift.

It's all of our food. We are all in this together. We give, we get.

The shift is slight, but meaningful.

I make mango salsa from flats of canned mango. I make Potatoes Dauphinoise from a couple cases of sliced canned potatoes someone drops off. Before the pantry, I would never think to buy canned sliced potatoes. I am a cook in the thrust of a super-local, everything-fresh, ingredient-quality-hype part of the food world.

And maybe I have fallen prey to it.

The food we are giving to poor folks does not have the same labels as food for the upper classes. Not seasonal. Not local. Not heirloom. Not GMO or non-GMO. Not organic. We use different words for food for people in different classes.

Food comes to hunger organizations in pounds.

Baked into talking about food in pounds is the disconnection between people and the food itself. It feels like the kind of food, the quality of food, the way it tastes—all of it doesn't matter because we just delivered someone pounds of food. The more pounds the better, and forget what it is, because it will help you stay alive in the short term.

Talking about food in pounds disconnects people from the kinds of foods they are choosing. It disconnects our fellow humans from the fun parts of food—that it can taste good, it can be filling, nourishing, and comforting. It can be healing. Cooking it can be a ritual, a source of connection itself, a balm for loneliness. Eating together can be restorative—standing around a butcher block, dipping breads in sauces, vegetables in dressing, chicken in its own fats—and can be a radical act of togetherness even in times (especially in times) of hardship.

Words like *heirloom, organic, local* may exude certain privileges, but the joy of food is not a privilege. We do not think people who are experiencing poverty should experience joy—or the full range of emotions—with their food.

Picking up forty pounds of chicken parts that you had no involvement in choosing feels hyper-disconnected from all the things about food that are cultural and intimate and important. Food is reduced simply to fuel.

Essential to survive, but more like the subplot rather than the centerpiece to anything.

I take the potato slices out of the cans. I drain off the water. I let them dry on paper towels. The cans are absolutely perfect for making this simple Julia Child recipe, in which the potatoes get sliced immaculately thin—they come that way in the can. I lay out the slices in a long hotel pan, pour in milk, slushy garlic cloves from a big jar of garlic confit, and splashes of the garlicky oil from the jar. Salt. Pepper. Pads of butter everywhere. 425-degree oven.

And because the slices in the can are par-cooked, this dish is a step easier. Fifteen minutes in and out, and the slices will be creamy underneath and blistered on top. I set aside some for the family and swatches of the dauphinoise get spooned into containers, labeled, and set outside. I take the rest of the tins of potato, pair them with milk, butter, salt, pepper, and garlic inside a giant ziplock bag and attach a hastily dashed recipe card.

I do a play-by-play recipe in the Facebook group for others to follow along.

Juana, a young newlywed, who is an exceptional home cook, leaves another recipe.

This one for a can of whole new potatoes that she drowns in shmears of garlic and oil and salt and roasts at around 400 degrees. Again, it's a quick recipe because they are par-cooked.

Folks on the Facebook page take note.

A cooking discussion breaks out.

I suggest Leanne Brown's spectacular cookbook *Good and Cheap: Eat Well on $4/Day*, a book that anyone can access for free as a PDF. In the book, published in 2015 as part of her master's thesis, she writes that she "designed these recipes to fit the budgets of people living on SNAP. . . . If you're on SNAP, you already know that the benefit formulas are complicated, but the rule of thumb is that you end up with $4 per person, per day to spend on food."

Four dollars a day, per person. And the recipes are really fun and delicious.

In a later cookbook, *Good Enough: A Cookbook: Embracing the Joys of Imperfection and Practicing Self-Care in the Kitchen*, Brown writes something that stays with me: "I noticed a pattern with folks struggling to feed themselves. Money is often a huge issue, but the deeper issue is believing they are not worth the effort."

We start posting information for eviction support. Other food and pantry drives. If someone drops food in the pantry, they post and tell others so they can come get it. More recipes are posted. What people make with a certain vegetable or meat gets posted.

We form a micro-community. It isn't perfect.

But what it does have is a fairly high level of social capital.

* * *

Marina pulls out into the street. She speeds away.

I go back inside. Raffi offers me a piece of quesadilla. It tastes like my mother's corn muffins. We stand around the butcher block, sampling Marina's cake.

"It was nice of that lady to give us this cake! And like for no reason," Raffi says, popping a piece in his mouth.

I take a bite.

"It sure is."

* * *

The first thing Coco does after hugging me is run through the front door. Through the house. And out into the backyard where the chicken coop is.

She does not even say hello to her fellow humans.

She is the chicken whisperer.

Coco is twelve, the exuberant daughter of Emilie and Chantal. Also a child who wears cool clothes and a rainbow of hair colors.

Emilie and Chantal are driving for a delivery service. They drive for all the big delivery services: Amazon, DoorDash, Uber Eats. Then, after their work is done, they deliver food to people who are in even deeper shit than they are.

They are always in their vehicle, a clunky Suburban with dents and scraped paint. Not pretty, but a warhorse. They cobble together the money for rent and keep the lights on in their trailer while eating from USDA food boxes. They come to the pantry often, usually bringing as much for others as they take for themselves. It's been rough. They are caring for their two kids along with Emilie's disabled mom. They hop out of their rough-looking Suburban with stories of clashing with the public.

"This lady sent me to buy $1,000 worth of groceries for charity." Emilie isn't even out of the car before she is well into the story. She is round and pale and badass, with her platinum crew cut.

"I bought all this food and delivered it to the place . . . and you're not gonna believe this . . ." She is pointing at me from the middle of the street.

"That bitch didn't even tip me. On a $1,000 order for CHARITY."

We give each other a masked hug.

"It's devastating. To do all the work, everything she asked for," she says, her hands flying in big thrusts as she talks.

Emilie counted on that nice fat tip for her hours of work. It doesn't come. In her attempt to gather food for charity, the buyer didn't think that maybe the person packing her order needs money, too.

Despite her hilarious delivery, the result is devastating for the family.

They pick up extra USDA Farm to Family boxes from various locations around the city. They bring some to the pantry. These boxes are supplied by the government. They are given out by food banks, tribes, community pantries, and churches. People are so desperate, they line up around streets and neighborhoods in long, winding lines to get one or two per family.

Emilie and Chantal have several boxes in the back for some families in their trailer park. They hand me four boxes. I unload them into the pantry.

This Farm to Family box has precooked meatballs, a bag of onions, carrots, potatoes, a bag of grated cheddar cheese, butter, two containers of sour cream, and a dozen eggs.

I take everything out. Not every family needs everything in the box. Not everyone needs sour cream. And some families need more to make dinner. A few families who come to the fridge have eight or nine kids. One has eleven. And now families have multiple generations staying with them through the pandemic. Moms move in with kids. Grandmas move in with grandchildren.

"You got anything for Gammy?" Emilie asks me.

I have been collecting a box for Gammy on the side.

"Foster, if I see another can of chickpeas," she starts.

Chantal gives her a knowing look and rolls her eyes in agreement.

"Do you have soup and cottage cheese? She likes the softer stuff with her teeth."

I go inside and pull the box from the inside fridge on the side porch. I combine perishable and nonperishable foods into a box. Apple sauce, cottage cheese, yogurt, instant mashed potatoes, canned gravy, some bottles of Ensure, instant oatmeal, bananas, and strawberries. I give her some ground beef I have stashed away. And some cupcakes for the kids. I hand her cans of pork and beans. Tuna. Canned pulled pork. Cans of black beans. And I put in a couple cans of chickpeas to get her going.

"Nope! Nope! Do not give me any chickpeas, Foster!" she says, tossing cans into the yard.

"I have eaten so many goddamned chickpeas!" Chantal is picking up the cans, laughing and setting them inside the pantry.

There have been a flurry of boxes with cans of chickpeas, and the chickpea surplus has grown so much I have to remove them. When I get them, I bring them in the house and store them. I put them out, a can or two at a time, as space opens. The government must have made some deal with a chickpea company. And a sour cream company. I end up having cases and cases of sour cream hogging up my extra refrigerator.

This is a common problem. Getting the same foods, or types of foods, in these boxes. There are only so many ways to prepare the same kind of bean, precooked taco meat, precooked shredded chicken, precooked meatballs. Potatoes and carrots.

I start posting recipes on the pantry Facebook page for dishes that use sour cream. And chickpeas.

We post Swedish-style meatballs in a sour cream gravy, Edna Mae's Sour Cream pancakes from Smitten Kitchen, cucumber salad with sour cream and dill. After we get some tongue from Tink, I make lengua burritos with cilantro lime crema.

And from the chickpeas, I make dishes to put in the fridge: hummus, falafel, a stew in the tagine of lamb, and chickpeas with turmeric. A slew of chickpea salads: some roasted and served with dill, cumin, and garlic yogurt, with pistachios. And others, like a Spanish-influenced chickpea salad with roasted peppers cumin, paprika, tomatoes, and spinach. And bowls with roasted sweet potatoes, crispy kale, chickpeas, a tahini sauce, and crispy fried shallots.

The recipes are simple enough for me to make for the pantry. But to make even the simplest dishes, a stocked pantry is key. And a lot of our community doesn't have the privilege of a fully fitted-out pantry. It is obvious and noticeable that the Farm to Family boxes have the same kinds of food over and over again.

I wonder if this repetition is something we can work on?

How can we make sure people have pantry supplies, so they can make the same foods they are receiving taste different over many meals?

Emilie pops open the back of her Suburban. I hoist in the big box for Gammy. We take out the boxes and load up the pantry. Coco, with Desi and Raffi in tow, run toward us. She has found a stash of eggs in the yard. The kids run off to get an egg carton to put them in. Chantal makes a Facebook video of what we have to offer at the pantry. She posts it to the Facebook group.

In minutes, cars pull up. They line both sides of the street. There are masked people bending over boxes. They make bags of fresh veg for themselves.

"¿Comen puerco?" I ask Manuel and his wife. They are new to the pantry. I give her bags of nixtamal to make tortillas. She is very happy.

"Si, puerco está bien," he says.

Manuel and Mona are caring for their grandkids. Their kids are essential workers. I give them a cake for the kids. Rice. And bags of beans. A bag of nearly ripe avocados.

"¿Tiene aceite?" she asks me.

I end up giving her my big container of canola oil, lard, and a big box of kosher salt. Mona can cook. She knows exactly what she needs.

* * *

The next two hours are as close to a party as we will have during the pandemic.

The weather has cleared. It's sunny, not warm or cold. We have reached First Spring in Vegas, that lovely temperate period from March to May. Second Spring will come, September to November, after some gnarly and blistering heat.

People linger. They talk in masks. They pull out jalapenos, and cabbage heads for their neighbors. Cindy comes over. Baby Angie is on her hip. She brings over a woman from her church to pick up food. Sherlynn runs to help with collecting eggs and sorting them into cartons.

Some of the folks haul boxes for me.

Manuel, David, Emilie, and Chantal take the last of the boxes from the back of the Jeep.

They set everything up with care.

I give out all the meat. Meat gets everyone excited.

Shannon comes with a bag of things to donate. More cars. More people come and go. The young people from Vegas Liberation—a group of twentysomethings who come together during the pandemic to rescue food from restaurants and grocery stores, and make sure it gets to people—show up with nearly expired foods they picked up from Trader Joe's. The folks from Juice Stars, a local shop, drop off bottled smoothies and sandwiches.

There is a big box of herbs from Tink. Basil, lemongrass, cilantro, sage, thyme, and oregano. They are still fresh and green. I grab a couple bunches to make dinner tonight. Desi and Sherlynn pretend they are bouquets of flowers and run into and out of the house with them.

It is busy in the front of the house.

People talk in roomy clumps. Raffi is running in the street with other kids who have piled out of cars. Edie is tailing Desi and Sherlynn. Bossing them around, with their occasional bickering and egg breaking.

The sun is setting.

The lights of the Stratosphere, on the Strip, one of the hemisphere's tallest observation towers, glow over the tops of our palms as dusk closes in. It reminds us that we are both desert people and city people. Everyone in Huntridge can stand in their yards and see the Strat. It is a part of our scenery. It calls us home when we are in Summerlin or Henderson or North Vegas. Or coming in from farther away, Reno, Los Angeles, Phoenix, or Salt Lake City.

If you see the Strat, you see us.

It is our dot on the map.

* * *

People take what they need. They come. They go. I walk in the house to find it a riotous mess. I have a few hours of work ahead of me. I put away today's donations. Try to straighten up the riot. We are living in a madhouse of cans, boxes, chickpeas, and discarded cardboard boxes.

But it's all good.

We aren't alone.

We are surrounded. And in hard times, that is exactly the best place to be.

6

FOOD + HOUSING, CONJOINED
+ INSEPARABLE TWINS

IT'S 117 DEGREES. Probably hotter in the Smith's parking lot.

"It's a dry heat," the tourists say.

Sure it is.

But if you can't escape to air-conditioning, it's like setting an oven at 120 degrees and crawling in.

The heat is a three-month assault, June to August. Air-conned car to air-conned house to air-conned grocery store to air-conned work to air-conned car to the pool to the air-conned house again.

I'm having an air-con to air-con day when I squeeze in a quick Smith's trip. There's a huge sale and I'm unexpectedly loading twenty boxes of sparkling water into the Jeep.

Which is when I see a man coming toward me.

This is the reason our neighbors don't like the Smith's. Our other neighbors, our poorer neighbors, are not so easily forgotten or invisible in this parking lot.

The man's forehead is raining sweat. He has been out in this heat for a long time.

"I was wondering if I could help you with those boxes for some extra cash," he asks.

Chris Preston is a big guy. He is tall, his head is closely shaved. He has muscle and girth. His son, Ty-Jon, popping up behind him, is thinner, lankier. Chris is slow and precise. Thoughtful. Ty-Jon darts quickly. Chris looks like he might be in his early thirties. Ty could be an older teen or a young adult.

Chris has mastered the parking lot sales pitch.

He is gentle and outgoing. Not the bravado and banter of a showman, he is sincere. You can see it in his eyes. He is someone you immediately trust. He approaches with his hands up. He lets me know he isn't there to hurt me, something Black men unfortunately have learned to do, so as not to freak out white ladies like me in parking lots. But it's also part and parcel of working a parking lot that is heaving with people desperate for cash. You have to present your best, safe self to beat the competition for work and cash.

"I'm a cook," he says, grabbing cartons.

Ty-Jon picks up cartons and heaves them into the trunk.

"I got laid off at my bar." Chris works at a locals' bar in North Las Vegas. A bar that's more about slots than the kitchen.

He introduces Ty. We shake hands. He has this huge, sweet smile.

"I'm tryin' to get enough money together to move my family out of Motel 6 and into a weekly motel."

I hand Chris a handful of donation money I have and my number. I tell him about the pantry.

We start texting immediately.

* * *

"That was a rough day for us."

Chris is talking about the day we met.

I am sitting with him, his partner, Melinda, and Ty at a picnic bench in a treeless North Las Vegas park. We cannot go to their house.

They have no house.

It's morning and the temperature is bearable. The longer we talk, the more the heat creeps in. I remove my light knit sweater and go sleeveless.

This family is now living with Melinda's brother. It's a necessity. They can't pay for the Motel 6 anymore. It's toxic as hell for all of them to live together. But the choice is the car or Melinda's brother.

When you can't pay rent or buy groceries, you move in with family and friends. Which means family and the strength of our intimate social groups make all the difference to our welfare when times are hard.

Yet again, social capital is everything.

But it can be hard to be dependent on family. For some, there is simply too much twisted-up, accumulated dysfunction.

Melinda's brother, Darryl, says he wants to help them, but decades-old hurts interfere. He is angry. And so is she. About a dog that ran away when a door was left open. About $200 that someone took. Or didn't. About who took care of Maw-Maw when she was dying.

She and Darryl are bonded. But they are also mired in old trauma that becomes a series of explosions when they live together.

Melinda is stressed the fuck out.

"My priority is this woman right here, my mom," Ty says, and puts his hand on Melinda's shoulder.

Melinda is pretty. In her thirties. But she is tired. She is afflicted with chronic diseases and untreated cancer of some kind. They reference the cancer. But they never get specific. It never feels comfortable to ask pointedly about it. So, I don't. They talk about cancer as something out of focus for them. It's there, but far away. They can't call it up right now, because they can't deal with it right now.

They can handle only one immediate problem at a time.

What they don't have is a place to rest. To think. To plan a strategy. To look to the future. Turns out even being able to tend to your sickness is a privilege.

Melinda keeps a balled-up tissue in her fist. Occasionally she has to get up and cough deeply a few feet away. She is fragile. But she still shoulders much of the family's burden.

"I hate the way my uncle treats her," Ty says. "She is too good for that, and so is my dad."

Ty and his dad are tight. The love and respect are obvious. They have the weariness and connectedness that grows when you've seen all the bad things together. And lived to tell the tale.

Everyone wants them out of Darryl's house.

But Chris and his family are stuck.

Because being poor keeps you stuck.

* * *

"I was born with a seasoned hand.

"I used to sell food, you know, in a cart," Chris tells me.

In 2019, they left West Virginia on a Greyhound trek that Chris says was "the longest, most horrible trip ever."

"I came to Vegas to cook," Chris says. "I heard cooks make decent money on the Strip."

In West Virginia, Chris had a thriving hot dog cart outside a Save-a-Lot. He cooked hot dogs with mustard and homemade onion cart sauce, fried cod sandwiches on a roll with cabbage slaw and homemade tartar sauce.

His fish sandwiches were legendary. As were his secret-recipe chili dogs. He sold smashed cheeseburgers off a flat top, with pickles, chips, and cold cans of soda.

"I use the same things in the parking lot as I used at my food cart," he tells me. "I get a conversation going, chat with people, tell 'em my story."

Chris brought in $125 a week in unemployment. Not nearly enough to keep them going. They were down to bologna sandwiches and cold cereal when we met in the parking lot at Smith's.

It felt like do or die.

"Pops coached me so many times, but I just haven't got the salesman thing down," Ty confesses.

They laugh about the awkward challenge of approaching strangers in parking lots. How hard it is to make yourself vulnerable.

"You can't be prideful," Ty says. "You have to let that go. Pops taught me that."

* * *

Pride is a big issue for people who are struggling.

This is especially true of people who have lost jobs, houses, and businesses. Who have never had to reach out for help. Those people might not know about the structures in place to get assistance or what resources are available to them. They also might be less inclined to tell people they are in trouble. They might try to solve things on their own. Or they might flounder for longer than necessary.

And then there is the messaging from hustle culture:

You fucked it up.

You failed.

You can't support your family.

You can't keep a job.

You had potential, and then you bumbled it.

You didn't work hard enough. Sacrifice enough.

You are lazy.

In reality, poverty is frequently not an identity-defining, permanent condition. It is often a short-term bump in the road.

"For the vast majority of individuals, poverty is a transitory state," economist Kathryn Anne Edwards tweets. It resonates for me while writing Chris's story.

Edwards defines poverty as "cash income below a certain level."

That level right now is just under $28,000 a year across the country, which is a little more than $2,300 per month for a family of two parents with two kids.

"There's an idea that people in poverty are some kind of permanent underclass, a fixed set of people who are different from us," Edwards tweets. "This is fairly inaccurate."

Edwards says that *Dynamics of Economic Well-Being: Poverty, 2013–2016,* a report from the Census Bureau, shows that about 34 percent of people in the United States have spent at least two months in actual poverty within a four-year period, but only a little less than 3 percent of people have experienced poverty for the whole four years.

People are up and down. In the money and out. Lucky and unlucky. And they are, in general, moving toward something—a career, finishing their education. They are preparing to make a solid move when their kids are old enough to be in school, so they can work.

"The median duration of poverty is 11 months," Edwards tweets, quoting from the report, "meaning the majority of people who become poor, are poor less than a year."

She also explains that people who are experiencing poverty are generally young. They are still getting traction in their education and careers. They tend to have small kids. They have not had time to save up. During difficult times like pandemics, these folks hit bottom faster and harder.

But they will recover.

Of course, some people are chronically poor. They seem doomed to never get out of it. It's often this subgroup that's treated as the "poster children" of poverty. These folks tend to have added challenges that keep them from moving out of their current situations, like addictions, mental health issues, physical and cognitive limitations, and intractable generational legacies of racism, family separation, and trauma.

But that population is the exception, not the rule, according to Edwards.

Politicians stand at electoral pulpits and talk about how these folks rip off the system. How numerous they are. How they suck the marrow out of the welfare system. The term "welfare queen" was coined by journalists responding to Reagan's antipoverty policies and rhetoric.

It stuck.

"She used 80 names, 30 addresses, 15 telephone numbers to collect food stamps, Social Security, veterans' benefits for four nonexistent deceased veteran husbands, as well as welfare," Reagan said, describing a woman named Linda Taylor, at a campaign rally in 1976.

Taylor did have a complicated, difficult life. She was born to a white mom and Black dad during a time when such unions were illegal and met with prison time in her home state of Tennessee. She came from sharecroppers, dependent on weather, booms, and busts. Always beholden to landowners. She lived an itinerant life after she left home. She was so accustomed to lying and hustling, she assumed characters and names like changing clothes.

"Her tax-free cash income alone has been running $150,000 a year," Reagan said of Taylor.

But did it?

This single story helped cement the false narrative that the poor were scamming the country. And possibly worse, it pitted white people against Black people, again.

It deepened racial divides.

From a 2019 article in *The New Republic*, "The Myth of the Welfare Queen":

As Ronald Reagan and other politicians ginned up anti-government and anti-poor resentment in the 1970s and '80s, the welfare queen stood in for the idea that black people were too lazy to work, instead relying on public benefits to get by, paid for by the rest of us upstanding citizens. She was promiscuous, having as many children as possible in order to beef up her benefit take. It was always a myth—white people have always made up the majority of those receiving government checks, and if anything, benefits are too miserly, not too lavish. But it was a potent stereotype, which helped fuel a crackdown on the poor and a huge reduction in their benefits, and it remains powerful today.

By the '90s, about 64 percent of Americans believed welfare contributed to keeping people poor.

Bill Clinton came into office with a promise to restructure welfare. He added work requirements. Sanctions for noncompliance. He also set time limits for people to get their lives together. Both Democrats and Republicans have advanced policy built on the idea that poverty and criminality are connected. Even inextricable.

But the research—a pilot program in Milwaukee called the New Hope Project—tells a different story.

This study tracked fourteen hundred families, half on the program, half off. Folks in the study already worked at least thirty hours a week. These folks still functioned under the poverty level.

The half on the program received a financial supplement that pushed them over the poverty line, a childcare subsidy, a health insurance subsidy, and a six-month paid community service job.

Importantly, the study tracked participants from birth into their thirties.

The data were clear—the New Hope families used what they needed to get a leg up. And their kids reaped the rewards. They used the services they needed and abstained from the others. So, if a family had a caregiver for a child, for instance, like a grandma or an auntie, they might not need the childcare subsidy. But they took advantage of another subsidy that helped them raise their families up.

This has caused economists like Greg Duncan, speaking about New Hope on the Stanford Center on Poverty & Inequality podcast, to advocate for families to get an increase in income by $3,000 per child, per year, for the first five years of the child's life, when environment is essential to child development.

If we did that, researchers think, the kids from that family would probably work 135 MORE hours a year when they are in their twenties and thirties. That's a $15,000 investment per kid that actually improves the entire life of a child, and that will make our economy more stable for the next generation.

This gels with even more current research published in the *Proceedings of National Academy of Sciences*, in 2022, that specifically connects increased brain activity with $333-per-month cash stipends moms got in the first year of development for their babies.

This is huge. The brain changes prove—beyond a doubt—that we can actually heal and grow healthier brains in the most important developmental stages of a child's life.

With cash.

It's really that simple.

But for Chris, it isn't just a home or a pocket full of cash that he has lost.

"The pride is what you give up," Chris explains to me.

"It takes a toll on you when you can't even care for your family, when you are in a parking lot asking for people's spare change."

Not being able to provide for your family is soul-crushing. It alters his self-esteem. It alters what he knows about himself. It destabilizes his confidence that he can make things okay. It reminds him that he can lose stable ground at any time.

That life—their life—is fucking precarious.

Chris, Melinda, and Ty have been through hell. They are the definition of housing insecure. First, they slept in their Saturn. Then they moved to Darryl's, where they have a room, and Ty sleeps on the couch. An unemployment check gets them to a Motel 6. Panhandling in the parking lot of Smith's gets them to a weekly motel.

This feels like an improvement. But Melinda isn't sure.

"We are in the ghetto," Melinda says.

The Roachland they are in is known for being the least expensive in the city. It's also filled with the most desperate of people. Many are coming straight off the streets. Or from living in their cars. Or just out of the Clark County Detention Center. Many are mentally ill and in real-time psychosis. Most are managing out-of-control addictions.

If these folks can't afford to get into this weekly, they camp out around the complex. In the evenings, it can get boisterous and loud. People in clusters drink and smoke. Meth circulates along the perimeter and inside the weekly.

Chris sees them. Human beings, no better or worse than him. They are not able to afford a roof and walls like he can. He and Melinda go to sleep in a bed that night.

Chris feels lucky, he tells me.

It is a testament to Chris that at some of the darkest moments of his life, he can see his own luck.

* * *

Being poor is not really about food or money.

It is about housing.

It will always be about housing.

Any solution for poverty, food scarcity, and hunger that doesn't involve housing is not a solution.

Housing is important because it soaks up a family's income. This is what connects it to food and stability. It's about what's left over. If you have an affordable rent for your income, then maybe you have enough for food and necessities. If you are struggling to pay rent, then you are also struggling to feed and care for your family.

If you look at Senator Elizabeth Warren's plan for family health, from her book *All Your Worth: The Ultimate Lifetime Money Plan*, she lays out a 50/20/30 plan for handling money. 50 percent goes to needs. 20 percent savings and debt. And 30 percent goes to things you want.

But this sort of idea does not work for the poor. And I'm sure it wasn't meant to.

For the poorest families, the Federal Reserve notes that the average amount of money left over after paying rent is about $500. That $500 has to cover monthly expenses for food, clothing, health care, and transportation. If the family has kids, make that about $450 left over. And for elderly and disabled single renters, that is around $600 left over.

It's not a lot of money.

This is exacerbated by the predatory realities of weekly hotels. Many low-income families like Chris and Melinda have to stay in Roachlands in this part of the country because there are no other options.

Chrissy and Jay. Charlie and Tessie. And Chris and Melinda. They are adults. They are considered "housed" inside a Roachland.

But the standard is different for kids like Raffi, who grew up in Roach-lands.

The McKinney-Vento Act, which provides certain rights to children in precarious housing situations, stipulates that children living in motels, as well as campgrounds, cars, public spaces, substandard or abandoned housing, are considered "unhoused."

This speaks to the transient nature of this kind of living. There is no real permanency in weekly motels for children.

We have, according to the National Low Income Housing Coalition, here in Nevada, about two available low-income rental units for every ten families who need them. Families who can't find housing are often in weeklies. They are cobbling rent together over days. They are often transient. They have to move from place to place to stay ahead of homelessness. They do not have the security of a lease.

I am reminded of Dr. Sapolsky's research here, where simply the threat of eviction and homelessness traumatizes the brain so fully that people make limited and reactionary decisions. They do not have the headspace to think things through. There is no reserve.

No calm.

Just fight or flight. These folks are responding to the most immediate needs.

Big picture, long-term thinking and planning disappear.

Brains in this level of scarcity and threat can't make good decisions, by definition.

This is reflected in Melinda and Chris's lack of focus on her cancer. They are so full up with managing the next meal, the next place to sleep, they have to push off huge, complicated things like cancer.

"Everything has to be reactive, in the moment," Sapolsky writes in *Zebras Don't Get Ulcers*. "Which increases the odds that you'll be in even worse shape to deal with the next stressor."

We have people who are stressed and scared. Their brains are on limited capacity. And we have for-profit companies lining up to give them housing, with over-the-top predatory pricing.

Extended Stay America is one, a chain from Charlotte that has hotels in some forty states. And there is Vegas's own, Siegel Suites, which operates some thirty-six flexible stay apartments in seven states and some thirteen extended-stay apartments, at this writing. These companies are growing. They are expanding rapidly into new cities and towns across the country. They have a business model that is cash-flush, profitable, and easy to replicate.

Built into the footprint is how to keep poor people poor.

Companies like Siegel buy up old, crumbling apartments. They spend minimally to bring them up to code. They charge much more than the market will bear for each apartment. They hire great PR and position themselves as standing in the gap for low-income folks. They offer solutions in the absence of low-income homes or voucher programs. They give out branded blankets to the unhoused and food drops at some of their motels. Actions that are performative, but not entirely substantive.

Here's how it works in Roachland:

Let's say you are a single mom with a kid, working a minimum wage, forty-hour-a-week job—that's $10.50 an hour in Nevada at the time I'm writing this—you are making less than $21,840 a year after taxes. More like $19,342. Which boils down to less than $53 a day and less than $372 a week.

To get an apartment, you need a clean arrest record. Decent credit.

Chances are you are one of the 40 percent of folks below the poverty line who have not been able to inherit wealth or establish credit. Add to this that paying rent on time, paying back a payday loan, or even making timely utility payments will not help you establish a credit rating. The big three reporting companies aren't interested in the metrics that help poor folks build credit or wealth.

You will also need first month's rent and a security deposit. That's probably a big stretch if no one is helping you out, or you have lived a life in which you have made mistakes—like not paying bills on time or having been evicted before. Maybe you have been arrested.

Add to that the fact that there aren't many apartments available in your price range, even if you could manage the upfront costs and credit checks. So, you avoid all that and go to a weekly apartment. They will take you with all your imperfections and hard times and mistakes.

A junior one-bedroom will run you about $514 every two weeks, so you save the extra $100 and take a studio, which will set you back a little less than $900 a month. You and your child will sleep on a pullout in the living room. In the summer, there will be roaches when the lights go off. On the bed. On the walls. Everywhere. You will cook your food with roaches.

There's a telling Yelp review of Siegel Suites, this one on Martin Luther King Blvd. "Run!! This place is disgusting. It's a roach infestation! I kill about 5 to 10 bugs a day. I don't feel comfortable staying here with my child. I'd rather sleep in my car."

Folks from the pantry Facebook group confirm this when I ask about their experiences with weeklies, specifically Siegel Suites.

"It's like that scene from *Joe's Apartment*," Ronnie says, referencing the hordes of cheerfully singing and dancing cockroaches in the 1990s MTV movie that take over a New York City apartment.

Then there's the mechanical stuff. Maybe the elevators work, which is meaningful if you are older or disabled. Maybe the air conditioner works well enough to cool the room. You may have pots and pans and silverware. You may not. You might have to buy paper plates. There are often no sheets. Bring your own.

But hey, it's a roof over your head.

And you have the option to pay $220 a week for that roof. You have about $160 a month left over. About $40 a week to buy food, gas, pay for babysitting, and necessities for the week.

Heat and air-con might be broken and need fixing. The internet is often advertised as a free item. But when you get in, it's often extra. You will be charged $5.00 to $7.50 per device. Per week.

But maybe the internet is frivolous? Maybe you can skimp on that?

"For a lot of people, the internet is the way to check for jobs, or potentially have a job," Mary Laverne writes. She is a member of the pantry Facebook group. But then she also says something very nuanced about what we need, and what we want, and how those things are negotiated.

"I have two friends, one physically disabled, and the other learning impaired. For them, online social contact, through a video game or social media, is a second life."

It's more than simply entertainment. It's a form of connection and social capital.

You will pay extra for the remote to watch TV. Remotes can be as much as $10. The rooms don't come with microwaves, but you can rent one. You can get a card to do laundry, but the card itself costs $5 plus whatever you pay for washing your clothes. Lots of these little costs require a debit or credit card. If you don't have either, you have to go to a bank to get a money order for the card. If you can't get to your bank, or you don't have an account, you will pay a fee, around $2 to get one at the post office.

To manage the nightmare of your situation, you start maneuvering.

This is stressful, but you do it.

Remember that poverty makes you reactive. Your whole body is just managing the next shitty thing that threatens to topple you. Your reptile brain is thrumming, trying to figure out the next move, and the next. This is one of the ways Roachlands contribute to poverty—it's not simply numbers. It's the way they keep people on terrifying treadmills that break them down, molecule by molecule.

You monitor your gas to make sure you have enough to get to work and also idle in the long line at the food pantry. You will pick up a box of food for you and your kid, if the hours work with your work schedule. You don't really get to choose what you receive. But it might be a good box.

Maybe you'll get milk, commodity cheese, iceberg lettuce, potatoes, a bag of onions, a bag of frozen cooked meatballs. Rice. A can of tomato sauce, butter, a dozen eggs, and a loaf of white bread.

This doesn't include treats. Or the snacks your kid is going to be asking for.

There's probably a convenience store nearby. You can walk there. You'll get her an inexpensive snack, like cookies, and something fruit-flavored and blue to make her feel happy and special. Normal. The cookies will make her smile, and that will make you smile. You need a reason to smile.

This will get you through a couple days. By Tuesday you will be scrimping to save food for your kid. You will start going without. You'll eat whatever she has left over. Just to make sure she is okay.

You've done it before. It'll be okay.

But your kid needs peanut butter for her lunch at daycare. You pay a reduced fee for daycare. But you are still forking out money every week. And you can't forget to get your paperwork in again. Or you'll lose the steep discount. Also, you left her lunch box behind when you moved out of your boyfriend's house. You go to the store. You buy salt. You buy roach spray. You buy tampons, pads, and diapers, which cost a small fortune. It's Friday and everything has to get you through the next six days.

Maybe you can score a beer at the convenience store. Or someone will share their weed. You cannot save money to get out of this place because there is nothing to save. That's why housing is at the root of it all—you pay more than what your apartment is worth, more than you can afford for rent every month.

And it holds you back. It keeps you poor and small and stuck.

When you get back home, you remember there are no pots and pans in your apartment. No silverware. One plate. Because the last tenant took them. Roachland has not replaced them. You cash your check at Smith's. You stand in a long line with the baby on your hip. You borrow extra money against it at your neighborhood payday loan place. Payday loans are high-interest loans that are generally repaid in two weeks or so. It's borrowed against your pay.

It is a debt creator.

Let's say you borrow $100 for two weeks. The charge will be approximately $15. That doesn't seem like a lot, but because the loan period is so short, that raises the APR to something like 400 percent. More than $1 a day.

When you are counting pennies, that is costly.

It is money wasted.

And this is if you keep your nose to the grindstone and you don't get entangled in the drama of your neighbors. Because if you do, you might end up slinging fists with another mom in the parking lot who called you something rude. And you should've just walked away, but this bitch is getting on your every last nerve. And you are at the very fucking end of your rope. And angry as hell. And if she doesn't shut up, you might have to shut her up . . . And someone calls the police.

Because the police are always being called at weeklies. Or CPS.

Then you are officially in the carceral system. You will not have bail. You risk losing your apartment. Your kid. And doing jail time, in which case you will lose the belongings you have in the apartment. Maybe have your car impounded. And basically, owe the courts whatever fines they decide to impose.

There is no room for you to make a mistake.

And when you inevitably do, because you aren't at your best and the whole situation is impossible, the whole thing can come cascading down.

When you leave on your own terms. Or by eviction. Or the imminent threat of it. The fees can mount.

In Nevada, we have something called summary eviction. If a tenant gets a notice for a seven-day eviction for nonpayment of rent, they have to immediately stop everything and file an answer with the court requesting a hearing within that seven days or they get kicked out.

"It is the only legal proceeding of any kind that I'm aware of that requires a defendant to initiate a court action by first filing an answer," Assemblywoman Selena Torres says in *The Nevada Independent*.

"It is akin to requiring someone to sue themselves for an opportunity to mount a defense."

Imagine not knowing that and losing your shelter because you didn't know you had to stop everything and file a motion with the court.

Weeklies can also assess charges for damages from previous tenants. Management knows poor folks don't have the resources to hire lawyers. Or the social capital to get free help from the community. So they can, and do, take advantage.

A friend of mine, Aleksandra, a chef on the Strip, has a story like this. She shares in the pantry Facebook group about living in a Siegel Suites apartment when she first moved here. She was pregnant. She and her husband were looking for solid work.

"They took advantage of us by charging us over $1,000 for damages that were already there," she wrote to me. "We are still, years later, disputing that on my credit report."

This seems to be a common theme.

"It was three years of living hell," Julie writes, recounting her experience in a Siegel Suites apartment.

"A drug deal gone bad right outside our window that erupted into gunfire. Months with no A/C with triple digit summer temperatures."

She writes about the extra fees for everything and then adds:

"We had exposed wiring across our walls and floors. The bathroom ceiling was falling in on us. When the A/C was finally fixed, it poured water into the shower and bathroom, so the bathroom floor sagged when two or more people stood on it. The kitchen cabinets were falling off the walls. I had to clean it before we moved in to make it even livable. They are still saying my son took the bed, when, in fact, we did a walk-through when we handed in the keys."

The reasons for evictions can get creative. Weeklies are evicting people for having unregistered guests, particularly when family members come to stay during the pandemic. Property damage is another, and accusations of criminal activity. They evict people for having too many pets.

The stories of the brutal treatment from weeklies is recorded in a 2020 *New York Times* piece, "Falling Behind on Weekly Rent and Afraid of Being Evicted." In the piece, a Reno woman, staying at a Siegel Suites motel, talks about the constant threat of eviction.

"For a time, they were waking me up and banging on the door every day," she tells the reporter. "One time, the manager came into the room without permission because I wasn't answering the door."

The paper goes on to say that in retaliation for owing them $300, "the management also withheld her mail and cut off the free Wi-Fi to her unit."

These practices happen all the time in Roachlands. People have been telling these stories for years. But we don't listen to the poor.

Finally, this behavior caught the attention of the House Select Subcommittee on the Coronavirus Pandemic. A July 2022 *Nevada Current* piece by Michael Lyle details how the subcommittee determined that Siegel, along with three other US extended-stay companies, Invitation Homes, Ventron Management, and Pretium Partners, all used abusive tactics to evict people during the pandemic.

They used loopholes. Deception. And coercive tactics.

These companies evicted people even when they had or were waiting on relief money to pay their rent. And the companies themselves received millions in rental assistance and PPP (Paycheck Protection Program). Much of that appears to not have been used to support tenants as it was intended.

To make matters worse, emails from Siegel executives and property managers reveal a pattern of disrespect, unlawfulness, and deception.

One email from a Siegel executive instructed a property manager to threaten a tenant with having her car towed. Another instructed property managers to enter a tenant's apartment when she isn't there and swap out her working air conditioner for a nonworking unit, as way to encourage her payment. Other emails told property managers to knock on doors multiple times a night and intimidate tenants. Perhaps most horrifying is the email in which they instruct a manger to call CPS on a family with kids, to secure payment.

Siegel also distributed paperwork that looked like eviction notices to force people to self-evict and did so after 5 p.m. on Fridays so people had no recourse or access to resources. Their only alternative was to pack up and leave.

What was truly jarring?

In the report from the subcommittee, there is one particular line that puts the problem in clear perspective for me: a Siegel regional manager wrote an email and said this: "I love getting to say that this means the eviction may happen sooner than expected and seeing the look on their faces."

The email ends with a smiley face emoji.

This person ENJOYED watching people lose their housing.

This, in a nutshell, is how people think of the poor. And the struggling.

We erase what makes them human.

We distance ourselves.

We disconnect from people in crisis.

We blame people who are struggling for why their lives are meager.

We subject them to our control and surveillance.

We are satisfied giving them charity, because it makes us feel good.

We convince ourselves this is enough.

And in the process, we damage our own humanity.

* * *

I stumbled into my own slum landlord situation by accident.

I'm a hopeless absentminded professor archetype. I am constantly banging the fenders of my car. I lost my debit card and forgot to replace it, so I just use David's card. I lost my driver's license and can't focus on the bureaucracy to apply for a replacement. I carry around my passport and a photo of my license on my phone.

I take Lucy and Edie to LA one weekend—Edie is a member of Le Petite Cirque, a circus full of beautiful and talented teens who do contortion and aerial trapeze—I take David's debit card.

I think, somehow, this will be fine.

We get in late, 10 p.m.-ish.

David, sensing I won't be able to check into a hotel with his card, has been calling every crappy LA motel in search of one accepting cash. He finds a Super 8 near LAX and Edie's training gym. The room is $140 a night. They ask for a $100 deposit.

The room is fine, despite the half-eaten bag of Doritos on the dresser. I'm concerned about the number of times someone has washed the bedspread. But whatever. It's one night. I take off the bedspreads.

In the morning, we shower. There is only one setting: scalding. We wash with wash cloths, and a sort of in-and-out-the-shower bathing technique. One foot in the tub. One foot out.

Then we can't turn off the water. The faucet spins around and around, not catching. Water is teeming out of the faucet.

I pop my head out the window. I see a housekeeper working her way down the rooms. She comes in to help. She can't turn it off either. The manager comes to the room. He and his wife live on the property. He sits on the edge of the tub and wheels the faucet handle around in circles.

"We'll have to get someone in to fix it," he says, looking at me.

I nod.

"And since you broke it, we will have to take your deposit."

The way he says it is still so memorable to me. He doesn't think about it. It's like he has done this a thousand times before.

"Um, we didn't break it," I say. "It was this way when we got in the shower this morning."

"No, it wasn't," he says. "Everything was fine before you came in. You obviously broke it."

It's dawning on me. He is in the process of scamming me.

It is so obvious this is his hustle.

I completely lose my shit. When conditions are right, I can ramp up—think the Shanghai Maglev train that can go 268 miles per hour. That's me. Before long, I'm standing in the lobby at the plexiglass safety window. I am screaming at the manager and his wife.

I say I am not leaving the window until I get my deposit back. A couple impatiently shuffle behind me, wanting to check out. I'm not budging until this is cleared up.

The manager is on the phone. Off to the side. He says he is calling the police.

"Go ahead, call the police," I yell back.

If it all goes down, I can afford bail. This is not about money. It's about letting this asshole know that he cannot fuck with people. I have never felt so fully charged with using my white female, cis, middle-class privilege to see this through.

It's just a sheet of blind rage behind my eyes.

The girls are off to the side, watching. I think they might be embarrassed. And maybe they will ask me to stop. Just talking to people can send them into a shame spiral over their loud mother. But when I look over, they give me a fist in the air. This fits their Gen Z activist agenda. I'm shocked they aren't videoing it, because they video everything.

On second thought, it's a good thing. I am a crazy woman.

This is a small injustice for me. We can afford to lose this $100 deposit. But what if we couldn't? What if this was my gas money? My getting around money? What if this was our food?

If Chris and Ty-Jon tried this, chances are that three LAPD patrol cars would arrive in moments. They cannot assert themselves this loudly and with this little self-control because they are Black men. They do not have the privilege to go ballistic without severe consequences.

But I do.

This happens so often to folks in these temporary living arrangements.

Something breaks, and management lays it on the tenants.

It's an aggression. An act of violence.

Tenants have little recourse. They can be buried in penalties and fines. They lose deposits that they are counting on. They get dings on their credit that keep them from renting or buying.

I do not move. No one else can check out or check in. I have stopped all progress.

"Move me," I say, eyes on him. "With my $100."

It goes on like this for a while. I let the manager know I'm gonna sit right at their window for as long as it takes.

Finally, he offers to split the deposit 50–50.

I don't want to, but I begrudgingly take the deal. Mostly because I'm keeping other folks from their day, and that, too, is a stressor on them.

But this does not feel like justice.

I'm rattled.

Thrumming.

We are fifty bucks light. I drive Edie to training. I take Lucy to visit her friend in Hollywood. I sit in the car and stew in my own anger. Hours later, I am still unhinged by the audacity of this manager. The easiness with which he tried to fuck me over.

For people in the throes of high-stress poverty, this kind of act can throw everything off. It's another chip in their basic sense of safety and security. It is another way these companies can chip away at the well-being and trust of people in communities.

I do not want to carry this anger around with me. I feel the anger weighing me down. How much it hurts me to be this angry. It feels so bad to be fucked over.

The only way to handle it is to be driven by it, like Chris.

Or drown it in booze or drugs. Like Charlie and Tessie. Chrissy and Jay.

Or let it eat you up inside, like Johnnie.

I can let the anger pass and move on. That is part of the privilege of not being poor. Of having social capital. I probably won't get hit with another injustice today.

For low-income folks, though, for people who struggle hard and are at the edges of their reinforcements, this is how life goes.

Day after day.

* * *

Chris goes back to work at his tavern in North Las Vegas.

He is making $11 an hour. His district manager offers him a shot to become a kitchen manager. He gives him a ninety-day trial at $12 an hour. The whole family is excited. This is nothing short of life-changing for them.

They set about making plans to move again.

The tavern is a neighborhood gambling bar. Their customers are mostly locals. The manager tells me that it's mostly the familiar faces. Regulars, who keep the bar going. He's happy to have Chris come back and to train him for the kitchen manager job.

"It's hard to find kitchen managers because of the pay," he tells me on the phone.

They don't stay long for $12 an hour.

"But Chris is eager to learn. I want to teach him how to run the kitchen, do the ordering, staffing, budgeting, so in a couple years, if he decides to leave, he can take these skills with him. I get excited about teaching him because he cares."

The manager talks candidly about the narrow margins of the business.

"We'd be happy to have the kitchen break even," he said. "We make our profit from gaming, and that keeps the kitchen running."

A statement that pretty much underscores the fragility of the business model for independent restaurants.

Ty lands the graveyard shift at a 7-Eleven.

Things are looking up. They find a small studio in a Siegel Suites on Bonanza Road. The same layout as the picture advertised on their site. But not as light, airy, or spotless. It's dark and mildewy. Dark because it's on the first floor. They often keep the curtains closed tightly so people walking by can't look in.

But they feel the possibility for another life here. They have momentum.

There is a small kitchen with a sink, stove, oven, and fridge. The living room has a huge foldout bed. And Melinda is sprawled there under blankets. Her head propped on pillows. The nightstand is cluttered with 7-Eleven cups and a CPAP machine. She is watching TV.

She was just released from the hospital. She passed out again.

"I'm going to get those tests," she assures me when I ask about her cancer.

Melinda is ambivalent about the healthcare system. For good reason.

She has been beaten down by paperwork, credentials and verifications, and records that are impossible to manage living in a car. There's the succession of motels and weeklies. Moving, settling someplace, moving again. She needs to make calls. Book appointments. Deal with bills.

She is exhausted by it all.

Like many struggling families, Melinda and Chris use the ER system for doctor visits. This is expensive, and financially unrecoupable for the hospital. It also means she is only treating the symptoms, not the disease.

This healthcare issue is huge for Chris and Melinda.

She has cancer on her thyroid, she tells me. A cyst on her pancreas, and a few chronic and serious diseases, such as diabetes. She is not getting better.

She does not receive consistent treatment. She is not managing her chronic diseases.

Chris and Ty are terrified to lose her. It is a constant stress.

For now, she has a bed to rest in. A TV to occupy the hours. Some peace. Some relief, so Chris can make his next moves.

But they are far from stable.

For his part, Chris Preston's goals for being a chef are eminently doable.

Or should be.

"I want to have a normal life. I want to make $50,000 a year. I want to pay my bills. Take care of my family. Have a place to sleep," he says.

"That's it. I just want to cook for people and enjoy my life."

* * *

I write a piece about Chris for Nevada's NPR magazine, *Desert Companion*.

In a hospitality-focused city, it's a piece about a homeless chef having to panhandle.

It comes out a couple weeks after I sit down with Chris and Melinda. I tweet it around. Celebrity chef Andrew Zimmern catches it on Twitter. He retweets it. My world explodes into a moment of quasi-virality.

A Vegas friend, Dina, organizes a GoFundMe for Chris and Melinda. The next thing I know, it's throbbing with money. She cuts it off before it hits $6,000. All the donations are small: $10, $20. Lots of people contribute a little to help.

This is really what community activism looks like—lots of people doing what they can.

The next day, Dina gives Chris and Melinda an envelope full of cash.

"I can't wait to buy you a completely useless welcome home present for your new permanent apartment," I tell them, handing them boxes of groceries.

I always save up the less widely known vegetables for Chris's box. Broccoli rabe. Celeriac. Yard-long beans. Nopales. And romanesco. As well as chicken breasts, pork butt, steaks, top round, chuck, and avocado, cheese, greens, pasta, oranges, and dates. I know he can cook whatever I throw at him.

He particularly likes the cans of pork.

"I make my special BBQ sauce and put all that pork in there," he tells me. "So good."

* * *

Chris has been to prison four times.

I'm sitting with Melinda, Ty, and Chris in that weekly apartment on Bonanza Ave. They have banked the GoFundMe money. They have plans to get out of Roachland and into something more permanent.

The prison stays happened in West Virginia. Chris was seventeen. He was selling crack. He was in jail by eighteen. As he tells it, he got out. Went right back to what he was doing, selling crack on the streets.

When his house arrest bracelet went off, he didn't check in with parole. He was sent back for another nine months.

Same story when he got out.

Selling crack.

But this time he got shot in the stomach. He lost half his colon and part of his large intestine. Around this time, he and Melinda started hanging out together. She was stuck in a loveless marriage that lasted nearly a decade. But even after losing various parts of his insides, he went back to selling drugs.

"I did it for the money," he says. "You got money, you can party, buy cars, take care of the ladies, do what you want."

The "do what you want" piece of this is powerful. Chris wasn't going to have a lot of freedom working a traditional minimum wage job. Poverty is its own prison. It's carceral. Poverty hems you in.

Given how small a life on minimum wage can get, it doesn't surprise me that he chooses dealing crack to avoid a compressed life.

"I had a good family, but the streets were stronger."

The next time he was busted for selling crack he went back to prison for more than two years. Melinda was there when he got out.

"My mom loved Chris. She said, 'This guy is gonna do something, stay with him,'" Melinda tells me.

Chris listens with his head bowed.

"My mom gave people chances," she says. "So, I gave him a chance."

But Melinda is no pushover. She didn't want a crack dealer raising her kids, Ty-Jon and his brother, Ekia, who is back East playing college basketball.

"No games," she said she told Chris. "It's the streets or me."

Chris was already rethinking his life. He was nearly thirty. He had nothing to show for it but incarcerations.

"I was going to die," he tells me. "I knew if I went back out there, I'd die."

He became a cook. It gave him a new kind of notoriety.

"He started working three jobs," Melinda says.

He washed dishes. He bussed tables. He moved up to being on the line. He worked at Burger King, a Thai restaurant, the restaurant chain Shoney's.

And then a place called Tidewater Grill made him a sauté cook. He supplemented his income with his cart parked outside the Save-a-Lot. He made chili dogs for the neighborhood.

This filled him with pride.

"I realized I had a gift for something, telling my story and making people feel good with my food."

* * *

Melinda is much healthier looking, although she never leaves the bed while I'm there. But she does roll out into loud laughs when someone says something funny. Like when I ask her if her brother ever read the magazine article about them.

"NOOOOOOO," she says, throwing her head back.

Chris and Ty join in.

"But he did try to make things better," she tells me.

Darryl's wife reached out to Melinda. She said he wanted to make peace. Melinda went to his house. He told her how much he appreciated her caring for their mom until she died. He admitted that she probably lived longer because of the care Melinda put in.

This makes her happy. To be recognized. To be seen by family.

But things were said that can't be unsaid.

"I don't drink because there is alcoholism all over my family," she says. "He drinks and gets loud and says things. They all say things when they drink. I don't like that."

In fact, this family has been pretty successful at warding off some of the temptations that could make their lives harder. Chris never did the crack he sold to other people. He is able-bodied. Strong. He is only forty.

He can push his way out of poverty. With brute force, I think.

But the better part of me knows that's not how it works. Pulling yourself up by your bootstraps can be a myth when the path is littered with booby traps. There is never a guarantee that Chris and Melinda can make it to a place of middle-class stability.

Their goal is $50,000 a year. That's a full-time $24-an-hour job (the minimum you need to make in Nevada to afford a modest two-bedroom apartment).

Chris is doing everything he can to make that money for his family. He is selling clothes and shoes on the street. He is thinking of taking a truck driving side job. He is working overtime hours at the tavern.

I remind him he hasn't given his chef career here in Vegas enough time.

But I know that some of those best jobs are on the Strip. His felonies will probably make the highly regulated casinos a tough option.

He tells me about how the customers at the tavern have been giving him love for his Reuben sandwiches. He gets bigger when he talks about it. Taller. Puffed up. He can't help but smile when he talks about the compliments, the tips. The love. It fills him.

"Don't give up just yet."

"I won't, Miss Kim. I'm not goin' nowhere."

* * *

Poverty is a policy choice.

We have poverty because we choose to have it. The government could throw money at the problem. A few billion a year, culled from cutting various other programs, along with requiring corporations and wealthy families to pay their share of taxes, and we could eradicate poverty in the United States in our lifetime.

It could happen.

There would be economic issues to navigate, like inflation. Some folks would worry that taxes would be too high as a result, or that we are supporting laziness in workers, something we heard people say after the Great Resignation in 2021. And our basic goods and services might be more expensive during the adjustments.

But those things are economically manageable. This isn't what's stopping us from eradicating poverty.

What we really want is to maintain a compliant, silent workforce that is dutiful, does the dirty work, and stays quiet, subservient, and works for cheap.

We need the Chris Prestons of the world to do their jobs.

How are we going to get our burritos delivered to our door if no one is willing to work at the taco shop on the corner and have someone deliver it to us in our bare feet and pajamas for a few bucks? How will we get our orders delivered to our door from Whole Foods without a low-paid employee to retrieve all the stock, make the purchase, and bring it to us? Who is going to DoorDash us an emergency cheeseburger?

Who is going to wait tables for tips? A strategy for restaurants that dates back to Reconstruction, when white people didn't want to pay wages to Black people for cooking and serving their guests.

Restaurants run, quite literally, on the charity of their guests.

Who will work at McDonald's for minimum wage? Who's going to pull a double in a hot, under-ventilated restaurant kitchen? Who is going to keep working under a boss who is sexually inappropriate or bigoted six ways from Sunday?

We—those of us in the middle and upper classes—need a certain part of the population to stay poor, because that's how we fill low-wage shitty jobs that we don't want to do. That's how our businesses stay afloat. That's how we make our own bank. And buy our own houses. And build our own wealth for our families.

On the backs of people economically poorer than we are.

Each of us, individually and collectively, has as much responsibility as Siegel Suites and Extended Stay America has for doing right by its tenants.

A solution to poverty does not simply mean Elon Musk and Jeff Bezos sharing their wealth, in the form of fewer tax loopholes for corporations and the 1 percent—although taxing the rich and requiring them to contribute is certainly required—but all of us shifting how we think of convenience, necessity, and leisure.

Does it mean carefully choosing what businesses we patronize? Sure. It might mean shunning Siegel Suites' Pink Box Donuts or Bagelmania, their popular Jewish-style deli, off the Strip. Why? Because they can't make a bagel good enough to justify the fact that it was made off the evictions of poor people during a pandemic.

But it's more than that. It's how we negotiate our needs and wants. It means asking ourselves about all the luxuries we have, and what it means to keep them in our lives.

We have to ask: Who is working their ass off in shit conditions for shit wages just to make sure our feet look good?

Our meal is served?

Our toilets are washed?

Our kids are cared for?

Achieving equity will not be painless. In fact, it might be uncomfortable for a lot of us.

But it could happen if we decided it was essential to American life.

* * *

It has been four months since the GoFundMe.

Chris and Melinda have $2,500 left and have been looking for a place. They are spending frugally and money is coming in. But expenses pop up.

My fear is that the longer it takes for them to find a stable apartment, the more of their GoFundMe money will need to be used. Car repairs, essential life expenses, and Melinda's health care are all things that could overrun them.

Chris, Melinda, and Ty go to see an apartment in North Las Vegas. It's a cash-only place. And they will not be looking at his credit score. They are doing the work-around.

The apartment turns out to be a house.

"Gorgeous," Melinda says.

She swoons a little, thinking about it.

"Yeah, too good," Chris chimes in.

There is a real estate combination lock on the front door handle. The guy showing the apartment doesn't have the combination. And has to check with some guy, with a heavy accent, on the phone.

"I have friends from Kenya," Melinda says. "Sounds Kenyan to me."

Another couple pulls up. They want to see the house, too.

The guy on the phone is texting Chris. Whoever Cash Apps the money to the Kenyan first gets the house. There is all this pressure to make it happen.

Who will get the house?

Who will get the money to the Kenyan first?

But Chris is street-smart. He doesn't get played easily.

"It's a scam," he says. "This guy doesn't have the number to get in," he says, laughing.

"He can't even get in the house."

They didn't send the $1,100.

I tell him about Destiny. How she lost everything through a rent scam. Her money. Her kid. Her freedom.

"It was gonna go down like that," Chris says.

They are still in Roachland. They are waiting for the right opportunity that will get them into a stable apartment.

I do not think this will happen before their money runs out.

* * *

One year later.

The money is long gone, as you would expect. $6,000 is a blip for any family. Chris, Melinda, and Ty are still in Roachland.

Same Siegel Suites.

Same room.

Chris is no longer at the tavern. The manager is no longer taking my calls.

Chris leaves me voice-to-text messages telling me they screwed him over.

"I didn't get paid for five weeks," he tells me. "That almost pushed us back into homelessness.

"I did everything they asked me. At the end of the day, they cussed me out like a dog. They put my family in jeopardy."

Ty kept the family afloat with his job at 7-Eleven.

I ask for details.

"The business I was bringing there was the business of color," he says.

He was bringing Black customers into the restaurant to eat his food. He was making a name for himself with his food, with his people.

"But management made the people I was bringing in feel uncomfortable, not welcome, you know? So, I'm over at the Wynn now."

He is talking about Wynn Resorts on the Strip.

Chris considers suing. But that also feels like an entirely new job to manage, and I doubt he can see it through. Melinda isn't well. She is hospitalized again. When I ask him about it, there is the same disconnect, the haze around her pain and her health.

"She isn't feeling well, Miss Kim," he says to me in his Southern lilt.

His sadness is right at the skin. He wears it. It's draped all over him.

This is all the detail he gives me.

But it's amazing to land a job in an upmarket resort on the Strip. The restaurant isn't casino-owned, so he can have felonies on his record and still be hired.

He flips burgers in a fast casual restaurant. From what I can tell he likes it well enough.

He is hustling outside of work, too. He has started a church, a street mission. He cooks for and feeds some of the unhoused around Bonanza Avenue. He posts inspirational memes on his social media. One, over a photo of Denzel Washington, says, "Difficult doesn't mean impossible, it means you have to work hard."

Chris has that down. The man works hard. Every day.

I'm not sure if it's enough to change the circumstances of his life.

Or to get him into a permanent home to live in.

But I hope so.

THE LIMITS + LIABILITIES OF LUNCH

"HEY, THERE IS a homeless guy cooking his lunch in your kitchen," David texts me.

". . . just wanted you to know."

Smiley emoji.

I'm at Costco picking up pork butts. As you do.

Smiley again. Chef's knife emoji.

I think he might be messing with me.

But sure enough, a man named Stefran is making eggs and warming up soup in my kitchen.

When I walk in, he is dressed in a cape.

A pink cape. And black jeans. A Nirvana T-shirt. His hair is braided in rows. His bike, with a huge rainbow flag hanging off the back, is leaning on some bougainvillea in the pathway to the house. I set down the first round of bags.

"Hi!" I say.

"This is Stefran," David tells me. Stefran waves back. Big smile.

Stefran is a stranger to me. A man who walked up to the pantry to take some food but is now somehow making himself at home in my kitchen. Stefran is standing at the butcher block with David. They are in a heavy discussion about a show. David is scraping fried eggs from a small sauté pan onto a plate.

"David here is going to help me with my show with Fabio," he tells me, smiling, scraping orange yolk with a fork and popping it in his mouth.

Fabio Lanzoni is the model known for posing on the covers of dozens of historical novels. His linen shirt is flung open to reveal his rock-hard abs and sprawling chest. His long hair flies in the manufactured wind of the studio. Fabio is also in some pretty funny I Can't Believe It's Not Butter commercials from the '90s. He is a man who spoofs his own reputation as a beefcake.

I respect this.

Stefran, I learn, knows Fabio. And if he can get his social security card, he can reach out to Fabio. They can finally work together.

I leave the boys to their conversations.

Which is mostly Stefran talking to David. And David nodding, and eating his own eggs, probably fried in duck fat and smothered in spicy chili crisp. Or the homemade carrot top pesto I make in a big mason jar and leave in the fridge for dabbing on eggs.

I don't know how Stefran cooks his eggs, but he seems quite happy with them.

Then they both leave their empty plates in the sink and bring in the rest of my boxes.

Stefran never stops talking to David.

David never stops nodding and listening.

* * *

Later, when I ask David about Stefran, David tells me that I wasn't offering food that unhoused people can eat. The majority of the food in the pantry requires cooking. It requires utensils for chopping. Prep work. Cooking techniques—steaming, boiling, frying, and roasting.

"He needs a can opener and a pan, and a place to heat everything up in order to eat food from the pantry," David explains to me.

My focus has been on feeding families hit hard by the pandemic.

"The unhoused have their places to eat," I say back to David. "There are services for them. They will weather the pandemic the same way they weather their lives."

To be honest, this oversight is by design.

I am worried about how the unhoused will change the pantry. Although I never say it out loud, to anyone, let alone myself, I never include them in my planning for the pantry.

I have seen how an influx of unhoused people can affect a part of a neighborhood when food is being offered. I secretly hope the chronically unhoused don't find out about the pantry.

I just have to think of the park down the street from our house to know what can happen.

* * *

Circle Park is a small park in the middle of a busy traffic intersection in downtown Vegas.

My kids can walk there in ten minutes. It's a little patch of trees and wide swaths of grass. There are bathrooms and a playground for the kids.

The park has been closed for years. It sits surrounded by fencing and cops who occasionally monitor it to make sure no one uses it.

But at one time, it was a place where movies were shown outdoors on a Friday evening every month. Families brought their blankets. And shared snacks. There was a man from the neighborhood who looks completely like an authentic Santa who played Santa every year for the kids. Neighbors made cookies and kids sat on Santa's lap.

This Santa was Desi's first live Santa. She still talks about the day she met him in person.

The community lost this park when the anti-hunger group Food Not Bombs (FNB) started feeding unhoused folks there. This brought homeless folks from all over the city. It became a place where agencies from other parts of town dropped off unhoused people. It became a place where gamblers took refuge when they tore through their paychecks and found themselves bled dry by the casino tables.

When I say unhoused people, what I mean, mostly, is white, drug-addicted men. Some were veterans. They leaned into the grass and shade in the park. These guys took over the bathrooms. They set up bicycle chop shops inside the park. They went out into surrounding neighborhoods and stole people's bikes. They worked on them and resold them for drug money.

A new community was created here—one that offered shade, water, bathrooms, rampant illegal businesses that generated drug money, with unchecked meth and heroin use. And free food delivered right to them. It was perfect. The park went from a few unhoused people seeking refuge to a community of hardcore vandals and addicted folks who made the park uninhabitable.

Statistically, crime in the neighborhood increased substantially.

There were needles everywhere.

Fat hairy penises with large sets of balls drawn on play structures.

Curse words scrawled on slides and swing sets.

Broken whiskey bottles littered the playground.

The mentally ill urinated and defecated out in the open.

Litter. Foil and plastic wrap from the food giveaways blew across the grass.

No one from FNB stayed around to clean up. The grassed areas where trees shaded the ground were given over to clumps of people who slept in tents and sleeping bags.

The bathrooms were now places for sex and drug use. They became so gross they had to be cleaned out by teams in hazmat suits.

The last time I took the kids there, a woman who was actively in psychosis had a long emotional conversation with an invisible friend the entire time we played. She sat on the bottom of the slide, blocking any kids from using it. She talked to the air and the wind and the trees while the kids ran around her. She barely knew they existed.

FNB, represented by the ACLU in court, won case after case when neighbors tried to shut down the feedings. What they were doing was not illegal. You can feed people anywhere. But as the park slipped into chaos, the community started frequenting other parks. The hardest hit were not the middle-class families in the neighborhood.

It was poor families who really needed the park and couldn't use it anymore.

Parks often provide refuge for poor families needing to get out of under-ventilated, hot apartments in the sweltering desert summers. The bathrooms provide running water. Places to wash up. Folks can refill water bottles. A lot of families on the edge came to the park. And while parents made calls for work, or hustled to get jobs, their kids played in the playground.

Circle Park was for them, too.

Once, we met two sisters, Luisa and Luna.

They were a bit younger than Lucy and Edie at the time. Maybe eight or nine years old. They were there, seemingly playing alone.

Luisa, the older of the two, sat on the bench next to me. She told me how she had been taken into foster care. Her eyes were big and brown. She had long straight dark hair. Bare feet. A Polly Pockets T-shirt. She told me about her mom, who was on drugs. And how she, her mom, and her sister lived alone in a big building with her mom and lots of her friends.

They didn't have food or water. Her mom slept a lot.

She was scared and sad a lot, she told me.

"But now I live with my dad," she tells me, sipping on a chipped, faded Hello Kitty water bottle.

"If he does his homework, he gets to keep me and Luna forever," she says.

That homework sounds like a reunification plan.

A while later, Dad came to the park with pink and yellow sandals, which he had just purchased at the 99-cent store, for each of the girls. He took the tags off with his teeth. Each girl took turns sitting. He carefully put the shoes on their feet. He kissed both their heads when he was finished.

"I fix computers," he told me, giving me his card. "If you ever need any help with that."

The rest of the time he sat in his Impala. He watched the girls play with my kids. He made phone calls.

"I'm looking for gigs," he tells me. "I don't have childcare."

I pass his name along to some friends in the business.

He gives Luna a bag of mini Oreos to share with the kids. It's like they've discovered gold. There is glee. And fun. And no more worry. Or talk of drugs. They were safe. And they knew it.

Circle Park stood in, like a babysitter.

The park—this free, green space—is theirs, too.

The fatal blow to the park happened in 2019. An elderly woman who lived on the edge of the park was beaten by a man living in the park.

Badly.

The city closed the park.

The neighborhood breathed in a sigh of relief. But the trauma of losing that park hasn't left us.

We have seen spaces we love and need taken over. Run down.

Trampled on.

Made dangerous.

And closed.

It is a psychic wound. A ghost in our neighborhood.

There is the fear that even a car abandoned on the street can become a drug hub for the unhoused. A living shelter. A gathering place. A site where the mayhem of addled, drug-addicted, and chronically broken brains coalesce into crime.

We know what happens when we feed the unhoused.

We lose the space to them.

They move in.

They bring their community.

They live outside of ours.

Of course, this won't be how I think of the unhoused always. They have their lessons to teach me.

* * *

I bring this apparition with me to the creation of the pantry. A certain wariness.

The pantry is for people with kitchens, I think. There is not one part of me that wants to manage the unhoused people of our community at the pantry.

And yet the unhoused community have other plans. Just as Stefran had other plans for David and his eggs.

"When he came to the door, I asked him if he wanted eggs," David says. "And he did."

"Wait . . . you cooked for Stefran?" I asked, laughing.

He didn't cook his own?

David does not cook, certainly not for me.

We have over the years divided our domestic responsibilities into who does the chore the best, and who hates it the least. I cook. He does laundry. We both do dishes. When I'm out and David and the kids are alone, I will find them eating from boxes of chain pizza.

"Eggs, I can cook eggs," he says, warding off any smart-ass remarks I might be thinking. He does, in fact, make excellent scrambled eggs, and he has a whole system about what kind of butter (Kerry Gold) and how much heat, and when to add the salt (at the end, never at the beginning). He likes a little labneh mixed in for creaminess. And half an avocado sliced and salted on top. Maybe a little sauce of some kind on top.

I put the food away. David washes Stefran's dishes and his own.

There is something that touches my heart about how this man I married cares for this stranger in our home. And yet I feel that something has broken open, something is changing at the pantry already.

"So, what made you invite Stefran into the kitchen to eat?" I ask him while putting away the food.

"I had the time," he says.

Lockdown opens up time for those of us moored at home.

"And I like his Fabio stories."

* * *

The day I meet Ms. B, it's cold as hell.

It's late summer. Dry and eviscerating some days. Monsoons on other days.

Heavy rains. Flash floods. The feel is nearly tropical as humidity and cloud cover take over. Water pools everywhere. Our phones bleat out flood warnings.

The skies in the West are greedy. Twisted and ominous. The wind kicks up. It blows down palms and Tipu branches with angry snatches. For those of us with shelter, a storm brings a kind of excitement in the desert. The kids are enthralled with the rare dark, sunless skies.

They run out and dance in the rain. As desert kids do. In their underpants and rain boots, along the curbs that are mad-rushing with rivulets of rain.

But the storm is still gathering itself.

Whatever is brewing over Mt. Charleston is not here yet.

But it promises to rip itself open all over us.

* * *

Ms. B has a stroller filled with blankets.

She has a box of Cheez-Its poking out of the top. It rests on the hood of the stroller. She also has a bag, which is full of plastic and things in cardboard, hanging off the side. I see sandwiches from the pantry wrapped in butcher paper and then a ziplock bag. She has laid them on top.

She has a Chihuahua named Princess.

Princess is shivering in the front seat of the carriage.

She wears a hot pink dog jacket. A tattered, diamond-studded collar. It, too, is Bazooka gum pink. She is a terrified little thing. She vibrates. She seems at home only when in her stroller hidden under blankets. Or when Ms. B carries her like a football under her arm.

Ms. B tells me that Princess—true to her name—prefers to be carried.

Ms. B takes a jar of peanut butter from the pantry. She puts it in her stroller.

"Where do you live?" I ask.

"I lost my apartment," she tells me.

"How?" I ask.

"Someone stole my money," she says.

The way she talks about it, it sounds like she lost her apartment recently. Since so many of the people at the pantry are being evicted or threatened with eviction, it doesn't surprise me.

It's all very vague with Ms. B. Our conversations aren't straight lines. More like bendy half circles and swirls that take us in and out of thoughts as they come to her.

The B stands for Boky. Pronounced Boh-key.

Ms. B is probably in her late sixties. She is petite. Korean. Her face is tanned brown from the sun. Her hair is short and gray, cut into a pixie cut, so "it's easy to manage," she tells me. It makes her look a little like a mythical elf, with her rosy cheeks and deep-cut, hard-earned lines.

Beautifully weathered is what comes to mind.

She is beautiful.

Not surprisingly, because she is pushing her stroller around Vegas, she looks more fit in shorts than I do, with my sad writer-butt sitting in a chair all day. Her calves and arms have lean muscles rippling through tan leather skin.

Ms. B tells me she hangs out at Baker Park. A few streets over.

Baker Park is in the opposite direction of Circle Park. It has a splash pad for kids. The city now has an iron gate around it, and anyone inside has to have a child with them. But during the pandemic the gate hadn't yet been constructed, and the unhoused sometimes hung out there.

I should've realized at this point that Ms. B is a lifer to the streets. The place she feels most comfortable. But I am taking people at their word at the pantry.

I put my hand out to Princess for her to smell. She does so with great caution. I hear a small, Chihuahua-size, guttural belly growl. Princess is not so sure about me.

She has street-dog skepticism. I can't blame her.

* * *

Ms. B is a woman vibrating with butterfly thoughts. She has what doctors call "flight of ideas."

Her thoughts come out to me like butterflies released from her mouth: one beautiful, one shy, one barking, one tragic, and they all flutter about.

Then as her focus changes and the topic shifts, their brief lives sputter out. They disintegrate. They make room for more thoughts to tumble out into the air.

I listen for as long as I can until I decide to just nod and murmur affirmatively. She doesn't seem to notice and keeps right on talking. I load some groceries into the pantry while she talks. But then she notices the plants in our front yard, and a kind of clarity moves over her.

She starts telling me about Korea. And gardening.

"The soil is better there," she says.

Her hands make a cup as if she is holding it. Feeling it.

"It is dark and moist," she tells me. And then sort of spits at the desert soil she is standing on.

I can't help but laugh. Being a gardener in the desert is not easy, but for Ms. B, gardening brings memories of her father in Korea.

They had a farm. She tended the vegetables and fruit with him. Cabbages, radish, persimmons, peppers, and onions.

The butterflies stop slipping out from between her lips now. She pauses on this memory. Her father is important to her. His memory brings clarity to her thoughts.

* * *

Ms. B tells me about kimchi making in her village.

She never names it. But I think she is talking about gimjang, where the community makes kimchi together in large batches. Many Koreans now simply buy kimchi at the store. But there was a time when whole communities came together to make kimchi.

The tradition of gimjang historically started by procuring small fish.

The women went to the fish boats in the spring. They harvested small shrimp and anchovies. Sea salt was harvested in the summer. Red chili peppers came from the gardens in late summer. They were dried and ground to powder.

And then in late fall, the community, largely made up of women, came together to make huge amounts of kimchi. Recipes were passed on. Mothers-in-law to daughters-in-law. Children were invited in. It was about tradition, transmitting recipes and techniques to new generations. And being in community together. The women lightened the load for each other by cooking, prepping, and cleaning together. They made enough to share.

It is as much social and cultural as functional.

These kinds of multi-person food preparation events helped all members of the community have food. In this case, enough kimchi for every family through the winter months. And it created social capital and connectedness among people in the community.

It's about the food, yes. But mostly, it's about survival over generations through being connected and present. And in many ways, it is no different than inmates making a spread in a jail unit. The making of the food is practical, but the camaraderie and connection are the point.

* * *

Ms. B makes kimchi at her friend Jenny's house. This is what she tells me.

I will meet Jenny. She is also Korean. She has an apartment with her husband. I see her often with the unhoused folks in our community. I am perplexed and intrigued by the way she moves between housed and unhoused communities.

But there are a lot of people who exist in this in-between space.

They have been homeless. They made friends. They created their own community of support. They miss it when they become housed. They sleep in their own beds. But meet in parks and in McDonald's to nurture old friends and past connections.

When Jenny and Ms. B make kimchi in her apartment, it serves as a microcosmic gimjang.

Jenny salts the cabbage and leaves it to sit for six to eight hours to draw out excess water. Then Ms. B sauces the cabbage. This is where the process becomes personal and familiar. Every recipe is different. Ms. B tells me there is usually some combination of gochugaru, salted seafood, and fruit, like Asian pear. There is always garlic and ginger. She adds delicate slivers of radishes. She makes a slurry from glutinous rice flour and water. Jenny cooks it all down on her stove. The slurry helps deepen and spread the fermentation.

Jenny and Ms. B slather each leaf of cabbage by hand so that the red juices slide in between and through. They make enough for Jenny and her husband.

And for Ms. B to store in her van for herself.

* * *

Ms. B is oddly specific about her cooking techniques. Her brain snaps into a kind of military-style precision when she talks about ingredients. It is intuitive. Bound up in girlhood with her father on a faraway farm. She speaks freely and joyfully. Always as if her father is with her and she is still a girl.

"I'd rather not have a phone," she says. She believes people can track her through the phone.

She has three sons. I ask her if she calls them. She does not call them. They do not call her.

"Do your sons know you are living in your van?" I ask.

But she doesn't like this line of questioning. She looks down at Princess.

"They don't know," she says.

I wonder if this is true. Is this self-protection?

How would they feel if they knew?

What would it mean to her sons to know their mom is living in a parking lot in Vegas? What if this is too much of a burden for them?

What if they feel shame that she is their mother?

What if they just don't know what to do with her addled, clickety-clack brain that stammers out thoughts and ideas?

What if they believe she is dead?

I will never be able to answer any of these questions. They rise up into the air and disintegrate there, butterflies, as if they had never been asked.

* * *

"The soil is much better in Korea," she tells me again.

She bends down and crumbles dusty soil between her fingers. She wants to talk about something else. I won't interrogate her anymore.

I tell her to wait. I go inside and get some daikon that I picked up at Tink's.

Two big white tubers, like giant pearly carrots. I bring them to her. A gift. And an unopened tub of gochugaru I have in my own pantry.

Her face lights up. She takes it. She wraps it all carefully in a canvas bag and hangs it on her stroller.

"I'll pickle this," she says.

"I have everything I need in my van."

* * *

I call my friend Sonja, a writer, cook, podcast producer, and all-around lovely human, who introduced Raffi to cricket eating.

She's also the kind of friend who brings little kitchen novelties when she visits. It might be an interesting spice blend from a curious little shop. Sometimes it's a smoky habanero sauce from the farmers market in some city she is visiting. Once, she brought me this large mesh box that hangs on my porch, to dry vegetables from my garden. Her gifts are always unique and really useful.

I have a hunch Sonja might want to meet Ms. B.

Ms. B needs to have as many connections to housed people with resources as possible. Social capital and all. The fact that they are both Korean is an excellent head start.

I'm right.

Sonja meets me at Baker Park.

She has not sidestepped her usual generosity. She brings several plastic boxes of gimbap, a Korean sushi-like roll with vegetables and rice rolled in slices of seaweed. She brings rice and congee, ready to eat in plastic-wrapped containers.

Horace, an older man with a wiry gray beard, is sitting on the picnic table with his dog Chip.

And another dog. It's Princess.

I'm sure this isn't right.

"Check by the bathrooms," he advises when we ask for Ms. B.

"She isn't so good today."

Sure enough, next to the wall that houses the pool, and across from the restrooms, in a little tunnel that resists the vortex of the damp wind, I find a blanketed lump.

I recognize her shoes. We call her name. She peers out from under the blanket.

The weather is taking its toll.

We sit next to her. Cross-legged like kids in morning circle. She stays in her blanket. She doesn't get up. She talks to us while lying down. I am not trained to recognize old age dementia versus mental illness of other kinds. But I recognize that she is not the woman I met at the pantry.

She rambles, even more than usual.

Her voice is feeble, sliced into fragments of words.

Whatever strength I saw in her is gone.

"Why aren't you in the van?" I ask.

"It has to be warmer."

"There's no room," she says.

I watch Sonja nod. Listen. Commiserate. At one point, she reaches out and holds Ms. B's hand.

Whatever their interaction is, whatever Sonja says to her when I walk away, it clicks.

She likes Sonja.

And Sonja becomes one more person in her social capital arsenal.

* * *

A few weeks later Ms. B will take me to the van and open the doors.

I will see that it is stacked with lamps, bowls, cooking equipment, gardening tools, clothes, blankets, and pillows. And a huge clump of scallions growing in a clay pot, that she keeps next to the driver's side window for sun.

It is miraculous. Nothing short of it. To see green sprigs thriving, longing for the sun, inside this hoarded out van. She has cared for them with the experienced hands of a gardener.

But the truth is clear. She is not actually living in her van.

Her life is picking up things, everywhere and anywhere, carting them in her stroller. She is always moving. Pushing big loads. Picking up things that could be something.

She is a lifer.

And she has been out here for a long, long time.

* * *

Becca travels in the same circles as Ms. B.

"Ms. B is totally crazy," she tells me, laughing. "Like really crazy, she drives me nuts when she talks on and on."

But Becca has a soft spot for her.

She lets Ms. B sleep in her safe space over by a lighting store on Sahara Avenue. The owner agreed that Becca could sleep there in a dark corner.

"I keep an eye on things for him," she says. "And I look out for Ms. B."

She respects Ms. B for her strength. For being out on the streets, an old woman alone.

Becca is a trans woman.

Many know her as Montana, a nod to her birth state. Others remember her when she first came to Vegas and used her birth name, Luca Navarro.

She is in her early thirties. She left Montana to body double Johnny Depp in a movie. But whatever happened, it didn't end like she'd hoped. She found Vegas. And like Nicolas Cage in *Leaving Las Vegas*, also found a desire to drink herself to death.

She wears tight-fitting black jeans and a brunette wig, striped with flaming purple strands setting off her face. Her own hair tucked haphazardly underneath. More like a hat than an integrated section of hair. She wants to be more kempt. She tries to stay kempt. But street life wears and tears on her beauty. Sometimes she comes wearing glorious shades of eyeshadow, black-painted nails, and high-heeled boots. But her nails are still caked with grease from

202 | THE METH LUNCHES

working on bikes. Other times, she comes in sneakers, a halter top, big glamor sunglasses, and ragged jean short-shorts that show off her gorgeous legs.

I suspect Becca is nicking bikes around the neighborhood.

We often see her riding. She always has a different one. She fixes them. Trades them. Uses them as equity. There's usually a handmade, metal-and-wood trailer attached, bouncing along behind her.

The trailer has the cardboard sign BECCA's MOBILE BIKES.

She fixes bikes, encampment to encampment, picking up ten or twenty dollars a pop for her trouble.

Because David is also a bike guy—back in New York, Lucy and Edie would cling to his bike's long cargo rack, the three of them weaving through Harlem traffic on the way to school; now he mountain bikes up and down the rocky desert mountains—Becca often pops in to borrow grease. Tire tubes. Or to talk drops and derailleurs. She unloads all her tools in the driveway and magically makes mangled bikes run.

We see Becca regularly. We will come to know her as we know all our neighbors, with or without walls.

* * *

The connection between bikes and the unhoused community is huge.

Bikes are useful for getting around. They are easy to store. They're plentiful. Easy to steal from homes and within encampments. And there's the freedom. Kid-me got to fly fast and free on my banana-seat bike, a tall orange flag on a pole attached to my wheel hub to alert traffic to my presence, a basket on the front with flowers. Handlebars with streamers. A working bell, too.

That Schwinn was my ticket away from hovering parents.

A bike is freedom.

For the unhoused, bikes are that kind of freedom and more.

Bikes are also a savings account and a currency. Like real estate, a good bike can be used for getting around, until you are in hard straits and need to liquidate. Your bike is an asset that can be traded for food, drugs and booze, sex, staples, whatever you need.

"I can't stand thieves," Becca tells me.

She has been imprisoned for car theft. Not to mention her bike business, which is founded on stealing bikes from the neighborhood. But it seems different when addicts steal from her, looking for that fix.

It is against the code or something.

She has been both thief and victim. She is aware that she has slippery morality on this. But she is resolute in these inconsistencies. She negotiates this paradox easily because the rules inside the community are different from the rules outside.

To steal in the neighborhood is one thing. Expected.

To steal from other unhoused people is total shit.

* * *

Becca says she quit meth a couple years ago.

"See? I still have my teeth," she brags, showing off a set of white and straight teeth.

Becca's face is still pretty. It doesn't look meth addled. If she did quit, she did so before the drug settled into her body and visited visible war upon it. Unlike Ms. B, Becca is easy to talk to. Her stories make sense. With beginnings, middles, and ends. She has a college degree, four years in business administration.

"I made bad choices. It's all me," she says, telling me about stints in jail for stealing cars.

But it feels like there is something more. Something heavier and darker is going on with her. I get this nagging feeling that this isn't just about bad choices.

"I landed in jail twice for stealing cars," she says.

"My choices. No one else's."

She is massively accountable.

We talk about her mom.

This makes her cry. Hard. Tears seep through her hands and wet her fingers until they glisten. Her mother makes her cry. She doesn't tell me why. And I do not ask.

I already know she won't tell me. It's all locked up and away. She has no desire to drag out her baggage.

She does tell me about her anger.

How black and deep it gets.

I've seen it a few times. Like when she can't get parts to fix her bike. She chucks wrenches across the yard. Or drops into aggravated sullenness. She lashes out at anyone who says anything. When she is in this place, she cannot move herself out of it.

It covers her. Smothers her. Drags her under.

And then there is Cecily Rose. Her twelve-year-old daughter, who died a year ago. In a traffic accident along with Becca's grandmother, who had custody of her.

"You lost them both?"

She lays her head in her hands again. Rubs the edges of the wig back and forth across her forehead.

"She took good care of her," she tells me about her grandmother.

"Her mom and I couldn't get it together, but Grandma was good with her. She was safe."

"Cecily Rose's mom is a meth addict," she tells me.

Becca does not know where she is. But she is sure she is in desperate straits. Becca says that the mother of her child is deeper into meth than she was.

Still, Becca is caught in a place where she wants to grieve for her child. But she can't really. Because she didn't know her well enough. She can tell me about her headstrong personality. How Cecily Rose was a lot like both her parents—an outspoken extrovert with opinions. But she can't really express what her day-to-day was like, who the child was in detail.

It reminds me of Chrissy and Jay. When they spoke of their kids, everything they knew about them was at the surface. They knew them only generally and abstractly, stunted into a memory, frozen at the age they were taken, wearing the same clothes, doing the same activities, having the same interests.

Knowing people—really knowing them—is formed in the ugly minute-to-minute of living together. Becca doesn't know Cecily Rose.

Becca grieves her inability to care for her.

To really know who she was.

She grieves the loss of parenting her.

Even though we both know she is in no place to be a parent to anyone. Even to care for herself. And then, after her child's death, Becca mourns the loss of hope that someday she might get herself together and parent her.

The grief is exponential.

Her darkness is fathomless.

It trails behind her, tarnishing everything she touches.

* * *

Becca rarely needs food.

Neither does Ms. B, really.

Whenever they take food from the pantry, it's "for later." Whenever that is.

If I have something sitting hot on the stove, neither of them ever wants it. And when they do pick up food, it never feels like there is urgency. This confirms for me that there is plenty of food for unhoused people in Vegas.

Becca just wants yogurt from me. She loves yogurt. We share a love for Noosa honey yogurt. When I buy some for me, I give her a big tub of her own.

When she is deep into that inky hellhole, it picks her up.

But other than yogurt and maybe ice cream, sugary things, she has her own systems for getting herself food. Becca and Ms. B know the ins and outs of the arteries of charity and food giveaways. They know which restaurants throw out good food at what time. What establishments leave the dumpsters unlocked. Charitable orgs that give out shelf-stable granola bars, crackers, chips, and cookies.

It's all cheap, mass-produced food that isn't fresh enough to need refrigeration.

Think of it this way—if you were evicted from your home today. If you found yourself hungry, you might not be able to ask a person you don't know if you can come inside their house and maybe make a couple of eggs.

But Stefran can.

A person who will listen to your stories and see you as a human being might also offer to cook you lunch. The level of intuition it takes for Stefran to size up David, ask him, and get the response he needs is truly impressive.

For Ms. B, Becca, and Stefran, you do not survive on the street unless you are resourceful by nature, adaptive. And resilient.

They are all of those.

* * *

The gateway to homelessness is crisis.

For Ms. B and Stefran, I would guess mental illness is the crisis. For Becca, it's meth and maybe other traumas that led to her using drugs to self-medicate.

There are a variety of ways a crisis can present itself.

Crisis may be driven by need, for instance; the lack of something.

Lack of affordable housing.

Lack of jobs.

Lack of a living wage.

Lack of education.

Lack of supportive family, especially when you are LGBTQ+.

Isolation, and lack of social capital.

Crisis may be driven by having certain issues in your life.

Like trauma. For veterans, childhood abuse survivors, and aged-out foster kids riddled with invisible, but intractable, complex PTSD. In fact, research on adverse childhood experiences (ACEs) can be directly connected to homelessness.

ACEs can include emotional and physical abuse and neglect, or having a parent with a mental illness, or addiction issues, or a parent who is incarcerated. It can include adverse experiences in the community, like bullying, racism, and removal from the family through CPS intervention.

Not surprisingly, poverty holds most of the risk factors for adverse events in childhood. Children who live below the federal poverty line are five times more likely to experience four or more instances of ACEs, according to the National Health Care for the Homeless Council, compared with kids in financially stable households, who might experience one or two of these events.

They found that more than half of all unhoused people have experienced four or more ACEs in their lives, while one in eight housed people have experienced four or more events. This means that childhood abuse, child removal from the family, and neglect put people at risk for homelessness.

Another kind of crisis that can lead people into homelessness is traumatic brain injury (TBI). This is a significant and often overlooked factor. Poor mood regulation, concentration problems, and memory loss caused by concussions and head blows are thought to impact as many as a whopping half of all homeless people, according to a 2019 study in *The Lancet*.

Stephen Hwang, MD, internist and homelessness researcher, as well as director of the Centre for Research on Inner City Health at St. Michael's Hospital in Toronto, tells the story of a patient acting out verbally and physically with staff.

The staff told him to watch out for the patient because "he can have these outbursts and be nasty."

Dr. Hwang investigated further.

He found this patient had a cerebral hemorrhage in his frontal lobe.

This was probably a contributing factor to his mood swings.

This finding helped Dr. Hwang let the patient know what was happening in his brain. He was able to send him to get therapies and medications that might ameliorate his symptoms and support mood regulation.

TBI works both ways for unhoused folks—having a TBI puts you at risk for homelessness, but being homeless increases your risk of getting a TBI, keeping you even more entrenched in poverty and insecurity and even more crisis.

Substance use disorders are another crisis that can drive people into homelessness, as well as mental illnesses, personality disorders, and developmental disabilities. These issues often make it challenging for people experiencing them to form consistent connections with family, and often these family members are keeping people out of homelessness. Chrissy comes to mind. Her substance use and her mental state contributed to her separation from her siblings, so when her life got hard and CPS came for the kids, she had no supports in place to help her keep her kids and get into treatment.

It is thought that perhaps a quarter of all unhoused folks live with schizophrenia, bipolar, major depression, or schizoaffective disorder (a combination of both schizophrenia and bipolar disorder) compared with the greater population at about 6 percent.

But this stat still feels light to me.

A lot of the chronically unhoused people who visit the pantry have obvious mental illnesses, like Stefran, Becca, and Ms. B. I suspect the number of unhoused mentally ill is much larger than we know. As with TBI, mental health issues work bi-directionally—they impact the risk of being homeless and also put people at risk for more mental illness while living on the street.

But with all of these factors, the biggest crisis keeping people outdoors is the lack of actual buildings for people to live in, either alone or in supported care environments.

When people need a place to live, we come up empty.

* * *

The kids don't let Ms. B in right away.

They know her. But with the pantry open for business, I've told them not to open the door for anyone. Except our immediate neighbors. It's something we have to do because so many folks are coming to the door now.

Raffi and Desi crack the door. They ask her to wait.

All I see is the shape of her head through opaque glass.

When I open the door, it guts me. A blast of chill hits me in the face. The wind is roiling. Rain spits at me through the open door.

She falls against my body.

I hold her up.

I walk her into the house. Kids gather around. They know her well enough now, but they have never seen her so small and fragile. She doesn't have her stroller. She is holding a drenched, quivering Princess in her arms.

I hand Princess to Edie, and she and Desi run off to get a towel to dry the dog and cuddle her. David and I bring Ms. B to the couch. We take off her wet jacket and wrap her in a soft fleece blanket.

Desi brings Princess to the couch, wrapped in a towel. I sit Desi next to Ms. B. Princess settles between them on the couch. Desi is thrilled to be entrusted with this important task.

Then she tells us. Words spill out.

She talks in circles.

About gangs of men. And people hurting her.

"They took my stroller," she tells me.

The one with her things piled into it. The one that houses her life. The one that Princess rides in, covered in a blanket, and drinks water from the hole where baby bottles are supposed to sit.

"My hands are dirty," she tells me. She holds them up. Her face is dirty, too. She has been in some kind of tussle.

I send her to the bathroom with towels. Soap. And washcloths. I tell her she can shower. But she chooses to give herself a sink bath. Lucy brings her fresh clothes. They probably wear the same size.

She sits on the couch. The end right near the fireplace. David brings her a fresh coffee. I take her wet jacket and clothes and run them through the washer and dryer.

"I can't eat," she says when I offer to make her something.

But she puts both hands around the cup and sips. Princess snuggles up between Ms. B and Desi. There's a fire crackling in the hearth. The flames make shadows on her face. The color in her cheeks is coming back.

The kids can't help but talk to her. They adore her.

I worry they will inundate her. Raffi is showing her drawings of monsters he made. Desi is babbling on about Princess and her pink collar and whether she might need food. But Ms. B is coming back into herself. It starts to show. She leans into them and their stories.

"This is scary," she says, admiring the details of Raffi's pencil work. He is pleased.

It is obvious as we sit there, we cannot send her back out to the streets. We also do not have a place for her to stay. Not one available bedroom. Even if that were a good idea. Which I'm pretty sure it isn't.

Still, Ms. B needs a place to stay. She cannot go back out onto the street, not sick.

But I have absolutely no idea where she can go.

* * *

Vegas has the usual array of social service organizations and shelters. But how do you find someone a place in an hour? It might be easier for a professional social worker, but that's not my world.

I drive to the Super 8 on Las Vegas Boulevard. It has recently been turned into a shelter. They don't take dogs. I know Ms. B is not going anywhere without Princess. I try a couple of shelters. No room. Or no dogs.

I write a post on the neighborhood Facebook page:

> Hi all-
> I ask this knowing it might feel like a gigantic ask, but here goes. . . .
> I have an unhoused woman who comes to the fridge a lot. If you

follow my IG, I've written about her there. Her name is Ms. B. She is older. She has a small chihuahua named Princess. She can definitely have some paranoia and dementia, but she is generally smart as a whip, and has very good boundaries.

She washes her clothes and showers at various agencies. She is an unmedicated diabetic and has been going through it with her feet out on the streets with all this cold. Two nights ago, a bunch of dudes roughed her up and took her stroller, which is sort of a carrier for Princess.

She will not part with Princess. I've checked everywhere to find her a place to stay. She has asked me if I could find her a garage or shed that she and Princess can sleep in, for a week or so, just until the cold goes away.

Does anyone know of a safe, not-so-cold shed, etc. for Ms. B? I wouldn't ask if she wasn't just the sweetest person. Thank you.

I deeply dread posting this.

Hours go by and I don't hit post. I expect people to be upset that I am asking them for favors I cannot give myself.

I expect: "Why don't you do something?

"Why are you dumping this on us?"

I post only out of desperation.

In minutes, my fears are proved wrong. The neighborhood rises up for Ms. B. The Huntridge Neighborhood page offers coats and blankets. People offer their sheds and back porches.

It's an onslaught of concern and love for someone these folks haven't met.

And one person does something extraordinary. Her name is Woodie. I know her as the woman in the group who always writes everything in capital letters, as if she is screaming.

She says she has a long-term solution for Ms. B.

* * *

Woodie and her friend Carol live in a dark, no-frills, broken-down weekly called St. Louis Suites. It's a few streets over from our home.

Woodie and Carol met at the Courtyard, a 24/7 campus where unhoused folks can go to shower. There are bathrooms, light medical services, and psychological support. Folks can use the bathroom and sleep safely in a secure, clean, open-air environment on mats.

Woodie and Carol hated it there. Woodie has nothing good to say about it. Becca also hates it there. Ms. B refuses to go there. Their reactions are immediate and clear. There is no hesitation.

Why do all the unhoused people I talk to dislike the Courtyard?

I go there to check it out.

The Courtyard itself is an airy, attractive structure with a roof and no walls. It sits in an area where there are other service organizations, like Catholic Charities and the Salvation Army. The area is called the "Corridor of Hope," and many of the unhoused line the sidewalks around the area.

But it doesn't feel as hopeful as the name implies. There are a lot of people who are inebriated. They walk like zombies through the surrounding streets. Along a chain-link fence, hundreds of homeless people sit and smoke pot, buy and sell drugs, and share food they have. I see a wildly psychotic woman, with an obvious case of tardive dyskinesia, a condition that often results from years of taking of psychotropic drugs—involuntary lip smacking, grimacing, eye-blinking, and twitchy, jerking arms. She walks across the street in front of my car. She stops and yells something to me or someone invisible. And moves on.

But inside the Courtyard it feels different.

People sit under the roof. At tables or waiting in line for services, bathrooms, or to plug in their cell phones. The Courtyard is a pavilion with tables and chairs. There are mats for people to sleep on at night. I have no idea what it feels like to be here in the summer at 117 degrees, but on this cool, low-80s day, it feels like being at an Oktoberfest beer festival, without the beer. I spy heating units on the ceiling. There are fans to move the air around.

There are security guards. Lots of them.

I watch a guard intervene when two men start getting heated in a conversation. The guard uses a soft voice, and by the end of the interaction, the guard has talked everyone down. The men talk things out. It feels like the guards are trained in de-escalation.

I sit down against a wall and talk to a woman named Claudette.

Her makeup is done, pink lipstick, dusty rose on ivory cheeks. She is in her fifties. She was an LPN for many years in Nebraska. But she was hit by a car—this is her crisis moment—and suffered a TBI. Her memory is shot. When she talks, she goes into long, fragmented tangents that make sense but are just a tad disorganized.

"My brain is not back yet," she says when she misses something or searches for a word.

It becomes obvious to me that even though doctors have her TBI on scans and have kept it in her records, they have been unable to keep her from losing her life. After her divorce, her life is aimless. Claudette shows up at bus depots to buy a ticket to someplace, any place, whatever bus is leaving next. Then she goes there.

Her brain is working. It's chugging along, but it's also not quite there. It isn't fully tethered to the world.

Claudette remembers her old life of stability. Her house with a garden. She tells me about lilac bushes and how you could smell them through her windows in the spring.

"I gave my husband the house," she says.

"I thought he needed it more than me."

She talks about college. About caring for people in sick wards. And about times when her life was in front of her, still to be determined. There was a time when Claudette was the caregiver.

Claudette is self-reliant enough to keep her private insurance, the cost of which is taken out of her disability payments every month.

"I don't want to go on Medicaid," she tells me as a healthcare professional, "the private insurance is better."

The rest of the money she gets she uses for food and when things are especially hard, maybe a motel room for a couple nights.

"Are you planning on staying in Vegas?" I ask.

"No," she says quickly. "It's too rough for me.

"I don't do drugs. There are a lot of drugs here."

I don't know if she means the Courtyard or Las Vegas in general. But I see in her the look of someone who isn't going to change their stance about whether they could live here. Like New York City, people either love it and get it, or they want to get the hell out of there.

Vegas is pure love–hate. Opulence and abject despair. A city of extremes. Probably the reason I have come to love it as much as I do.

* * *

When I leave the Courtyard, I am struck by how positive it all feels.

How professionally run. The guards are even compassionate. There is humanity expressed out loud the day I am there. But it's one day—a beautiful, temperate day—and I'm only there for a few hours. To be clear, the Courtyard is not housing. It's not a voucher to get housing.

It is a state-of-the-art Band-Aid.

The Courtyard itself will never solve the problem of homelessness in Vegas. It will never be a home for anyone.

Woodie and Carol saw that, as did Ms. B and Becca.

They knew they couldn't live in a place where even going to the bathroom or charging your phone requires standing in a line. The Courtyard is not a substitute for having your own place. Your own things, your own room. Your bed or the nightstand with all your stuff on it.

A mat on concrete is good for a couple nights, but it can't stand in for your own bed.

What is missing from the Courtyard is freedom.

This is why almost everyone who I meet at the pantry cannot see the Courtyard as their solution.

Instead, Woodie and Carol pooled their benefit money and paid an over-market rate for a three-bedroom apartment on the third floor, in Roachland.

They are now family. Woodie calls Carol her sister.

Woodie cares for Carol, who is older and a little senile. She is sweet and mostly quiet. I don't think I've ever said more than hello and goodbye to her. I don't think she could care for herself without Woodie. Or at least this is the impression Woodie gives me.

And now they've offered to allow Ms. B to stay.

Woodie is an ex-army cook. Cooking is among her many talents. She is a tough cookie, to be sure.

She has a bristled silver brush cut and strong arms. She is from Hawaii.

"I have cancer," she tells me.

"It's gonna kill me."

I am not sure what kind or where or if she's received treatment, but she tells me she is dying slowly. She medicates it only with street marijuana she buys from one of the handymen who floats around their Roachland. She tells me she is in pain all the time. A steady influx of pot helps keep much of it fuzzy and manageable.

This is, I think, her own kind of palliative, end-of-life care. On her own terms.

She dreams of Hawaii. She dreams of returning with Carol and living on the beach. What Woodie wants is to die in Hawaii. But there is no real plan for that to happen.

It stays in its dream-encased longing.

She talks about water lapping the sand. The breadfruit you can pick off the trees. Plate lunches with fat mounds of Kahlua pig, mac salad, rice, and pickles. Poke made with tuna, hours out of the sea. And Japanese breakfast—steamed rice, grilled fish, miso soup, pickles—whenever you want it.

I don't know if she will ever make it back to Hawaii, except in her longing.

* * *

I make trips up and down the stairs with Ms. B's stuff. The rain is lashing. The wind is bending back trees. I love this season so much, but not for moving people's stuff up and down three flights of stairs.

The elevator has been out for weeks, Woodie tells me.

Ms. B has a lot of stuff in bags and boxes. I wonder why they are important to her. But it is none of my business. Ms. B can have whatever makes her feel safe.

I let her talk and get to know Carol and Woodie. I make trips up and down from the car.

Woodie is cooking.

We gather around her in the tiny kitchen. A simple, no-frills galley kitchen that Woodie has made into her lab. There are dried spices and fresh herbs. A bread box, which makes me think of my mother.

Does anyone use a dedicated bread box anymore? I ask myself quietly.

But if you have roaches and mice, like in many weeklies, a bread box might come in handy.

I unpack boxes of food I've brought from the pantry to get them settled. Lots of meat, which I configure inside her freezer. Veg in the crisper. Snacks neatly lined up on top of the fridge.

She tells me where to put everything while working around the counter-top, with intuition and expertise. She makes a bruschetta with roasted peppers, pesto sauce, a soft cheese on top, drizzled with olive oil, and speckled with salt. She hands me toast on a plate to try.

It is very good.

Ms. B tries some, too.

This attention to cooking feels like a good fit for Ms. B, who has gone to her van, which is just down the street, and picked up the pot of sprawling green onions. We place them on the windowsill of her new bedroom, so they get light. The green is a miraculous sign of things growing, coming into being. These spring onions are hope for the future and better lives.

"Mahalo," Woodie says.

"I'll take care of her," Woodie says, and puts her big round arm on my shoulder.

As I'm leaving, Sonja comes with goodies from the Korean market.

Ms. B hugs her.

I get a text that someone from the neighborhood is bringing a bed for Ms. B. The apartment is sparking, flint on steel, with camaraderie. Sonja is eating a bruschetta before I can even leave.

I hit the stairs with Ms. B's life coming together into something new.

"As long as we have a home, so does Ms. B," is the last thing Woodie says to me as I close the door.

I take the three flights of stairs down to my car.

I am pretty damned happy with the world.

* * *

The follow-up Facebook post to the Huntridge neighborhood group:

First, I want to say thank you for every single response here. Seriously. You all make me proud to live in Huntridge. Look at all the comments and offers to help! Amazing.

Ms. B and Princess have moved in with Woodie on St. Louis. She has her own room and will be contributing to rent with her SSI. I left them settling in and will bring them more food and supplies tomorrow. They have two dogs, so I will be reaching out to folks here, who have access to dog supplies and food to give them a hand.

Woodie is a retired chef (among other things) so when I dropped her off, we all got to taste some of her beautiful homemade food and Ms. B was very happy, tasting and talking about cooking. I left feeling so happy that she found a place that might work long-term (or short-term, whatever) for all of them (fingers crossed).

Anyway, thank you for offering money, messaging offers of help, offering sheds and coats and blankets. You all are just wonderful people. Thank you.

I check in after a month. It's a thing of beauty, this arrangement.

Ms. B comes to the pantry to pick up groceries several times a week. She tells me what Woodie would like to make for them. I try to come up with the groceries to make her dishes happen.

"I have three dreams I'm working on," Ms. B tells me as I put carrots, head lettuce, beets with long bushy green tops, scallions, rice noodles, tofu, and soy sauce into a bag.

"My father's dream, mine, and Woody's."

She holds up three aged fingers.

"The first is for my father, who wanted me to live in the US," she says, smiling. "And I am."

"The second is for me," she tells me.

"Did you know my father only had me, a girl, and he couldn't have me be his heir?" she explains. "So, he adopted my cousin, and he was my father's heir."

"I'm so sorry," I say.

"This is how it was in Korea," she says.

"But I am living my own life now," she says. "That is my dream."

"And the third?" I ask.

"Woodie's dream is to go back to Hawaii to die," she says.

"That's her dream. I am living now to help her make her dream come true."

I start calling Woodie, Carol, and Ms. B "The Golden Girls."
I have high hopes for their futures.

* * *

Ms. B will stay at the apartment on St. Louis for three months.

Whatever love there is sours with time.

Woodie texts me about Ms. B's erratic behavior. About her penchant for picking up things on the street and bringing them into the house. Woodie is suspect of all the food she brings home. She can't be sure what's fresh and what's been decaying in her cart.

We set up a procedure in which I give Ms. B food from the pantry. I text Woodie and tell her Ms. B is on the way. Then I make sure Ms. B goes right to the apartment with the haul.

Woodie is convinced that Ms. B is trying to get inside Carol's head and steal her away. She texts me in big, screaming capital letters about it. Ms. B pops by the pantry to share the goings-on. She says Woodie is abusing and dominating Carol.

Ms B. is, in fact, plotting with Carol to run away from Woodie.

I listen to both of their stories and nod caringly. I try to offer bits of advice. But I see where this is headed before it heads anywhere. I suspect the truth is somewhere in the middle. Woodie is possessive of Carol. She enjoys being the functional one, the caregiver. It gives her purpose in her life. And companionship.

Ms. B has taken that and fed it through the loop of her delusions. Ms. B tells me, with Princess low-growling in her defense, that Woodie is trying to kill Carol. And how she likes Carol and wants to get her out of Woodie's care and back out into the streets with her.

But I know Carol would never be able to make it in the streets. She would die there. She would have no care or context for her life. So, it doesn't surprise me when their living situation implodes.

Ms. B packs up her spring onions and makes trip after trip to move out her things. Up and down the stairs, until not a speck of her remains inside Roachland. She puts some of it in her van. Some of it in her storage facility. And some of it at our house, which she forgets about, and we end up carting to the dump.

She goes back to the life she knows best, the one that is her own dream for herself—to live her own life, on her own terms, right here in the United States.

It strikes me that dreams, even when they do come together, don't always come together as we have imagined them.

* * *

Becca is at the door.

She comes every few days now. To check in. Fix her bikes.

To charge her phone and battery.

This is Raffi's job. He plugs in all her battery packs, bike lights, and cell phones so they are fully charged.

"I feel like I'm a good person," he tells me after helping her.

"You did good, buddy," David and I tell him.

I'm happy that he is discovering caring for others. He is looking outside of himself. This is huge for a kid who came to empathy late in his boyhood.

I plan to offer dinner to Becca. She has been down lately. She had to do ten days in ICU with the flu. Her boyfriend abruptly left her. I had met her in a nearby parking lot after she texted me about the breakup. She cried deeply into my shoulder over the loss of him.

But before I can make the invite, Raffi is screaming for me and David.

Becca is on her knees. On our doorstep, crying.

We all pour out into the path. I sit next to her. She weeps and rocks. I can barely understand her.

Between gulps of air she tells me about how a security guard at a local taco shop flung her bike repair cart into busy, rush-hour-clogged-Maryland-Parkway traffic. Many of her day-to-day possessions are strewn and blowing between cars. The wheels of the cart are mangled, twisted. In pieces.

I grab the keys. I tell her to get in the car.

We are at the taco shop in five minutes.

The guard changes his tune a bit.

"I'm a good person," he says. "I wasn't giving her a hard time."

I'm friendly.

"I get it," I say. "Help me collect her stuff."

I am able to offer Becca the privilege of my housed status. Just by showing up in a car and appearing housed, the guard gives me respect that he will not give Becca.

Becca is so angry that I think she might hit him. I make her sit in the front seat like a petulant, grounded teenager. She tries to scream at him through the closed window. But I tell her to be quiet.

"Do not make this worse," I say in my firm, no-nonsense parenting voice.

Dodging cars, I scour the street for clothing, supplies, anything I can grab.

She is not purely the victim here.

She has launched a chemtrail of cusses and epic put-downs at the guard, who is just doing his job.

I load her stuff into the back and peel off.

At home, she lays all the things we've collected out on the driveway.

Becca and David spend a half hour picking through everything that is left. They decide the cart is unsalvageable.

This is devastating for Becca. It's her livelihood.

I happened to have salmon and tuna sashimi laid out for a make-your-own-lunch situation on the back patio.

Sushi rice, avocado, pickles, seaweed, and fried peanuts.

I invite Becca in. She makes herself a rice bowl. With splashes of soy sauce and sriracha. She sits on our patio, with David and me, Raffi and Desi.

Becca ponders how to put her life back together. Her hands shake around the bowl. Her foot doesn't stop tapping against the stone floor.

It's all so familiar.

I can't help but think of Charlie.

I can pop her name in for Charlie. It's seamless.

*We have seen **Becca** through a lifetime of crises.*

*Every day brings some kind of cruel surprise, some hardship that would pummel me. But it is just business as usual for **Becca**.*

Her life is a tedious wreckage.

And it never becomes clearer than when we eat lunch together.

It's like sitting around the table forces us to look at everything. See it up close.

Meth.

Becca is actively using meth again.

It all makes sense.

* * *

After losing the cart, things get worse.

It is a crisis that begets more crisis.

As a trans woman of Mexican descent, Becca is especially vulnerable to crisis. One out of every five trans people have experienced some kind of homelessness, a number that is huge and a testament to how much misunderstanding, prejudice, and discrimination exist toward these folks. One in ten trans people have been evicted because their identity was disclosed to their landlord.

Add to this that shelters and service providers might not be versed in creating culturally relevant services and spaces to meet their needs. And this also means sometimes trans people are forced to be in gendered spaces, with binary bathrooms and shower facilities that make them vulnerable to bigotry and acts of violence from other members of the program.

During the Trump presidency, the Department of Housing and Urban Development (HUD) considered rolling back Obama-era safety regulations that protect trans people from being kicked out of shelters for their gender identity. Obama's 2016 legislation mandated that shelters had to admit biological males to women's shelters and biological females to men's shelters when they identified differently than their assigned gender.

Rolling back this legislation would've meant that a shelter that received HUD money could turn away anyone based on gender identity. This matters when you consider that trans women are incredibly vulnerable to attacks and abuse. A 2015 survey reported that 70 percent of transgender women have been "harassed, sexually or physically assaulted, or kicked out" because of their gender identity.

The abuse transgender women face on the street becomes real, and in our faces, when two days later Becca shows up at our door. Her ex-boyfriend, a man prone to anger, who never has an actual name in any of our conversations, tries to burn her to death while she sleeps in her tent outside the electric supply store.

Becca gets out, with some singed clothes on her back, her backpack. Everything else is either pummeled or incinerated.

I have never seen her so broken.

Her ex slices her bike tires. Ruins her makeup and her wigs. Breaks and stomps on a fancy makeup palette of eye shadow she was given. All her clothes except what she is wearing are torn, destroyed.

Red Nike sneakers, a T-shirt, and Daisy Dukes—that is everything that she has.

She has lost everything.

But he meant to kill her, so the fact that she is here is something.

"Even the meal badge I use to pick up food every day," she tells me in between sharp breaths.

"I can't get any food without it."

And then her head falls into her hands again. She weeps.

Raffi appears at the door.

"Don't worry," he says. "We will always have a plate for you."

He says it almost without thinking and looks at me to see if I approve.

I smile and pull him in for a one-arm hug.

In the months since the pandemic, Raffi has grown to see Becca as someone who represents, in a way, his mom's life. He knows Chrissy was often unhoused or, at best, insecurely housed. She jumped from couch to couch trying to stay in front of her homelessness.

Feeding Becca, for Raffi, connects abstractly and profoundly to taking care of Chrissy.

It is what he would want people to have done for her. So, when he cares for Becca, he is also caring for his mom. Something that warms and hurts my heart on his behalf.

He is nine now. He struggles with issues and behaviors that will no doubt be his burden for the entirety of his life. Serious things. Trauma and deficits that can still implode his life.

Our son is not out of the woods yet.

But what is shaping up beautifully is his heart.

"Raffi's right," I say to Becca.

"You can always come here to eat."

* * *

But Becca and I both know losing her food source is devastating.

Even though everything she eats is packaged and sugary and heavily processed, it's HER source. It's her rituals and customs and her favorite cookies.

It's her freedom.

Becca can't go back out there. The unnamed man will try to kill her again.

"I am so alone," she tells me, unable to stop hyperventilating.

"I have no one, nothing.

"Do you have any idea what this feels like, to be in this city, and to have absolutely nothing, no one?"

She isn't asking me.

She is asking the universe, the skies. The spring air. The gods she doesn't believe in.

"If I die out here, they will just cremate me and no one will ever know I existed," she says.

"That's not what I want for my life."

I recognize this place. This special, painful place might be her rock bottom, if such a thing exists. The very idea of having a rock bottom is controversial in addiction circles—Does it really exist? Do you have to wait for some terrible low point before getting clean?—but I recognize this place as a fragile point where something could happen.

"I'm using," she confesses.

I know, I say.

"I want to use more."

I know.

Becca is hungry. I go to the kitchen and ladle sopa azteca into a bowl. It has smoky ancho chilies and chipotles in adobo, and a whole chicken in there with stewed-in tomatoes, onions, garlic. I add garnish: crunchy tortilla chips, dripping with oil and flecked with salt, fresh out of the fryer, a lime wedge, shaved radish slices, a crumble of cotija cheese, a spoonful of crema, and a pile of avocado slices.

I give her a big tub of Noosa honey yogurt from the pantry fridge, which makes her smile. A couple cans of cold soda water. I know the yogurt will be a much-needed treat.

Becca craves sugar. It's the meth.

Meth highs and sugar highs invoke the same parts of the brain. They each get the dopamine flowing, and each provides a kind of euphoric rush. Becca carries a bottle of pancake syrup in the drink holder on her bike. Not to be confused with maple syrup, Becca's syrup is pure corn syrup and maple extract. Pure sugar.

She chugs when she needs a little dopamine rush.

Raffi grabs blankets and a pillow. David tells Becca she can sleep in the back of one of our Jeeps. The red one, which isn't running right now.

Raffi opens the back of the trunk. He helps Becca settle in.

"She is exhausted," Raffi tells me.

He is right. And I am glad he sees it. Becca eats, sleeps. I tell all the neighbors she is staying so no one calls the cops. All the neighbors are cool.

We have broken a rule about housing someone. No one is more surprised than me. But this feels necessary. And she is no longer a stranger. No longer someone I can ignore. The unhoused are part of our community now. They are part of our lives.

Becca stays for three nights in the back of our Jeep.

* * *

In the morning, I make a ham and Swiss omelet. A little salad, and curvy strips of bacon.

My bacon is never straight; it's all curly and twisted. My brain doesn't have the capacity to lay bacon out in neat, linear strips.

Raffi brings breakfast out to Becca as if we are running a bed and breakfast in our driveway. Raffi always wants to bring the plate to Becca. He gets mad at me when I do something for Becca that he could do.

It's one of those sunny, warm days that pull you out of the house. The monsoon has mostly let up, but the air is tinged with humidity. A rare thing here. It feels like a true shame to sit inside.

Becca is sitting on our stone path organizing the few things she has left. Just seeing all she has lost makes her weepy and sad.

I bring a couple chairs out. Raffi grabs a couple cans of nearly frozen Diet Coke.

"I wasn't honest with you for the book," Becca says.

I had interviewed her extensively, but I knew she was holding back. Now, she is raw. She has nothing left to lose. This begins a story of an upbringing so tinged with abuse, and abandonment so intense, that she cannot get through it without it ripping her up as she stammers out the words.

Becca's crisis into homelessness starts with ACEs, adverse childhood experiences.

"I said no to my father," she tells me.

"That's it."

It had something to do with school.

"I got a C, I'm not sure, but I know I was never an F student."

Her father breaks her collarbone. Her forearm.

CPS removes her from her mom's home. An aunt takes her in.

The next years are a blur of aimless, rootless living—from Mom, and all of Mom's boyfriends moving in and out, to her aunt's house, back to Mom's, to her half sister's, Dad's house, to Mom again and the new boyfriend, who seems to stick.

The first ten years of her life, she is everywhere and nowhere. It appears to me that homelessness has been the dominating theme of the first decade of her life, something that has settled into the nooks and crannies of her brain. Instability is her stability.

She talks about her mother's boyfriends. How they talked to her, touched her. Their violence. Their fingers. The smell of their bodies on top of her, sweat and smoke and control. How her mom never stepped in. How no one ever came to save her.

But Mom's new boyfriend is different.

"This guy tries hard," Becca says, explaining that the new boyfriend coaches baseball and football. She figures she is ten or so. The guy comes in wanting to be a father to Becca and her sister right there in Montana.

"I feel bad," Becca says, sniffing back the tears.

"I wouldn't accept him because I knew it would make her happy."

"I will do anything to make her pay," she says. "We had it out for our mom, my sister and I."

"Your anger was legitimate."

"I have to be accountable. I could've made better decisions."

"You were a child."

"I was defiant. I was looking for the attention she didn't give me. I wanted her to pay for the pills and the booze and the constant men coming in and out, all the ways she ignored me while they hurt me," she says, wiping tears out of her eyes.

That is the force that compels everything Becca does. It's this unnamed thing that makes her want to ruin her life, to piss off her mother so much that it makes her pay attention, jar her into a place where she takes care of her children.

"My defiance, my hatred for her, just burns me up inside. I live on it."

I rub her back. Like Johnnie, it eats her up. She turns the rage in on herself.

"I won't let it go. It's like a friend. It's always with me.

"I hate her. I hate her so much." Her fists are rolled into little stones.

"I've got to be able to stop that. It's not fair to me. I still care about my life," she says.

"It's why I think I'm not dead . . . I could be dead and she wouldn't know. I don't even think she cares. I'd be another person in a body bag.

"I think about going there and killing her," she says in an unguarded moment.

"She didn't protect me."

We sit quietly for a few minutes while our pug, Smudge, pads out onto the sidewalk and plops himself in Becca's lap.

"I don't know how to help you," I say honestly.

"I don't know how to help myself," she says back, scratching Smudge behind the ears.

We laugh, but it's a truth that sits between us.

"I only know chaos," she says.

"Right. You have to normalize no chaos."

"I don't know how."

"I know."

* * *

I take my shot—I start talking about sober living.

About change that feels uncomfortable. How doing the comfortable will only get the same results. I talk about getting out of street mentality. She knows she has been sunk under by it.

She talks about doubling for Johnny Depp and how that was her dream. And how she can impersonate Johnny Depp on Fremont Street again.

"If I were a small-time Vegas celebrity, I'd call my life a success."

What she wants for herself is eminently doable, just like it is for Chris Preston. Their goals are accessible.

"I don't have someone like my mother to tell me I'm doing better," she says quickly.

"She should've been there."

I am in awe of the power of parenting during this conversation. The importance of the hand-wringing and worrying and considering and overthinking—all the aspects of it.

I give her a squeeze. The kids see, and Raffi and Desi pile in for the hugs. This pleases Becca. She can't help but smile.

"Am I doing better?" she cries in my arms.

"You are doing great, sweetheart." I say it with the experience of a mom who has comforted more than a few babies.

I look in her eyes.

"You can do this. We—all of us—believe in you."

We let her go, and she adjusts her wig, wipes her eyes.

"I need to take a bike ride to see how I feel about all this," she says. Raffi gets one of our mountain bikes for her to ride.

And she is off. I know she'll be back. She would never steal from inside her community, and I think that's what we are now.

Raffi asks about her periodically through the day. He wonders if I think she is okay.

Becca stays on all our minds for the rest of the day.

* * *

The next morning, after her last night sleeping in the Jeep, Becca comes to the front door.

She rings the bell. Raffi yells for me to come. I consider that I'll need to get breakfast on.

"Becca isn't Becca anymore," he says to me before I can see who is on the other side of the open front door.

I see a man who looks like a younger Johnny Depp. No wig. No makeup. No high-heeled ankle boots. Men's clothes. Jeans and a cap on her head.

"I can't go to rehab as a woman," she says. "It makes everything more complicated." I think to myself that it shouldn't complicate anything, but I know she's right. She is supremely adaptable; it is the way of living on the streets.

"Is Becca gone forever?" Raffi asks. He seems a little sad. Becca picks up on this.

"She is going for a little while," she says to him. "For now, it's just Luca, okay?

"Becca will be back soon," Luca says to me.

"I am so proud of you," I say.

"You are doing so well."

She leaves with a small backpack.

I do not see Becca, Montana, or Luca again for a very long time.

INCONVENIENT PEOPLE + THE STARVING BRAIN

GLORIA HAS SEVERE schizophrenia.

She is, I'm guessing, unmedicated. She sleeps wherever she is. She seems to be in permanent psychosis. She cannot utter an ungarbled sentence whenever she comes to the pantry. I talk to her. I listen when she talks to me. I try to be open. I smile. A lot. Nod my head.

I see her walking down the street and know there won't be a connected moment. That there is no way in for me, or out for her. I know she will want to sit down on our next-door neighbor's grass, yell at the tree, and the leaves. And the air. And that they will all yell back at her. In words I can't hear.

Sometimes when I talk to her, she hesitates.

I wonder if someone I can't hear is talking to her. Or if she is listening to me. Then she goes on babbling.

Gloria makes me feel powerless and full of pity.

I am the giver. She is invisible.

I am well. She is unwell.

I am okay. She is the other.

This is my bias, my problem. Not hers.

* * *

Homelessness and mental illness have been intertwined historically.

The intractable problem of homelessness grew out of the equally intractable problem of mental illness.

When we see tent cities on our streets and people walking aimlessly and talking to themselves in our cities, this is a direct result of policy from decades ago. Namely, President Kennedy's Community Mental Health Act of 1963.

Kennedy called for freeing mentally ill, autistic, and developmentally disabled people from their institutionalized lives. He envisioned a world where families took care of their mentally ill and developmentally disabled family members. Their care would be bolstered and supported by a chain of community care centers that would support the families and help the formerly institutionalized members of their communities live productive lives with their loved ones. The idea was that patients would lead the best, free lives they could.

It was a compassionate and optimistic idea.

And one that was never backed up by specifics or research.

Could we build the care centers? Would there be enough of them to support patients? What does the day-to-day look like for these families? How does this work in rural areas? The inner cities? What about people from diverse cultures? Will this generation of medications keep people out of psychosis—the fragile, often terrifying condition where people lose touch with reality?

None of those things had been determined. The questions are myriad.

Kennedy could not have foreseen that the community care centers would never materialize. That the money to fund them would never be there. That we as a country would not have the stamina to create and fund long-term care centers to support families and mental illness.

He also could not have foreseen that people would not be able to care for their family members. Or even want to without support. That there were few resources to assist families. That they were unable to meet the challenges of the mentally ill and the developmentally disabled.

We never made caring for the most vulnerable of our people part of American culture.

* * *

Still, no one believes the asylum system that existed before the 1963 act was benevolent or therapeutic.

Psych institutions were often abominable holding cells for people considered to be untreatable. The asylum system was never about treatment or healing. It was always about control and submission.

Warehousing humans.

Its goal was to solve a single problem that we are still managing today: What to do with inconvenient people?

Art, as usual, was the first to inspire a change in public opinion.

The Snake Pit, a 1948 movie starring Olivia de Havilland, portrayed the treatment of a young woman thrown into a cruel psych ward. *The Shame of States*, a book written by journalist Albert Deutsch, was an examination of the brutality of mental hospitals. Add to that *Life* magazine's "Bedlam 1946," a long, clearly told exposé that outlined the atrocities happening inside mental institutions.

These pieces told stories of patients strapped to beds and chairs in leather handcuffs. Sometimes for days or months without being allowed to use a bathroom. Straitjackets. Confinement in bare rooms for long periods of time, the rooms themselves reeking of piss and shit. Clitoridectomies and absurd techniques for muting the sexual desires of gay people and women. Rats feeding on the corpses of patients in basements. Electroconvulsive shock therapy used to control and punish. Rampant lobotomies.

One of the most stealthy weapons—used to keep people submissive, quiet, and controlled—was food.

"At its worst, which we see daily, the plate takes on the appearance of what usually is found in most garbage cans. . . . I have seen coleslaw salad thrown loose on the table, the patients expected to grab it as animals would. . . . Tables, chairs and floors are . . . many times covered with the refuse of the previous meal," reads an excerpt from "Bedlam 1946."

The exposé goes on to accuse the asylums of posting menus by dietitians and logging them into hospital records.

But the actual meals were a much more meager offering.

"One morning in August 1944, when the patients' breakfast menu called for Maltex and soft-cooked eggs, the patients got merely Maltex," the article reads. "That night instead of a menu-listed ration of 'macaroni, tomatoes and cheese' their supper consisted of nothing but lima-bean soup. A few days later breakfast was supposed to have consisted of 'orange halves, corn meal and scrambled eggs.' The patients got only corn meal."

This is important. The hospitals knew what they were supposed to do for patients. There were treatment protocols in place. But they also knew they were dealing with a population that had no recourse.

Who would believe the mentally ill anyway?

The differences of who got what kind of food was obvious.

If you were the slightly infirm, lucid-enough white daughter of a wealthy businessman, you might get to dine with the director and staff at a formal place setting, eating with silverware, surrounded by people pleasantly conversing. You might eat "prime rib roast beef with gravy, broiled potatoes, roast corn on the cob, bread (white, whole wheat, rye or raisin) with butter, salad of cucumber, lettuce and celery, apple-apricot pie and coffee, tea, iced coffee, iced tea, or milk."

You may get to eat there if someone has taken a special interest in you. Or your illness is not pronounced. Or if you were from the upper classes and white. The civility of a proper meal was analogous to being healthy and well.

On the day the staff ate prime rib, the greater body of patients ate "hard boiled eggs, lima beans, beets, white bread without butter and milk or black coffee."

The food you ate told you where you were in the strata.

It marked your place.

And your worth.

* * *

Modern psychiatric hospitals have clearly improved dramatically. And what is considered therapeutic has gone through sweeping change.

But even now, wellness is valued differently than insanity.

Patients who are more well—more lucid, more connected to the world—often get treated with greater respect and dignity than those who are suffering more intensely. The value we place on wellness translates to a tangible difference in a patient's lived experience.

In her book *The Collected Schizophrenias*, Esmé Weijun Wang talks about the hierarchy that puts wellness at the top and lunacy at the bottom as it relates to her schizoaffective disorder. A diagnosis that combines bipolar disorder's treacherous mood swings, reality-distorting mania, and depthless depression with schizophrenia's tricks, voices, catatonia, and delusions.

Wang describes "the horror of being involuntarily committed."

"First, there is the terrifying experience of forcibly being put in a small place from which you're never allowed to leave," she writes. "I believe that being held in a psychiatric ward against my will remain among the most scarring of my traumas."

There is also the question of where she fits inside the metrics of sanity.

"I . . . was perhaps even ranked as highly as the depressives, because I came from Yale," she writes about one of her hospitalizations. "High-functioning patients had the respect of the nurses, and sometimes even the doctors. A nurse who respected me would use a different cadence; she would speak to me with human understanding."

Wang talks about the patients with schizophrenia and schizoaffective disorder being excluded from group therapy because the staff were unable to make meaningful therapeutic connections with the most unwell folks. As Wang sees it, the people who need treatment and understanding the most in psychiatric settings are the folks who are the most removed from sanity.

And also the most removed from the ability to make connections with other people.

Unlike in the past, when psychiatric hospitals were engaged in the control and removal of a person from society, modern psychiatric floors operate like a vacuum. They are secure, blank holding spots for shorter stays. People stay until they are safe to be around other people. And themselves.

They attend therapy. Have their meds stabilized. And it creates time to let any suicidal or homicidal thoughts pass. But like jail and other places that hold people outside of society, even for short periods, meals, three times a day, mark the time.

And push people through the twelve hours of waking.

* * *

"You're not allowed to choose what you eat and within the limited choices that do exist, you're forced to choose only between things that are disgusting," Wang writes about food. She notices that her eggs are "reconstituted" and her stomach "lurches." Yet she is ravenous and needs to eat. There is no choice. No freedom. She has to ingest the eggs, reconstituted or not. Lurching or not.

An article in *Vice* by writer Penelope Q raises the same issues.

"They [mealtimes] are spaced incredibly close, and are completely unaccommodating to the insomniac, the manic, the psychotic, the orally fixated, addicts, the depressed," Penelope Q writes. "We're directed by the staff to shuffle in at 8 AM, 12 PM, and 5 PM, though the time of service often depended on the whim of the worker serving."

She goes on to talk about meals being late because of something as trivial as staff watching sporting events on TV.

She writes of an intense lack of control for patients around their food.

Although there are luxury psych wards with private chefs cooking whole foods and gourmet dishes for clients, that's not a typical experience. Certainly not in state-run facilities for the indigent and poor, or even middle-class folks dependent on insurance. And food in these wards is not used as part of the treatment protocol, even though food can be healing, comforting, and therapeutic. Instead, it is a proliferation of foods that are innocuous, harmless, bland. Like the hospitals themselves. All the comfort has been stripped out.

"Some folks cry into their food while others parse it into microscopic bites to create the illusion of consumption," Penelope Q writes. "Mostly, I stare at mine until I can't, then eat saltines until I feel full."

It is not lost on anyone in a psych ward that jail feels kind of the same. As Wang writes:

> There are inevitable parallels between hospitalization and incarceration. In both circumstances, a confined person's inability to control their life and their body is dramatically reduced; they are at the mercy of those in control; they must behave in prescribed ways to acquire privileges, and eventually perhaps, to be released.

From this Wang confirms the crisis—that jails and wards overlap, and that millions of mentally ill people are managing and not managing their illnesses in jails and prisons.

"For those of us living with severe mental illness," Wang writes, "the world is full of cages where we can be locked in."

Like prison, confinement breeds a similar kind of creativity, rebellion, and self-expression with food.

Penelope Q writes about obsessing about eating pie while on the ward. So, she makes the mental-hospital version of a prison spread.

She goes to the microwave table, where they keep a bowl of aging fruit. Some cheese sticks and crackers. Not everyone has microwave privileges, she writes. Once again, wellness is valued and translates into more perks, more sidelining the rules. More freedoms. More good food.

More opportunities to be overlooked while making pie in a psych ward microwave.

She tells us she takes packs of graham crackers and cracks them up with her fingers. She is experiencing a delusion that her hands are in the process of rotting. This means she has to work the ingredients just so, to prevent her hands from falling to pieces. She microwaves pats of butter to pour over them. Adds a couple single servings of maple syrup. Mushes it all together. This is the crust.

For those on microwave restriction, presumably those with more intense psychiatric issues, she suggests asking staff for hot water and using that to melt down the butter.

Then, she recycles something from dessert—it could be pudding, ice cream, or yogurt. She puts the leftovers on top of the crust in a single layer, chops a couple bananas into slices. Careful to cut out any bruises.

Penelope Q freezes her work. She assumes the presence and privilege of a fridge and freezer.

Two hours later, she still has her hands.

They have stopped rotting.

And she is eating the pie she craves.

* * *

The asylum system was still winding down in 1972 when Geraldo Rivera famously broke into Staten Island's Willowbrook State School. His undercover video revealed naked kids and adults, many more than staff could manage, sitting on the floor. They rocked back and forth in their own filth.

It galvanized the nation that change was needed.

Most of these institutions were finally closed. But without the care centers and Kennedy's visions and funding and stamina to assist these families, these humans were released into communities, untethered to anyone.

And then nothing changed. Reagan-era politics left the mentally ill behind. They became a policy issue.

A problem for us to solve.

"Once deinstitutionalized, those individuals created their own communities of isolation, alienation, hopelessness and despair," wrote Dr. Richard Wyatt, chief of neuropsychiatry at the National Institute of Mental Health, in a 1986 editorial. We got used to having people be out in the open without housing or support. We numbed ourselves.

"By law, the former residents of structured institutions became public policy."

Meaning deinstitutionalized patients became everyone's problem.

Inconvenient.

And now, we have tent cities in neighborhoods and bikes stolen from backyards and folks breaking into abandoned buildings for shelter. And this is typical. An accepted way of being.

Most of the public just want these people to go away. Which is why cities across the country have been accused of giving the homeless bus tickets to other cities. A common practice known as Greyhound therapy.

Our neighborhood park was a destination for other people's Greyhound therapy.

It doesn't take a PhD to figure out why Becca steals cars and bikes from the neighborhood to survive. And why her sense of ethics around stealing corresponds to who is inside or outside her community.

If we cannot find places for people to exist and thrive in our communities, then we can't be surprised when the unhoused don't respect us and our lives and our possessions.

We abandon them.

They abandon us right back.

* * *

I want to write that schizophrenia steals language from Gloria. That it deletes her words and her ability to connect with people over time.

Wang, in her book, rejects this.

She observes that this centers The Well. It's a judgment on how The Well—namely, everyone not living through a similar experience—define sickness for people who are sick.

Her words echo new beliefs taking hold around the edges of modern psychiatry—the idea that patients struggling in the most desperate ways with voices, delusions, and psychosis can manage their disease with a minimum of meds. And without involuntary psych holds in wards and a litany of other therapies that don't work at all for them.

This is highly radical. There is a lot of dissent in the psychiatric community around this.

But the overarching idea is that patients want and need to connect to other people who have the same diagnoses. They do not want to be told what to do by professionals who have no idea what it's like to be in psychosis. They do not want to take a medley of drugs that not only aren't working but have side effects that further debilitate them. They want a say in their own treatment plans. And safe places to go where they can, for instance, talk about having a suicidal ideation with someone who also experiences them, and without being thrown in a psych ward for saying out loud that they do ruminate on suicide.

The World Health Organization (WHO) underscores the importance of this approach in their Special Initiative for Mental Health. WHO is asking for a radical rethinking of how we treat, diagnose, and manage severe mental illnesses. The initiative calls for an end to the pharmaceutical dominance in treatment and an end to forced and involuntarily treatment protocols.

WHO wants us to challenge the psychological establishment. To recognize that what we have now is simply a standard of treatment that will be debunked by future progress and a better understanding of disease. Much in the way that Willowbrook and the other asylums of the midcentury were outed, debunked, and closed.

In fact, the online schizophrenia community is incredibly activist on this point. And food seems to play a major role in not just the treatment of the disease, but in the activism, too.

In several online support groups I've attended, patients with schizophrenia and sometimes caregivers talk a lot about food. And how it is integral to managing the ups and downs of the disease. In fact, an informal look tells me that some eight out of ten posts in schizophrenia support groups center on food and its impact on the disease, along with meds.

Sometimes it's simply a proliferation of food memes—one I've seen has a photo of a grocery store snacks aisle and the text: "Pretty insane that 90% of foods in grocery stores didn't even exist 100 years ago . . . (and neither did 90% of the diseases)."

But many are deeply researched and based on scientific evidence. The admin of one group comes to the page with quotes from papers and studies. Someone asks question about controlling the disease with just diet and not meds. She comes back to them with a heavily informed post. This is a part of it:

> Diet is not enough. You are carrying 200x more bad bacteria than the average human in your microbiome and need to consider a cleanse to reset your gut as well as investing in the products that will help you maintain a healthy gut and keep your bacteria ratio leveled out and at the numbers they are supposed to be at to prevent symptoms from flaring. . . . Diet is but one of the many angles you have to use to take to get this under control.

The connection between gut health and schizophrenia has been studied for decades.

Researchers know there is a connection. But the research is still in its infancy. Still, scientists think schizophrenia could be an autoimmune disease in the same way celiac disease is an autoimmune disease.

This means control of the trillions of microorganisms that sit in our intestines—called the microbiome—could play a significant role, along with genes, the GI tract, the immune system, and the brain, in the development and treatment of the disease and management of symptoms.

That means that food is one of the ways to make schizophrenia treatable. Manageable. It means that all those years of warehousing the mentally ill and serving them barely tolerable food probably made them sicker.

It also means the people with schizophrenia in these online support groups are fighting. They are reading the research. Searching for answers and common experiences. They are talking to each other and finding solutions with people who "get it."

They are turning a nightmarish diagnosis into something they can live with.

They refuse to be warehoused and tucked away from their communities because their disease is inconvenient. They demand a rich, well-lived life despite their diagnosis. They are demanding to steer their own treatment and have the autonomy to make decisions about what they need.

They are demanding that The Well rise to meet them.

That feels deeply revolutionary.

* * *

In 2005, a second-year psychiatry resident at the University of Medicine and Dentistry of New Jersey named Dr. Sun Yum Young wrote a piece for the Residents' Voices column in the *Psychiatric Annals*.

It is called "The Starved Brain: Eating Behaviors in Schizophrenia."

In it, Yum makes a case that the onset of schizophrenia is the result of a "starved brain."

Yum thought that people with schizophrenia often talk about food, sex, and religion with a particular intensity and connection. These conversations, Sun noticed, sometimes get tossed aside by therapists as a kind of flight of ideas that is not productive for therapy. His belief is that patients gauge the response from the therapist and stop talking about those things to give the appearance that they are more well than they are.

The more you read about this, the more you begin to see all the reasons why someone who is severely mentally ill might want to keep certain symptoms and thoughts to themselves for fear of therapeutic repercussions.

Food conversations might be perceived as obsessive. They get put away.

But that food obsession also might be linked to a physiological starvation that is occurring in patients. It can trigger behaviors like food compulsion, overeating and gorging to the point that it happens nearly subconsciously. And outside the control of the patient.

"Eating behaviors in schizophrenia often have been described as voracious gorging due to the lack of control or even as a form of environmental automatism," Yum writes.

Automatism is doing something without realizing you are doing it.

"Some patients gulp down an entire tray of food and then begin to fight others for more," Yum writes.

He describes a man who steals the donuts and coffee from a startled family visiting another patient. That same man obsesses about fruit. He asks for fruit regularly. He has had dramatic tantrums when he isn't given food when requested. Yum describes this as fairly common with his schizophrenia patients. He writes about people sleeping "with oranges in their hands or hid[ing] food inside their underwear."

Instead of ascribing gorging and food theft to a loss of control, Yum raises the possibility that the behaviors around food aren't aberrant at all, but possibly a coping strategy for a brain that is starved.

Yum does this by referencing the Minnesota Starvation Experiment that took place from 1944 to 1945.

In it, people volunteered to go through periods of calorie deprivation and starvation. The idea was to study the physical and psychological impact of starvation on healthy humans. Researchers observed the changes in the participants as they starved in hopes of learning how to rehabilitate starving people and bring them back to health.

Everyone in the study was a volunteer with full knowledge of the scope.

The study started with a twelve-week control period of approximately 3,200 calories, based on body type and metabolism. This was followed by six months of semi-starvation at around 1,560 calories a day. Then twelve weeks of various rehabilitation diets, with eight weeks of unrestricted eating to follow.

What the experiments confirmed, according to Yum, is that the effects of starvation mirror many of the characteristics of schizophrenia. These include depression, hysteria, and chronic obsessions about the study participants' health.

They experienced a substantial loss of emotional regulation. The study participants experienced a severe lack of sex drive. They didn't take care of personal hygiene. They withdrew mentally, and their ability to make sound decisions diminished. They couldn't concentrate. Their thoughts wandered. They sometimes became psychotic. They couldn't articulate their wants and needs. All kinds of physiological changes happened, including reduced body temperature, heart rate, and breathing.

The effects of starvation are catastrophic to a human body on almost all fronts.

One of the participants in the study, Sam Legg, chopped off three of his fingers with an axe. When questioned, he couldn't say whether he had meant to do it or had done it by accident.

"Hunger made the men obsessed with food," writes Yum in a later paper, "Eating Disorders in Schizophrenia."

"They would dream and fantasize about food, read and talk about food and savor the two meals a day they were given."

The participants of the study played with their food and made strange concoctions out of it that were nearly inedible. This has been defined as a form of pica, the eating of inedible objects. Something that can sometimes be seen with schizophrenia patients.

There was also a lot of compulsive hoarding behaviors that occurred during the starvation and rehab phases. Participants were found rummaging through trash to find food.

In his work, Yum asks us to consider whether the schizophrenic brain is so constantly starved of what it needs that what seems to be disinhibited eating is really a "physiological and compensatory effort."

Certainly, the online anecdotal evidence of real patients supports this. One online chat room participant wrote:

As soon as my son has any kind of junk food or near of sugar his entire being in this world changes. The symptoms come on like a freight train.

When he's eating healthier, life is easier to accept. It's a work in effort though.

For her as a caregiver, the connection is immediate and direct.
Still, there is so much to be answered.
But food seems to play a role in the solution.

* * *

I knew another Gloria once. She had schizophrenia, too.

My very first job out of college was as the night manager at a step-up house that helped adults with schizophrenia transition into the community. I worked there part-time as respite help during college. And then full-time as a night manager after graduation.

It was one of the best jobs of my life, really.

There were step-up houses throughout the small city of Troy, New York. The idea was to provide a place for adults with schizophrenia to live in communities. They lived in the residences or moved up through them—with fewer and fewer supports—to independent living. Independent living simply meant living their best lives in the community, with a caseworker dropping in occasionally to offer support along the way. Caseworkers made sure meds were taken. That they had food in the fridge. That they were making and keeping appointments, getting around okay.

But at Seventh Avenue, the name of the house for the most severely impacted patients with schizophrenia, the caseworkers were there round-the-clock. They took residents to doctor's appointments. They made sure they had what they needed. Handed out meds. Residents were free to come and go around the community.

It was at this job that I learned to cook for large groups of people. Because homemade, healthy meals were a part of the protocol.

My friend Marta, who then worked at Unity House part-time while also working for adult social services, taught me how to cook. As did some of the residents. I had no clue before this job. Later I would move to New York City and truly learn to cook from my across-the-hall neighbor, Chinese chef Kian Lam Kho. But Unity House was where I learned the foundation, the basics.

Together, Marta and I made the kind of foods that come together for family-style dinners for twenty or more people.

Marta taught me how to braise a brisket. Roast a whole chicken. Put together a meatloaf with garlic mash. She taught me how to use chuck to make pot roast. And why it needed to be simmered in the oven, low and slow, in tomatoes and onions. She taught me how to stuff shells and make lasagnas. Store spices. Supply a pantry for a full house. She taught me that the stuff forming on the top of the soup stock was scum. And all I had to do was skim it off.

Revelatory shit.

I made big platters of mac and cheese. Huge wooden bowls of salads that we put out with every kind of bottled dressing in the fridge. We did seafood boils with new potatoes, corn on the cob, clams and mussels. We made chili. Roasted root vegetables. Simmered pots of Italian wedding soup. And made fried chicken. For years, I couldn't cook for two. I was better at cooking for twenty.

This is where I met the first Gloria, in her thirties. With brown curls. A penchant for colorful skirts and Marlboro Menthols. She swung her arms furiously when she walked, so that she always looked like she had a purpose, a place to go. Something to do. An urgency. Her words were mostly garbled. Her mouth contorted by the effects of too many antipsychotics. I remember the exact way she held a cigarette. She kind of curled two fingers around it before she took a drag, and then balanced it in her lips so that it tilted up.

I learned from the original Gloria, Carmine, Judy, Dwayne, Virginia, and Jimmy—all the people I worked with at Unity House—that several mentally ill folks can do just fine in the community, if they have some supports.

Take Carmine. A short, sweet Italian guy in his fifties, with schizophrenia and some significant developmental disabilities. I was his case manager and loved him immediately. He was sensitive and cried easily, a hair-trigger of emotion. He had a full, thick head of silver hair. Because of his cognitive disabilities, he saw young teen boys as his equals. He bought them booze and cigarettes to get them to like him and hang out with him.

He wanted to have sex and fall in love with them because they were his peers. He wanted to not be lonely. But the teens also knew how to play Carmine's game. They led him on to get him to buy them beer and cigarettes.

Unity House caseworkers talked to the local bodega and shop owners about Carmine and his relationships with teen boys. Together, they made plans to help Carmine when he was around kids. A caseworker would walk with him to the store. The shop owner had eyes on Carmine and eyes on the teens. The teens couldn't trick him into buying them booze. He couldn't approach them to have sex.

Amazingly, the community didn't brand him a pedophile or a creep. No one locked him away, despite a complex situation and the temptation of labels and simplistic knee-jerk action. It's like he became Norm from *Cheers*. Folks looked out for him.

They yelled "Carmine!" when he walked in to buy smokes.

He died of a heart attack while still on my caseload.

The community came to his funeral. The bodega owner. The staff. His fellow residents. The community grieved the loss of him. Carmine died living a supported but independent life. He died loved. And not alone, despite some challenging differences.

Carmine was part of the community. Unity House gave him that.

* * *

Robert Kolker, journalist and author of *Hidden Valley Road: Inside the Mind of an American Family*, the story of a family of ten siblings, six of whom had schizophrenia, believes in light of current research, even places like Unity House might not be going far enough.

In an article for *Elemental*, Kolker challenges the idea that just stopping at housing people in communities and managing their meds amounts to a life well-lived. He talks to a woman named Valerie Rosen, someone who also used to work at Unity House, who now works on a project in Westchester called OnTrack.

The focus of the program is family involvement from the beginning. It is the opposite of warehousing—it's about the family supporting and being involved while the person managing the disease takes the reins of their own care. It's not about sending people away.

Instead of plying people with antipsychotics, Rosen advocates for starting with meds on low and ramping up and adding as necessary.

"Rosen has two concerns," Kolker writes, "the cumulative effect of the years of medication and the day-to-day state of being overmedicated, which only adds to the sense of disability." The idea is not to sedate and create compliant people. It's to help people thrive and be alive in their communities.

The program also focuses on getting involved as soon after the first psychotic episode as possible.

"Researchers have the evidence now to confirm that each successive psychotic break causes more permanent damage to a brain," Kolker writes, "a further loss of gray matter necessary for processing information."

So, getting to a person early, when they are young, before a lot of damage is done and a lot of bad habits set in, is key.

The program also has people further along in the treatment process working with people newly diagnosed. This means the person giving you advice has been there. This makes the information more meaningful and practical, and staves off loneliness and isolation that so often plague folks with this disorder.

The goal is to manage this disease the way people manage diabetes.

The goal is to help people live out their dreams.

To support them while they kick ass and live as wild and hard as they can.

That, it seems, is the very definition of equity.

* * *

The woman I think of as Gloria here in Vegas is not actually named Gloria.

Or it would be a gigantic load of kismet if she were.

I don't know her name.

She can't tell me.

So, I give her one.

It's silly, but both Glorias have long, beautiful brown curls.

I want her to have a name.

But that's just for me. She has her own name. And it is hers.

My discomfort around Gloria centers on the fact that we haven't found a way to weave her into our community. There's no place for the severely mentally ill and the non–mentally ill together in downtown Vegas. No way for connection to happen.

So, there's discomfort.

And disconnection.

This is on us, The Well.

Solely.

* * *

I go out to stock the pantry at lunch and see Gloria walking toward me.

We had a heavy monsoon rain last night. The air is wet and moist. The grass is still soft and damp. Petrichor, the smell after a good hard rain, is in my nose.

There is a mulberry tree next door with a large shade canopy. There are still cicada shells stuck to the bark from the first spring many years ago. From the first year we moved to Vegas and Lucy and Edie collected the shells in pails and taunted me with them. They are old enough now not to care for collecting such dirty little things.

We are lifers to the West now.

We will never go back to New York City to live. We will love her from afar only.

Nevada means home now.

Gloria walks in curvy lines down the street.

I see her coming.

I want to hand her a small container of fried pork wontons I made. But I worry she will leave them in her bag and eat them when they are rotten.

Instead, I run inside and cut up some fruit.

I grab a small container of Greek yogurt, a spoon, and a small box I fill with hulled strawberries. I wash them. The chickens will happily gobble up the green tops for dinner later.

The yogurt is a probiotic utopia. Not that I think I can cure her schizophrenia with my stupid yogurt. Just that it might feel good to eat it.

Hi, I say. She has her back against the tree. It's a spot she loves.

"These are for you," I say softly.

"Can I sit with you?" I ask. I know she won't answer.

I do not get too close. I don't actually want to sit down. I want to be able to leave easily if this becomes futile. But I force myself to make a little home for myself by the tree.

I pop open the foil on the yogurt and get a bit on the spoon.

"Want some?" I ask.

I try to get her to take the spoon but she won't. So, I make a gesture like I want to feed her.

She doesn't stop me.

I brush the spoon against her lips. Her head jerks away, but then she gets the taste.

She takes the spoon herself now. I hold the yogurt cup and let her spoon the yogurt into her mouth.

She eats. Scrapes the cup with the spoon for the last bites.

And then it's over.

She drops the spoon in the grass. Her arms are moving. She mumbles things I don't understand. I put the box of berries into the top of the bag that is over her shoulder and resting on the roots of the mulberry.

She sits under the tree for the longest time.

Then she gets up and weaves her way down the street. Away from the pantry. She talks to me. To the air. To the street. To the sky. To the mulberry with the cicada shells stuck to it.

She slaps my neighbor's gate as she passes. She talks. Stops. Talks again. Talks. Stops. Walks again.

Yells at a mailbox. Yells at the air.

Becomes smaller and smaller. She vanishes onto 11th Street.

Next time I see her, I swear to myself I'll try to make a connection again.

I don't even know if it mattered to her.

But it mattered to me.

The Well can always do better.

9

SLIPPAGE + THE DISCOMFORT OF FOOD

"You don't perform gursha with just anyone," my dear friend Messeret says, laughing.

Messeret became a friend when she taught Joseph, while he was with us. And then, later, Raffi and Desi in a nearby preschool program. I trust Messeret with my most vulnerable kids. No one is better at managing their special circumstances and moving alongside their hard edges.

She comes to everything with love. It is both personal and cultural.

Gursha is the Ethiopian practice of feeding people—physically feeding them at the table. You take a bit of the food. Maybe kitfo or doro wat. You wrap it in a bite of warm spongy injera, the bread of Ethiopia, and scoop it from the plate into someone's mouth.

"There are a lot of people I don't want to feed!"

We laugh about feeding people we don't like. Or know well. She makes a silly face. Even talking about it makes her feel uncomfortable. Although this is the point.

"Gursha ena feker siyaschenik naw," is the saying she uses. I look it up later. It's an old Amharic saying that means "love comes with a bit of discomfort."

This is an apt description of "the table" for me.

Connection exists alongside the uncomfortable.

Intimacy sits next to dysfunction.

If there is no tension, no discomfort or disagreement, then how will we know the ins and outs of each other? If there is no challenge. No friction. No mess or chaos. Then how can we get under the skin to the good stuff?

How can we pry down into the things that are real between us if we are afraid of the uncomfortable?

How can we have intimacy with the people we love if we can't look into the ugliest parts of them and ourselves?

How can we know the people at our table and ourselves if we won't go to the dark places and look around?

Feeding people—like gursha—is often beautiful and hard. And when we do it, it isn't just warm and comforting and nurturing the way sometimes we like to present to the world. It's actually a myriad of complicated things.

The way Johnnie and Raffi need to have extra food left over in the pot to feel secure.

The way Johnnie, Charlie, Raffi, and Becca crave pure sugar to right their brains and feel comfort.

The way Destiny's cellmate was left to detox alone, with only the cookies Destiny saved for her. How they must have tasted to her.

The way not having good food felt synonymous with being forgotten for Destiny.

The way Charlie talks about his children at our lunches, as if they were not affected by his addictions. As if they were still in his life.

The way cooks like Chris feed others while struggling to feed themselves and their families.

The way tens of thousands of people have to make something good and wholesome, and nourishing and not entirely hopeless, out of a bag of potatoes and a box of precooked meat and can still find the joy at their table.

The way people have access to ingredients but can't cook in their kitchens because of the roaches, broken ovens, and no pans.

The way a foster parent friend of mine has to have dinner waiting on the table for her four-year-old foster son because he worries there is nothing to eat and needs to see it on the table the minute he walks in the door from daycare. That dinner is security, love, and the beginning of building his trust in the world again.

The way Gloria comes to the pantry for food, and our connection is muted and distorted and not perfect. But it's there. It exists. It is something.

The way we think some people deserve good food. And others not so much.

Feeding people is love.

And nearly always it is never just love. There is also discomfort.

* * *

It's fall now for a lot of people. Second Spring for us.

The idyllic weeks when the flies and the insects die off or slither down into underground root systems. The air cools to something closer to 95. Doors and windows get thrown open. And neighbors can be seen standing on curbs, chatting with each other, coffees in hand. There is a kind of rebirth in Vegas during these weeks, where folks transition from the outrageousness of summer to a more lenient season. We eat on patios. We have dinner parties under twinkle lights in the backyard. We nurse our beers into the evening. We wear short sleeves around our outdoor fire pits.

Las Vegas becomes a West Elm commercial overnight.

90 can be flimsy sweater weather. A warm bowl of congee with crispy fried shallots, pork floss, a soft-boiled egg, and spicy chili crisp.

80 is the heat on full blast, and numbing, toe-curling, Sichuan-style boiled fish is cooking on the stove.

70 is comforters on the couch. One of David's ripping fires, beef cheeks simmering with guajillo and ancho peppers on simmer.

I enjoy this time of year most of all.

* * *

The pantry has been going for months. We have a cadence, a mission, and support from the community.

Before the pandemic, there was a group of mostly women (and a few men) who met monthly at our local independent bookstore, the Writer's Block—an exquisite shop in downtown Vegas helmed by one of my closest friends, Drew, his husband, Scott, and their fourteen-year-old daughter, Paige. The Writer's Block is an artful, lush word-haven, complete with a plump store bunny named the Baron.

On any given night you can hear literary giants like Leslie Jamison and Claire Vaye Watkins read their work there, next to a young Mexican poet in his senior year of high school doing his first reading. Or watch a formerly incarcerated Egyptian activist read his work after seeking literary asylum in Vegas. In a state known for neon, ghost towns, and legalized brothels, the Writer's Block is a sanctuary. It represents our deepest, smartest, most-engaged selves in a city famously known for being none of those things.

Every month, our cookbook group—called Please Send Noodles—met in the book shop before the pandemic.

We made buttermilk fried chicken and oyster po' boys from Toni Tipton Martin's *Jubilee*. We made Hawaiian plate lunches with Alana Kysar's *Aloha Kitchen*. Think rice, macaroni salad, and pork lau lau, fatty pork and salted butterfish wrapped in green taro leaves and steamed in little packages. We cooked from Samin Nosrat's *Salt, Fat, Acid, Heat* and made miso-cured eggs, soy-braised short ribs, buttermilk roast chicken, and herby Persian-ish rice with tahdig.

Sometimes we had chef demos, like the time Chef Nick Aoki from Piero's, a well-known old-school Northern Italian Vegas restaurant, came in and taught us how to make his signature poke. As a Hawaiian chef, he took the mission seriously, and Piero's generously overnighted yellowfin from Hawaii for us.

We are poised to dabble in Israeli and Middle Eastern–style flavors with Ottolenghi's *Simple*. But we never get to it.

Pandemic.

So we start cooking together and talking about cooking and eating on Zoom.

We meet every two weeks during the pandemic. New people join. Old-timers stay and some leave. A new group forms. Through Zoom we learn how to make and fold dumplings with Hsiao-Ching Chou, author of the *Chinese Soul Food* books. And to season our woks with Grace Young, James Beard Award–winning Chinatown activist and author of *Stir Frying to the Sky's Edge*, and the book that has meant the most to me as a home cook, *The Wisdom of the Chinese Kitchen*. With one of the chefs in the group we do a fish deboning demo, where everyone, including Raffi, gets to debone their own fish.

But there is a need for food all around us. The group wants to do more than just socialize.

We start organizing a community dinner every month. We make 250 meals, boxed and ready to be put into someone's car when it pulls up, on the last Saturday of every month. The idea is to get people through the end-of-the-month stretch with a hot meal. Families can order however many meals they want. We give them a pickup time and our address. There are no IDs required, paperwork, and no limitations on the quantity. We encourage ordering for leftovers. We offer twenty-five dinners that are vegan.

We ask longtime chef Luke Palladino and local restaurateur Kim Owens to oversee food safety. They teach the group how to prepare and package food that is safe for delivery. We make labels with instructions and allergy information.

We are "sold out" nearly immediately almost every month.

We make pulled pork with arroz negro, jicama slaw, and warm tortillas. Garlicky chicken thighs with lemon-anchovy sauce, herby parmesan potatoes, and haricot verts with grilled lemon. A Hawaiian plate lunch of chicken tonkatsu over rice, macaroni salad, and some sticky sweet and sour sauce in accompanying cups. Brisket slow-roasted in lemongrass, coconut milk, and tomatoes with coconut rice and Melissa Clark's broccoli salad. And an Ethiopian meal, led by Messeret, of beef sambusas, stuffed jalapenos, braised beets with jalapeno, kik alecha, gomen, misir wot, and tikil gomen on injera.

When neighbors start getting checks from the government—if they are doing okay—they give them to us. With that money and whatever we get from Venmo donations, we add more dinners for more people. We call it 100 Dinners, even though we've now made far more. We served the greater community, and through CPS we also served about seventy-five foster-kinship families. These are the aunties and grandparents raising their kin and keeping them out of the system.

When we pass out meals, we hear from the people we serve that they are struggling to get the pantry basics needed to make their dinners taste different every night.

So, Please Send Noodles gathers together on Zoom around this issue.

We organize a monthly pantry giveaway. We set out tables in the street in front of my house, and people come and take what they need to fill their pantry. The idea is to give people the staples that will help them make diverse and interesting dishes with the commodity foods being handed out by the government.

We offer necessary basics like salt, pepper, oils, butter, and vinegars. Flours, cornmeal, cornstarch. Sweeteners, all kinds. Starches and grains. All the rice. Pasta, lentils, tortillas, breads, and crackers. Shelf-stable snacks, like nut butters and jellies, dried fruit, applesauce, nuts, and healthy hot and cold breakfast cereals.

Also, foods like pickles, kimchi, chutneys, anchovies, olives, canned tomatoes, and boxed broths. Canned meats and fish. Dried herbs and spices. All the condiments. And bottled dressings, hot sauces, soy and oyster sauces.

Tink is getting more and more grocery stores to give us veg and meat, so we are flush with beautiful products for people to choose from. The community is cooking for themselves. They are getting supplies from the pantry and coming to pick up ready-to-eat dinners and pantry supplies once a month. Please Send Noodles is becoming a close-knit team of workers and friends.

We cook and grow close.

We cook and give each other shit.

We cook and feed our people.

We feed each other.

Everything is going off seamlessly.

Until it just doesn't anymore.

* * *

The pantry Facebook group is going nuts.

"I saw a woman take all the meat out of the fridge," Rita writes. She is not writing about Sasha, but someone else, who I don't know. Whatever this is, the hurt is fresh.

"I was standing there waiting my turn and this woman came in and took everything," she says.

There is no meat left for her family.

A heated discussion breaks out on the page.

Jose, a young guy who contributes to the pantry much more than he takes, is the one who has dropped off the forty pounds of sectioned chicken meat from a local hunger charity. The charity has a name. But I refer to the director, in my head, as "the Pepsi Lady" because part of her mission is "Soda Day," where a semi filled with two-liter soda bottles pulls up and people queue up in trailing lines to take free soda by the pallet.

The Pepsi Lady is a member of our Facebook group. She is none too happy that Jose has taken some chicken from her pantry and donated it to ours, even though that chicken came from another food bank. An unwritten rule of giving has been broken. It is my first hint that hunger work can be competitive, divisive, and not entirely about the people who need the food.

"Please do not give food from our food pantry to this pantry," the Pepsi Lady scolds Jose.

I ignore her and focus on the group of people who are freaking out in comments. One person taking forty pounds of chicken triggers everyone.

It is the perfect example of the war on the poor—how even things designed specifically for struggling people, to help them, like our pantry, sometimes don't work at all.

"That's freaking ridiculous," writes Lateema. "I had someone try to see what I had in my bag that I was dropping off, before I could even put the items in the fridge."

Teresa talks about waiting to see what would be left after the people in front of her finished.

"They grabbed it all," she writes. "I waited patiently to see what they would leave me."

The very act of watching this woman take every bit of food in the pantry is a trauma trigger. A reminder of how scarce things are. How precarious. It does not matter that the woman might've had a big family. Or might be picking up for others. It only matters that people watch as the resources are taken and stashed away in a car that is not theirs. Going to feed a family that isn't them.

It is a viscerally painful moment for Rita.

It is exactly what I didn't want the pantry to be.

I explain why I haven't been "policing" the pantry, or what and how much people take, because I want people to have the freedom to choose what is right for them. To make sure they aren't just getting pounds of meaningless product.

Pounds again.

Not heirloom. Not organic. Just pounds . . .

The comments continue. It feels like therapy. Or a support group. Or an activist protest. The injustices and times when people feel shortchanged or ripped off are endless.

People write about the competition for food. And how it feels to be on the losing end of the grab for resources, which I suspect is also how they experience the world in the larger context of simply living their lives right now. It's a bloodletting. This isn't just complaining. It's venting about the fucked-up, chronic lack of interest in their well-being. And it's all coming to the surface.

"Okay, I understand people are struggling," Lateema writes.

"It's hard out there and I really do get it, but it bothers me that people are CLEANING OUT THE FRIDGE before anyone else can get there. Like seriously y'all, please think of others because someone thought enough of you to even do this!!!!!"

We need to change the policy.

Together, we make a plan. Everyone has input. The pantry Facebook group decides we will offer veg and grocery supplies 24/7 at the pantry, as usual. People can come and take whatever they want. I will refill as often as possible. We will continue making 100 Dinners for pickup for the community once a month. And we will continue pantry giveaways as needed.

But I will keep the meat frozen in my extra freezers on my side porch.

People can make appointments to come get meat for their families, when it is convenient for them. Everyone will choose from the meat, selecting what they want and how much for their families.

I post these new rules in English and Spanish to make it official.

This brings a calm to everyone in the group.

Rules are safety. Rules are consistency, particularly for people who have been through hell. I'm happy to make everyone feel safer.

But I can't help but feel that something unsettling is happening at the pantry.

* * *

Cardboard boxes are taking over my life.

I am putting out box after box of vegetables from Tink. I throw the empty boxes on the side porch. I get so many boxes of meat and veg now that Raffi has created his own little business. On trash day, he tears down the box mountain. He puts a few of the flattened cardboard squares into each of the neighbor's recycling bins.

He is a cardboard ninja in the dark on trash mornings.

David pays him $5 every Tuesday night. He is thrilled, rolling in the dough. But Raffi bitches vehemently about the task. David prods him along. I see him get wide-eyed. He surveys the stack of boxes.

"Mom, go easy on the boxes. This is too much work."

My full-time job is managing the donations from neighbors, whatever I buy with donation money, and the stock I pick up at Tink's house. Everything that comes in must be sorted.

I am grateful for all the new sources of food, the donations. The way people are thinking about their community. But it's starting to feel out of hand. The news coverage has spread word of the pantry near and far across the valley. And it is becoming harder to manage. A lot of people are cleaning out the backs of their pantries and leaving me with grossly expired food, things that have sat and festered in the back of their cupboards from a decade ago.

Saltines that expired in 2008.

Bread crumbs in 2010.

Cases of instant ramen in 2014.

I check and double-check everything that goes out. While some people lovingly stop and personally shelve the items they picked up for the pantry, other people treat the pantry like a contagion itself. They drive up. Stop. Open their car door. And drop bags of groceries in the dirt. They pull out like they are complicit in a homicide, and the police are in hot pursuit.

I can no longer control what is going into the pantry before someone comes and takes it.

Aisha, a member of the pantry Facebook page, tells me her daughter is sick. She is vomiting after eating ramen she got at the pantry.

She checks the expiration dates. Instant ramen from the '90s.

The little girl is fine.

But I'm not. This scares the shit out of me. Food safety has always been a huge concern, and here we are poisoning children.

I post signs on the pantry requiring folks leave grocery donations by my front door only, so I can go through everything before it hits the pantry.

At least once a day, I worry that the Farm to Family boxes from the government have not been properly refrigerated, as they go from distributors to food banks to a pantry to the next pantry and the next. A lot of the boxes are being handed out by churches and regular folks, who may or may not understand food safety. Sometimes these boxes are so many, they have to live in parking lots in all kinds of weather conditions until they can be distributed to the people who stand in line for them.

I stop picking up the boxes and just use product from Tink. Her food is mostly from local groceries, and the chain is short, a supermarket to Tink to me.

I am also disgusted at least once a day by the things people leave for other people to eat.

A half-used jar of off-brand mayonnaise.

Expired cottage cheese. Molded.

Sometimes I find specialty products like jars of honey, bee pollen, cornichon, olives, and things with truffles suspended in them, only to find out they were produced in the early 2010s for a corporate gift basket. I refuse to even feed the contents to my chickens for fear of making them sick.

I also notice that unhoused folks coming for food in droves are now leaving their mark on the pantry.

Sometimes people eat directly from the fridge. Half-chewed food and wrappers pile up. In the dead of night, someone drinks milk from a half gallon jug. They cap it and put it back in the fridge. Scraps of food. Plastic and paper wrappers tossed in plants and trees. Old shoes. A lamp.

Someone starts dropping off men's clothes. I stop them and tell them "Thank you but no."

"Are you sure?" she asks. "'Cause you know, they were my husband's before he died and they are in great shape."

"Thank you, I wish I could," I say.

But that's a lie. I don't wish I could.

Because if I take clothes, then other people will drop clothes, and I'll be in the clothes business.

Or the kitchenware business.

Or the flea market business.

Someone drops off old golf clubs.

My policy is—if you leave it, it goes in the trash.

If one person drops a T-shirt, I will have a hundred T-shirts to unpack from garbage bags for the remainder of the evening, along with the on-slaught of groceries to sort, store, and curate into the pantry.

It will become a free-ass yard sale. A clusterfuck of things no one wants that will grow to be the size of a Northeastern-size snowbank. A tall useless pile of chaos. The mess of my community's dysfunction. Their anger. Their disconnection.

Their desire to be helpful and to be a part of this, on my doorstep.

I am a hard no on anything that isn't food.

People need guardrails.

* * *

I feel the pantry slipping away.

I think about King and Straub's slippage, the nearly microscopic, nearly invisible, almost untraceable collapse into decay that happens to bodies. To dwellings. To objects.

To souls and hearts.

To haunted houses.

And to food pantries.

The change is minute, but steady.

We are nearing the end.

* * *

I'm standing just outside my front door. It's morning.

But it has been a long night at the pantry.

Two people are sleeping across the street under a neighbor's tree. In sleeping bags.

A man and woman I have never seen before.

I walk over. I say good morning. I let them know they are safe, welcome to have some breakfast.

"You can't sleep here," I say gently, slight smile on my face. I let them know that after breakfast they should go before a neighbor calls the cops.

They assure me they will leave. I tell them not to hurry. That it's all good.

That people are sleeping here is a harbinger of what is to come. The beginning of a community is forming around the food source.

A potential tent city in the making.

Under the California pepper tree, I notice someone has dropped a box of about forty pounds of dried beans. Mostly yellow split pea. The beans are stacked in a flimsy cardboard box. But the box has cracked open and bags of beans are falling out everywhere, into nearby agave, nestled into the sides of a barrel cactus, lost in a tangle of bougainvillea. Whoever donated the box discarded the food as if it were garbage.

Something to rid themselves of. Like chicken nuggets. Like Raisels.

In the pantry itself, everything is gone, as it usually is in the mornings. On this morning, the fridge door has been left wide open and the shelves have been taken out. Whatever food is left is lying haphazardly in the curb, along with squashed cans that once had beer in them. And a lot of cigarette butts.

The shelves are gone. I look everywhere.

So I grab the racks from my oven and a couple milk crates and build some makeshift shelves inside the fridge. This seems ingenious—I might have congratulated myself—but milk crates carry things, and several times a week, my milk crates will get stolen.

Tink starts giving me extra milk crates when I pick up groceries.

Cars are pulling up now for breakfast items. I am cleaning up and reloading.

I can't help but think of my first therapist, Gwen, who told me years before in therapy that when people trash a public restroom, when they leave behind their bloody tampons, their dirty pads, wadded up tissue stuck to the floor, mounds of shit in the bowl with no need to flush it away, that these people are expelling their anger.

They leave their anger at the world behind, anonymously.

It is a big "fuck you"; do you hear me?

Listen to me.

Fuck you, whoever is next.

See me.

See my anger.

See how badly I feel.

Deal with that.

You think I'm not here. I am.

I am.

The people with the most chaotic lives are now people who are at my house. Eating out of the pantry.

I feel the weight and anxiety and brokenness and chaos of their attempts to survive.

I feel their anger.

They leave it everywhere. It's mine now. I get to hold it for them.

I will not be able to contain the slippage now.

It all gets played out in our yard. At our front door. In our actual day-to-day lives.

The pantry is a public toilet.

* * *

There are people who come to my door all hours of the day and night now, asking for food. Whatever boundaries we have created have mostly been obliterated. People are so desperate; the niceties are done.

I open the door all the time to strangers. They ask for things. I give them things. I close the door, but they stay with me long after they are gone. I feel them. I take them to bed with me.

They stick.

There's one woman, Shaina. She comes at least once a week. But never during the day. Always with "three families" waiting in the car. They are always in a rush. Always with the car idling outside.

"Hi. I know it's late," she says, putting her body in the door like a lever, so it has to stay open.

I have been dozing on the couch after taking an edible to put me to sleep. I'm fuzzy.

"You have soup!" she says, eyeing the makeshift shelves in the foyer filled with canned food. Bags of baking supplies. Jars and boxes.

"Can I get some soup?"

"Um sure." She doesn't wait for me. She is halfway into my foyer and dropping cans into her box.

I want to lie down and go back to sleep. But Shaina is in my house.

I can say no. But I know she would roll over me anyway. I'm too tired to put up a fight.

The next thing I know I am padding to the side freezer in bare feet. I take out packs of meat to load into the box she is making. I grab eggs, cheese, and cold cuts.

"Um, okay, what else do you need?"

"Everything."

We are now at the point of the global pandemic where any food is good food.

She tells me again she has three families in the car. Which means she wants more. I see the lights. I hear the engine. I wonder if she is lying. I recognize the telltale etchings on her face. How the drugs have hardened her. I have no idea if it's true that she is feeding three families. Or how they all fit in the damned car.

But man, she is persistent as fuck. I give her everything she asks for.

Week after week, she pushes herself in the door. Same car. Same three families that may or may not exist. Maybe she picks up food to sell for drugs. I don't know.

It's not my business.

I never ask her to prove it.

Because we shouldn't ever have to prove anything to have food.

* * *

It's getting bleak.

Farm to Family boxes from the government are now on their fourth or fifth round. The last few rounds feel less helpful. It feels like the government isn't planning things with actual humans in mind.

This cycle of food boxes gives people a couple bags of dried beans. But no one is cooking dried beans much now. Supermarkets are open, government checks are getting mailed out to supplement people's income. Dried beans are still hard to find in grocery stores, cleared from the shelves by people's panic buying, but no one is missing them.

How do I know this?

I have seven hundred pounds of dried beans in my living room.

I like beans. But maybe not this much.

In his comprehensive book *Beans: A History*, culinary scholar Ken Albaba writes, "More than any other food, beans have been associated with poverty. . . . In any culture where a proportion of people can obtain protein from animal sources, beans will be reviled as food fit only for peasants."

It's similar to how Robert Sapolsky writes about poverty—when everyone is poor, there is no poverty. It's the same with beans. In India, where 40 percent of the country is vegetarian and beans are a staple, everyone eats beans. Beans are good for everyone across class. But in cultures where beans compete with animal products, beans often get relegated to poverty food status.

Take Brazil as an example.

Folks in Brazil, Albaba writes, eat feijão, or black beans. But how you eat them says something about who you are and how you live. For the middle and upper classes, the beans can become feijoada, a clay pot full of pig parts, beef, onion, scallions, tomatoes, and bay leaves, served with rice, greens, hot sauce, wedges of orange, and farofa, a toasted cassava powder. For the lower classes, where meat is scarce, the dish might be cooked simply with manioc flour.

Beans are so hardwired into cultures that they are sometimes used as ethnic slurs toward groups like Italians and Mexicans who come to the United States to live. "Bean eater" marks people as lower class, different, poor, foreign. Albaba acknowledges that beans are "a blank canvas for our political beliefs."

My favorite and most prominent bean memory is of my father eating kidney beans from a tin, slathered on Wonder Bread. A sight that used to make me weak just watching him. But for my dad, it was a cheap, filling snack for a poor kid from a backwater country mill town with lots of siblings for his mama to feed.

This is the image I have of beans: a way to manage hunger on a budget.

But beans are more than cheap. They are also versatile and culturally significant.

In China, beans become doubanjiang, a spicy fermented bean curd made from broad beans, chili peppers, soybeans, salt, and flour that is used to make dishes like mapo tofu. Non-fermented beans make foods like dried bean curd and bean milks. Soybeans are the base of the ubiquitous soy sauce.

In Egypt, ful medames, a kind of fava bean, make fúl, a hearty breakfast stew with parsley, onion, garlic, onion, lemon chilies, and cumin bathed in olive oil and tahini.

And then there are all the beloved rice and bean dishes. Think Bahamian peas and rice. Louisiana red beans and rice. Persians have sabzi polo, a fava bean and rice dish with dill and turmeric. Puerto Ricans have arroz con gandules. And Ghanaians have waakye, rice and beans cooked with dried millet stalk leaves. The examples go on and on.

As more people in the United States consider the impact of their diets on the climate, and on animals, bean companies like Rancho Gordo have given beans a new prominence. Rancho Gordo beans tend to be triple the price of regular beans, still inexpensive, and they sell all kinds of heirloom beans through the mail.

But what really drives people is the exclusivity. There are celebrity chef sightings and Hollywood actors, like Andy Richter and the late great queen of Italian cooking herself, Marcella Hazan, who buy these beans. And according to the *San Francisco Chronicle*, thousands of people are on the wait-list for Rancho Gordo's subscription-based bean club.

It is now urban home cook legend to wait years to secure a spot in the bean club.

"When people want to claim solidarity with the poor or working class," Albaba writes, "eating beans can be construed as a literal and physical way of overcoming one's inborn prejudice."

In an article in *The New Yorker* about Rancho Gordo, I noted some of the words used to describe various kinds of bean eating. "A bowl of moro beans is speckled black and gray like a starling's belly," while the black beans have an "inky depth," the flageolet is "grassy," and other beans are "meaty" or have a "dense fudgy texture."

We aren't talking Goya brand pintos or a tin of lima beans. Or the bags of beans precariously piled up in my living room. Steve Sando, founder of Rancho Gordo, knows why: "If your point of reference is the canned kidney bean at a salad bar, I totally understand if you hate beans."

For people who are struggling, these lofty joyous bean descriptions are absent. The upper classes have product that is superior, fresher, more nutritious. More care and thought goes into its creation and to how the food is discussed. It is the difference between an elusive Rosa de Castilla bean from Michoacán that gets written about in *The New Yorker* and trashed chicken nuggets being kicked around on the floor of a fast-food restaurant.

At the pantry, the Mexican abuelas take the pinto beans and make frijoles de olla, beans lavished in onions, garlic, and epazote. Messeret takes the yellow split peas. She makes kik alicha, a staple Ethiopian split pea dish with turmeric.

"I will have enough beans to make kik alicha for the next year," she tells me.

I make daal for the pantry in little disposable containers, with coconut rice and mango chutney. I label the ingredients on the top.

And when I have some left over, I'll mix the daal with the leftover boiled potato and wrap it in little triangle-shaped egg roll wrappers. I'll fry them until they are dark, crunchy, leathery parcels. Lucy and Edie will eat them all in the middle of the night when they roam the night kitchen.

Beans can be cooked simply. With time. And made to be tasty and brothy, with very little in the way of precious or overly expensive ingredients. But you can't just absentmindedly throw together dried beans last minute. They require a long bath overnight to soften them, or a protracted cook time. And the beans you find at the supermarket might be old and tasteless anyway. Some can sit in warehouses for a decade, while nutrients and taste have disappeared by year five. And started to wane by year two. Those beans need all manners of distraction—brown sugar, bacon, ham hocks, you name it—to give them some taste.

But no matter what I cook. How much or in whatever quantities. I cannot keep up with the supply from the government. The bags of yellow and green split peas, the garbanzos, pile up.

No one wants them.

Except Raffi. The bags of beans are his new toy. He wants as many as possible.

He stockpiles the bags to make a hideously large fort in the middle of the living room that we all have to walk around. He is stacking the bags on top of each other like sandbags around a foxhole.

Like a machine-gun nest awaiting Nazi tanks.

My living room is the set from *Saving Private Ryan*.

Raffi and Desi pile up the sides and float a blanket over the top and sit in there watching their iPads for hours. They bring in snacks. They eat their breakfast inside the bean fort. Once, I get them to eat refried pinto beans inside the bean fort. I make a joke about how meta that is.

They just stare at me as if I'm stupid.

Raffi takes his project a step further. He makes a bean bed for himself.

On our living room coffee table.

It takes him days to get it just right. He adjusts it over and over. He takes one side down and repositions everything. Stretches out across it. He tests its heartiness. He notes the mass and weight of how dried chickpeas stack versus split peas. Then he stretches himself out on top. Places a blanket over himself. Head on a pillow of lentils, he puts in his earbuds and fires up his iPad.

None of this seems weird to him at all.

"Lentils are the best pillows," he tells me, not chickpeas, which are "knobbier and less comfortable."

We live like this for weeks.

We binge-watch TV in the evening, with the bean bed in front of us on the coffee table. We have strict orders not to dismantle it.

Still, I try to secretly cook down his bed.

He hates this. I am relentless in my attempts to cook his building materials.

A donation of black lentils sets me on a course for making dal makhani, a smoky Punjabi dish that has kidney beans—two beans for the price of one is my thinking. While I do this, he is trolling around the pantry bringing more beans inside.

"We'll take your beans!" I hear him say to some lady who has a box of them from another pantry.

"Do you want to see my bean bed?"

He is inviting strangers off the street into our home to view his bean bed.

The bed gets bigger and comfier.

I make more bean dishes.

The Please Send Noodles cooks make bean dishes, too.

I think they pity me. I have turned the computer camera toward the hideous display in the middle of our living room.

The group gets on Zoom and brainstorms bean ideas. God bless them, they pull inspiration from their family's cooking. Instant Pots are at the ready. We hunt through internet recipes and cookbooks looking for dishes that will be nourishing and taste special.

We make ribollita with kale and thickened with slices of sourdough. Smoky, sweet, slow-braised baked beans. Black bean soup with avocado crema. A cold chickpea salad with arugula, blood oranges, and shaves of parm. Chicken chorizo chili with salted garlic yogurt. A long-cooked cassoulet with confit chicken legs. And a navy bean and escarole stew.

We leave them in small containers, labeled and dated, for the community. People take them as soon as they go out. Raffi snags containers for himself. He came to us a bean eater and remains one to this day. Sugary Boston baked beans and Mexican-style refried pintos are his favorites. Lucy takes every bean dish that is vegan, particularly the Indian and Ethiopian dishes.

People love beans when someone else cooks them. When someone else has the time and space to think about them and what they can be. They disappear from the pantry fridge as soon as I put them in, as long as I have done the soaking and the cooking and the simmering.

One day, I'm talking on the phone and absently pull a couple bags from the side of the bed, for a Spanish tapas-style dish with smoked paprika and celery. The whole bed starts to slide. I try to stop it.

I know my son is going to be furious, so I try holding the bed up. I call for David to assist. But nothing can stop it. I watch bags and bags of beans avalanche out of my reach across the floor. Once one side fails, the whole thing is compromised. It fails in other places now. Bean walls break down. My arms are not wide enough to hold everything. In minutes the motherfucker crumbles and collapses in on itself.

Several bags burst and black-eyed peas roll under the couch, across the room, and into corners, where I keep my dust bunnies.

Raffi cries.

I can't blame him. I've destroyed his bean bed.

* * *

Throwing away food feels wrong. But I know it's time.

I have to get the beans out of my house. I'm not going to drop unwanted food at bigger pantries and food banks because that just gives them more work with less outcome.

I'm not going to pass them along and make them someone else's problem.

I am creating plausible deniability for myself. Talking myself into what I know I have to do.

If I am being honest with myself, this is a protest. A silent one, where I can express my own anger at being loaded up with everyone's refuse.

It's a silent protest against the boxes in my yard.

And the spoiled food people think is good enough for other people to eat.

And the lady with the meth-lined face demanding food for three families at 11 p.m.

A protest against the fact that I have to wake up and give her food because no one should have to beg for food from a stranger's house and be turned away.

And there're the texts.

And Facebook messages from people sleeping in their cars.

Or worried about losing their kids to CPS.

Or down to an apple and a cheese stick for dinner.

Or about to be evicted and wondering if they should pay the rent since they might be getting evicted anyway, because the Roachlands are evicting people even though there is a moratorium in place.

I am so tired of feeding people. Because I shouldn't have to.

I start to think that every food pantry, including my own, is simply enabling the government to not take care of its people. We do it so they don't have to enact legislation.

I rage against it all.

The fucking beans have to go.

Raffi and I load them in the car. He has come to terms with their demise and is now focused on our newest game—pitching bags of beans into the back of the Jeep.

I keep fifty or so bags to continue making bean dishes for people who need the food. Raffi and I take the rest of the quarter ton—a quarter ton—to the dumpster at his school.

We start hucking them into the dumpster.

"Do chickpeas fly faster than pintos?" Raffi asks me.

"I don't know . . ." I say, picking up a bag of each.

"Let's find out . . ."

* * *

It's Halloween.

Folks buy candy and wonder if kids will trick-or-treat.

They mostly do not.

When they find themselves with huge bags of leftover candy, people decide they shouldn't keep it around because they might eat it all. They might gain weight. Too much candy is unhealthy. Too much candy is not good for your teeth. For your body.

So they bring it to us. In dozens of pounds.

"Can I drop off my Halloween candy?" people I love text me.

I know their hearts. They have good hearts. But I pretend not to get the message.

They bring it anyway.

"Because someone will eat it," they say to themselves. In the car. On the way to dropping it off at my house.

And someone does eat it.

Mostly meth addicts looking for a dopamine surge.

And my kids.

Raffi takes more secret adventures to the fridge than ever. He stuffs his pockets with Snickers and Nerds. He is always chewing things. Snacking. Raffi has a collection of chocolate now hidden underneath his mattress, melting into the fabric.

I have every leftover Almond Joy in the valley.

The addicts who crave sugar the way they crave drugs—and Raffi, who craves sugar with a similar urgency—are scrounging for candy at the pantry. I find wrappers in the yard (addicts), in the cushions (Raffi), blowing down the street (addicts), hidden in little cracks and fissures in his bedroom walls (Raffi),

hoarded (both) and

coveted (both) and stuffed into

mouths (both) and relished (both).

I remember having my own gigantic leftover bag of Halloween candy in the years when Charlie worked on the house. I bundled it up in a bag and stuffed it in the extra freezer in the casita. I promised the girls I wouldn't throw it out, but I didn't want them eating it all, either.

The theory was: "Out of sight, out of mind."

Charlie ate it all while working in there. I remember being shocked he could eat that much candy in such a short amount of time.

But now I get it.

Sugar. Dopamine. Momentary happiness.

Food. Dopamine. Momentary happiness.

Meth. Dopamine. Momentary happiness.

I am worried the pantry is jostling the most primitive and reactionary parts of our son's brain.

The pantry might help the community, but I worry what it does to him.

Slippage.

I feel it.

* * *

It's February 2021. We have survived the triumvirate of holidays.

It went something like this:

Halloween: candy, candy, more candy. I hate everyone who chooses to give me their candy instead of hucking it in the trash where it belongs.

Thanksgiving: We gave out turkeys as we got them. And we got a lot of them because people were receiving Farm to Family food boxes that came in set quantities. This created waste. A family might need one turkey, but lots of other kinds of ingredients for mashed potatoes, stuffing, casseroles, sides. So they get a bunch of Farm to Family boxes to cover what they need for sides. And then have five extra turkeys, which they don't need.

And those turkeys come back to me.

But unlike candy, I can work happily with turkey.

Please Send Noodles recognized that food banks and charities were sending holiday dinners to people, so instead of 100 Dinners in November and December, we held pantry giveaway days. We also cooked some thirty to forty birds.

I kept the turkeys I received from the community in my extra freezers. Then I handed them out to group members to be cooked, and I roasted a bunch myself. Two at a time. We made gallons of stock. And container after container of schmaltz. I handed out turkey butts like the gold they are for making fatty stocks. I boiled and fried some of the tails. And served them up at the pantry with rice, veg, and a spicy, lemony, garlic-yogurt dipping sauce.

I made gallons and gallons of turkey pho, and wonton soup, and subbed turkey into every dish I could think of—turkey pot pie, turkey lo mein, steamed ground turkey with ginger and salted fish, a turkey porchetta, and embutido, a Filipino pork-based meatloaf that can handle a turkey substitution. We handed these dishes out to people at the pantry in quart containers.

I ate the necks standing over the kitchen counters. Heavily salted, the way my dad did every Thanksgiving. I love a roasted, crunchy, salt-flecked turkey neck.

Christmas and New Year's Eve: cases and cases and cases of leftover candy canes. No one likes candy canes (except my editor, who, inexplicably, has a jar of them in her office well into July). Even people who can eat one still generally don't see them as a go-to.

Raffi and I make a candy cane–themed trip to the dumpster.

* * *

I wake up in the morning in February. I pad outside, in bare feet and a wool sweater I hold around me.

I wonder what has gone on with the pantry during the night. I never know what I will find. It's like Christmas, but more hellish and unpredictable.

People must've been feeling out of control last night—I find it trashed.

The milk crates are gone again. The fridge shelves, which are technically racks from my oven, have been taken out, thrown into a tangle of orange jubilee.

Food has been taken out of the fridge. It's lying around the yard.

People have dropped off boxes and boxes of packaged foods that require refrigeration. But they don't actually put it inside the fridge. So now it's garbage.

Someone has opened every bottle of liquid and poured it everywhere. The fridge is sticky and gross.

The smell of urine smacks me in the face.

My yard is post-apocalyptic.

Robert, Sylvia's husband, who lives down the street, sees me outside and comes to me, breathless. He sat outside on his front porch last night with

Sylvia, beer in hand, enjoying the sky spin colors over the stratosphere. They watch the stream of post-midnight drug addicts make their way down the street.

Then more.

Then more.

After they go to bed, someone trashes their mailbox. They are looking for uncashed checks.

"I'm worried that the fridge is changing the neighborhood," he says.

This is the moment where we stop slipping and simply free-fall into reality.

"You know I didn't want to move east of Las Vegas Boulevard," he tells me.

"But things weren't that bad on this street."

Robert and Sylvia have always supported the pantry. I listen to them when they say it is time.

I know it, too, on some level.

Later in the afternoon, as if the universe is summoning all of its communication abilities and hurling them at me so I will listen, an official City of Las Vegas "Notice of Closure" is posted on the pantry. It demands the pantry's removal, detailing potential fines.

Fridges are not allowed in the front yard apparently.

Someone has called the city and turned in our pantry. They, too, must've known it was time.

David and I discuss it.

I post on the Facebook page that the pantry is closing.

* * *

It isn't easy to tell people that we are closing.

The pantry has become a trusted, albeit imperfect, place for connection. Discussion. Food. Resources and social capital. It has been our lives for over a year. These are the people who got us through a pandemic. We have all given to the pantry and received from it.

If I am tallying, and I'm not, we've received a thousand times more than we've given.

We exchange social media information and many of us stay friends. I keep the Facebook group open. We post food resources in other parts of the community. Please Send Noodles will continue to make dinners for the community once a month. We continue to sell out.

I am thrilled when people who struggled hard during the pandemic come out of it with new goals, dreams. I see them kicking ass in the community. Emilie goes from working DoorDash and Uber Eats to a steady job at a Smith's grocery store.

She loves Smith's. Loves the people, as Johnnie does. She posts pics of herself in her uniform and about how much she enjoys the work.

Chris Preston flips burgers on the Strip for a while. But he leaves chef work to drive a long-haul tractor trailer. He is hoping this is the gig that gets his family out of the Siegel Suites. God knows his restaurant gigs won't do that. They still live in the same apartment.

I don't worry about the unhoused folks. They are used to change and, sadly, things they depend on are taken from them all the time. They will miss us. But they'll also move on and forget us.

Becca, Ms. B, Gloria, and Stefran will stay in our lives, in various ways. I know this is true because I see them often enough while writing this book.

I drive out to Henderson to pick up the last of my groceries for the pantry. I tell Tink what happened and that we are closing.

It is not lost on either of us that I am lighter already.

"It's like a foot has been lifted from my neck," I say, laughing.

I'm exaggerating for effect, but there is some truth to it.

The burdens of the pantry are not about too many beans. Or how many times I stock the fridge. Or the cleanup after particularly chaotic nights. The hard and glorious and exhausting part is just constantly being engaged in and confronted by the conditions of our own humanity.

Tink and I say our goodbyes. And then, back at home, one by one, standing on the curb, I say goodbye to the people who I've come to love this year.

"Everything must go," I say as people come into the foyer of the house to pull anything they want from the shelves.

Cindy and Sylvia wash down the pantry and the fridge. The guys from Rebar come for their beer fridge.

The pantry closes at the end of the week.

* * *

Instead of food, David loads the library with books again.

People come. They add more. They take some.

I am no longer in the pantry business.

There is no physical marker that it ever even existed.

It will take weeks for word to filter its way back around to me. But several sources tell me that the call to the city to close down our pantry came from the Pepsi Lady.

I don't know whether to be mad at her. Or hug her.

LUNCH + THE BRAIDED-UP LIFE

"Destiny wants to talk to you." I get a call from Brandon, David's assistant.

I never thought she would speak to me again.

"She moved to Detroit," Brandon says. "She wants to talk to you."

I hang up and call her immediately.

The first thing she tells me is that she and Joseph are all right.

And the first thing I say is that I'm sorry.

For making a bad situation worse. For cutting her off from all the support systems. For being a part of the problem.

"It's okay," she says.

And then, just like I remember, as if no time at all has passed, Destiny launches into a whole thing about Dre.

"Do you know that fool said he was there to pick me up the night I got out of jail?" she says.

"He wasn't there," she says.

"You were there.

"You and David were there for me and Joseph," she says.

"I know you did what you thought was right."

"It wasn't right," I say. "I've regretted it every day since."

"Our situation was not good enough for Joseph," she says. "I can't blame you."

I think she can, but I'm grateful she is giving me grace.

She tells me how the controlling behavior got worse. How Dre took her money and IDs. How he wouldn't let her out of the apartment. How he wanted her to pay the rent by pimping her out.

"He choked me," she tells me.

She tells me all the details. Dre got mad because Joseph peed on the couch while he napped. They fought. He put his hands around her neck. He choked her until she almost blacked out.

She had him arrested.

"But then I let the fool come back," she says.

One night, they are fighting about money. Who is going to pay the bills?

"He wants me to get out there and trick," she says. "And I'm telling him to get off his ass."

It gets physical. Destiny is no pushover.

Dre calls the police on her.

"But when they get here," she says, laughing, "they found his outstanding warrant for choking me and they arrested him for felony battery. They took his ass to jail!!"

That's when she leaves him. For good.

She packs up Joseph. She is in the wind. She does not look back.

Joseph is now seven. They live in a comfortable rented apartment in a good neighborhood.

"Life is slower in Detroit," she says. "I mean, I know it's still a city, but you can stay home, you don't have to do things.

"I want to be out doing things in Vegas."

Vegas is—and Destiny gets this, really gets this—a city of failure and redemption. You can fuck it all up in Vegas and win it all back again.

But it takes its toll.

"I think Detroit is better for us," she says on the phone. "I know this place. I was raised here. I can get around."

Joseph gets excellent grades in school. He is tall and lanky. With that still-sweet boyish smile. He calls me Mommy Kim, and David is still Daddy David. He still introduces us as his godparents.

A job that is close to our hearts.

Destiny makes sure he is college bound. She has a job working at the GM factory. It's a good, solid job, until they cut back her hours. But she knows how to hustle and pick up hours at Family Dollar. She is not going backward.

She has a new boyfriend, Darius.

"He is not super-connected to Joseph as a father figure," she tells me. "But he also doesn't hurt him or mess with him."

She tells me that even though she and Darius live together, Joseph comes home from school and makes his own snacks if she is working. He has a phone for gaming and for calling her while she works.

"Darius has his own kids," she says.

"I raise mine and he raises his with his baby mama.

"It's fine that way. It works."

They seem like they have a smooth easiness with each other. There is less drama in her life now. The fights are minimal and never violent.

"He's a good man," she says. "We're good."

Raffi and Joseph met when one was coming in and the other was leaving. They grew to know each other when we babysat for Destiny. They still think of each other as brothers.

And this call brings that all back.

They play Roblox together, Detroit to Vegas. They talk on the phone while they game. In the summers, Joseph comes to Vegas to stay with us for a week. Destiny and Darius enjoy the Strip.

I snap their photo. The boys are shirtless in swim trunks. They go back to running through the sprinklers. Next year or the year after, Raffi will fly back with him. He will stay with Destiny and Joseph in Detroit.

We hope that these back-and-forth excursions stick permanently. That these will be the summer memories Raffi and Joseph can build on.

"He's my brother," Raffi says, and Joseph puts his arm over Raffi's shoulder.

"Brothers, forever."

* * *

The pantry has been shut now for almost a year. But we still have many of the people from the pantry in our lives. They are friends and acquaintances now.

Frederico, in his motorized wheelchair, waves as he dumpster dives for cans. Miguel is on his bike around the hood. We talk in our broken Spanish-English combo. When he came to the pantry, he was nursing a weakened heart. His doctor advised him to eat more vegetables. We hooked him up. With vegetables. Pantry supplies. With ways to make vegetables tasty and varied.

We turned him on to a jar of spicy chili crisp. He uses it all the time now. Marina still drops by for eggs. And to offer quesadillas to Raffi.

He never forgets. And he always asks about the cakes.

Johnnie is still at Smith's. She was an essential worker all through the pandemic and never endured the scarcity of the hunger. And this has changed her.

She is no longer the person who is thinking of killing herself on the regular. Instead, she is a testament to the fact that her coping strategies work. Things fell apart for people during the pandemic. But not for Johnnie. All the rituals around making sure she has food, extra leftovers, a stash that makes her feel less anxious, her cookies, her safety food. It all works.

She comes through the pandemic with an understanding that she knows how to care for herself.

How to calm herself.

How to be okay.

She is strong and resilient.

It shows. In the self-checkout where she works now, in the same neighborhood Smith's, she gives me a huge bear hug. Edie does as she always does and pretends her mother and a cashier are not hugging in public. Johnnie runs our groceries over the belt. Edie tries to pretend we aren't embarrassing losers.

"I really have never been better," she tells me.

Like Johnnie, many of the folks who came to the pantry are doing great now.

Folks are fully employed again. They are going back to school. Eating at restaurants. Moving out of their families' homes and back to their own. They have left jobs during the Great Resignation and found better ones. They are marrying. Breaking up. Having babies. Living their lives even as generations of the virus buzz around us, ever-present.

From where I sit, these folks remind me that poverty is, in fact, mostly transitional.

There is life—and hope—after everything turns to shit.

* * *

Of course, for some folks, things are harder to change.

For some people, the complexity of their experience and their trauma runs them down. It mires them into complete paralysis.

Rosalina calls me out of the blue. I know her and her partner, Aaron, from when they came to the pantry. They are a complicated couple. Rosalina is stuck in a kind of existential paralysis: Poverty. Mental health issues. Family separation. Addiction to meth.

Rosalina and Aaron have been together for years. They have been addicted to meth for most of them. Separately and together. She has two kids in their teens from previous relationships. When she met Aaron, she tells me she stopped fighting for the kids. She let them be taken in by a relative.

"Does that make me a bad person?" she writes to me in Facebook Messenger.

She does not speak to her oldest kids anymore. They exist in some fuzzy memory bank. She sends me photos of them. But they are small. On big wheels. Wrapped in baby blankets. They are eternal babies, frozen. She only mentions them as an afterthought, like she is penciling in her story.

"I let them go," she tells me. "I know it's not right, but I decided to start over, and have a family for Aaron."

She and Aaron and their meth addiction created five more kids. Two boys and a girl, now eight, seven, and six, have been taken from her and adopted by a family member. She no longer sees them. They are gone.

Instead, she messages me about her two youngest children.

Rosalina trusts everyone and confides the most intimate details, all her foibles and mistakes, to anyone who will listen. Aaron is different.

"His mom always told him to trust no one. She drilled that into him," she tells me, trying to rein in the hyperventilation that is just a few breaths away.

"Aaron keeps everything very close," she tells me. And so it was an annihilation, and a complete shock, when he left Rosalina behind.

Aaron is AWOL. He is either back on meth or tired of her shit.

She calls me from her phone while she is walking around Stations Casino. She is just out of jail for harassing Aaron's boss, an arborist with a landscaping business. Her mother got her car out of impound after she went to jail.

This is a gift.

Rosalina is living in her car.

"Have you gone to your court dates for the kids?" I ask, as memories of Chrissy rush back.

"Aaron went to all the court dates because I have to be in bed," Rosalina tells me, and then launches into a discussion of the utter terror she feels almost all the time.

Tomorrow, she starts fifty hours of community service. And that's not all—Rosalina is facing down parenting classes, anger management classes, and classes on domestic violence.

She does not know how she will get out of bed to attend them. And it occurs to no one that maybe treating her depression and mental health issues before anything else might get better results for everyone.

This reminds me of Chrissy.

Chrissy couldn't—not wouldn't—work her plan. She needed a different plan. One that met her where she was. Not where we wished her to be. A plan that created meaningful supports for relationships and connections with her kids, even if she wasn't the primary care provider.

Maybe she would still be alive if that sort of support existed. And make no mistake—this matters to my kids. Even Desi, who has no real memories of Chrissy, clings to stories about her. She pores over photos of them together.

"I miss my Mama Chrissy," she tells me. It comes out of the blue while we walk the dogs. When there is nothing to distract her or entertain her.

The ache is there for her and Raffi always.

They are proof that you can love your adoptive family and still feel the bottomless ache of missing something vital that you never had.

This is a singular truth for many adopted kids, even if they never say it out loud.

What if the job of foster care was to support the child having meaningful connections with their family? Knowing their origin stories? Their medical histories? Being able to decide for themselves who they want in their lives and who they don't, even when mental illness, addiction, and poverty make that complicated as hell?

What if we supported families staying together even when the raising was complicated and imperfect?

What if our systems could handle complexity?

It is easy to think about Rosalina as not deserving of her kids. She is so clearly unable to take care of them or herself. She is a disaster in her relationships, with Aaron, with her family, with her kids.

When I talk to Rosalina, I think of Sam Quinones's book *The Least of Us* and his writing about new synthetic strains of meth pushing people into mental illness. His book is controversial. But his findings don't really surprise me—meth, trauma, mental illness, poverty, addiction—they all feel intertwined around each other.

Our solutions feel like they need to be as complex as our problems.

For instance, offering housing to Ms. B could change her life. Housing means she has a place to hold her hoarded goods. A safe comfortable space to sleep. She can make kimchi in her own kitchen. Maybe have a small pot garden to grow the veg she tended with her father. A window for her scallions to grow. She and Princess could still find her friends on the street. Spend her days with them. A caseworker who pops by once a week could make sure she gets to appointments. Help her clean, take her diabetes meds. Make sure the bills are paid, and that she has fresh food in the fridge.

Ms. B could be housed if she were able to live on her own, on her own terms. With a little support.

But for people like Becca and Rosalina, the childhood trauma, the meth. The way the streets suck you in and make you a vague apparition of your former human self. These folks need more than just housing. They need wraparound services over long periods of time. Without proper supports, an apartment for Becca or Rosalina will be a place to safely do meth with their friends.

An apartment can easily turn into an uninhabitable indoor tent city.

Building actual apartments and residences and homes for people is the only way forward.

We need supported step-up residences, like Unity House, in communities across the country. These residences must come with a focus on people managing their lives themselves, when and as they can. Supports that allow families to stay together, children to reside with parents in recovery. People playing roles in their own treatments, making their own decisions about which meds work and which don't. And being able to access support groups, where people with the same lived experience help people beginning the treatment process.

We need to integrate these supported houses into our neighborhoods and communities so that The Well, and the people with resources, can offer others the benefits of our social capital by being involved in each other's lives. We need to have neighborhoods that are integrated beyond class, beyond wellness, beyond race. Diverse neighborhoods enrich us all.

This is critical.

An August 2022 article in *The New York Times* underscores this.

The piece introduces us to a new study published in *Nature* that looks at the Facebook friendships of seventy-two million people between the ages of twenty-five and forty-four. Researchers determined that poor kids who grew up in neighborhoods with wealthier kids and formed cross-class relationships increased their future incomes by about 20 percent compared with poor kids who did not have these connections.

One woman interviewed for the article talked about how her working-class parents instilled in her the ethics of hard work and striving. But it was her friend's upper-middle-class parents who signed their kids up for SAT prep classes that changed the trajectory of her life.

This signaled to her what she needed to do for herself. She brought that knowledge back to her family. Her mom then signed her up for the courses. She took the tests.

She is now a lawyer.

"The findings show the limitations of many attempts to increase diversity," the researchers say, ". . . like school busing, multifamily zoning and affirmative action. Bringing people together is not enough on its own to increase opportunity, the study suggests. Whether they form relationships matters just as much."

This means in neighborhoods across the country, middle- and upper-class communities can impact and improve the lives of people in the lower classes simply by having a friendship. People who are doing okay need to get out into our communities and be there for people who are in crisis, even if those relationships are uncomfortable, messy, and difficult.

How?

Food is always a solid gateway to making this connection happen.

So, I do the only thing I can and bring a package of food to Rosalina.

I pack everything into plastic boxes and stack it in a cooler with lots of ice. I am taking it all to her Oldsmobile. I have sandwiches with a coconut chicken salad and arugula. Cold cans of sparkling water. A piece of cheese-cake. A small selection of crudité: peppers, celery, carrots, and broccoli with leftover homemade hummus. For dinner, I pack her crab cakes with a small salad, and a pickle-filled, zingy remoulade for dipping.

Her car looks like her brain. Chaos.

"Is it still possible to get my kids back or should I just let them go?"

She is ruminating and obsessing. Her thoughts are scattered. Leaves twisting in wind.

"I don't think you can get the babies back legally," I say. "But you should never stop fighting to be in their lives. To be at their baseball games and their recitals. You can still visit them at your mom's and show up and be a parent to them."

But all this blows through her as if I am transparent. She talks *at* me, not *to* me.

"I feel like he feels the same way I do, just broken, like our family is just broken apart," she says, crying. "In the beginning when the kids got taken away it was like we just hit a wall and we're not going to break through it. We're never going to be whole again, like a whole family, wanting to do what was best, raising our family, our kids. But I take full responsibility and blame that it's my fault for calling the police six times on him. I feel horrible. I let my kids down. I let Aaron down. I let myself down."

She interrupts to apologize for vomiting all of this on me.

But then she continues.

She tells me she wants to kill herself.

"I won't have to worry about getting arrested, if I'm dead," she says. "I won't have to worry about my kids getting taken away. I won't have to worry about paying my bills on time. Or if I'm going to make rent. Or if I'm going to get my car taken away, you know? I won't have to worry about anything. I won't have to worry if something's going to happen to me while I'm sleeping on the streets. I won't have to worry about nothing. It would be so much better."

She is young, but she no longer looks young. Late twenties, but, like Chrissy, her body has been through so much. Babies. Bad food. No food. Meth. And trauma. And a lack of care. Rosalina looks closer to forty.

I tell her about Raffi. And what it means to him to never be able to have Chrissy in his life.

How it rips him apart.

How he and his best friend, Dante, who both lost their moms to addiction, talk about it openly to anyone who will listen. Dante, who is half Black, is being raised by his Filipino grandma. Lola, which means "grandma" in Tagalog, is so scared he will become like his drug-addicted, unhoused mother and father, that she never lets him out of her sight. She holds on to him with a strangling fear. Every moment of her parenting is cut with the terror that if she lets him go at all, Dante will turn into his parents.

And she will lose him forever.

She knows that pain. Lola, will not have it again.

Becca once chillingly described unhoused people like Dante's parents.

"It's like talking to ghosts. . . . They are already dead," she told me.

Rosalina is a ghost, too.

I tell Rosalina she needs to stay in the world. And be there for them in whatever way they might need her, and in whatever way she can be useful.

She gives me the night. She says she will stay.

She won't kill herself.

But I have no idea what will happen the day after.

Or the one after that.

All the people who have lives so messy they cannot be unbraided so easily.

* * *

It makes me think of Charlie and Tessie.

I wonder how they are. What happened to their braided-up mess of a life?

Did they make it out?

I text Charlie. I wait to see if he will text me back.

* * *

"Charlie, it's going to be okay," the voice says to him.

It's a gentle voice. Familiar, loving. Full of hope and safety.

Charlie wakes up slowly on the floor of a Roachland in Tyler, Texas.

"Tessie! Tessie!" he screams out, rolling over onto his knees.

He crawls along the cold tile into the bathroom.

She has to be here. He heard her.

But he is alone.

It's all tumbling in on him now. He remembers. She was here. He got her high.

He looks around. She's gone.

He cries out to God. Charlie begs God to fix him.

He cries the way crying happens when it forces itself up from the darkest, shittiest, most broken places inside of you.

"I begged Him for a way. A path," he tells me. "I will go down any path He gives me."

Charlie has overdosed. Again.

Tessie has left him. Again.

Not only that, it was Charlie who got Tessie high. He ruined her sobriety.

Tessie takes Helena, their one-year-old daughter. She leaves him on the floor.

He is toxic.

He will never get clean.

He will always pull her down.

He reaches.

The Bottom.

* * *

I'm on the computer with Charlie.

He has quite surprisingly agreed to speak to me on Zoom.

"With meth, unlike heroin, you don't usually die, when you overdose," he tells me.

It's been four years since we spoke last. Over the gate of the house next door. But he texts back almost immediately when I reach out.

Really, I'm shocked. I didn't think he would ever talk to me again. Tessie hasn't spoken to me since the publication of "The Meth Lunches" in *Desert Companion* magazine.

I wrote an essay—that is now the first chapter of this book—that outed some of the most deeply personal events of their family. It got national attention. It was nominated for and won awards. In many ways, that essay launched me as an essayist. I reaped the benefits of writing about their lives.

I never asked their permission. I changed their names, details about their lives. I hid their identities. But none of that ameliorated opening a link to find the very worst of yourself laid out in a magazine for everyone in your hometown to read. Sexual abuse. Incest. The removal of their children. Their infidelities and indiscretions. I hid none of it, and since I wasn't outing my own trauma, it wasn't hard to do.

I can't blame Tessie for not wanting to talk to me.

The truth is: I thought they would never survive. I thought they were dead. I had no hope or faith. I had never seen anyone come back from that kind of pitch-black darkness.

It never occurred to me they would know the piece even existed.

But this time, Charlie is telling their story.

Charlie and Tessie want people to know.

* * *

When Tessie leaves Charlie, she ends up going to Tyler, Texas. At Father Heart, a home for pregnant and addicted girls and women. It is a devoutly Christian program. Opposed to abortion and dedicated to the Word of God.

Charlie follows behind. He checks himself into Hiway 80, a rescue mission in Longview, Texas. He is working. Sober.

Father Heart helps Tessie get sober. They help her keep her baby, Helena.

I see the photos pop up on Facebook. Tessie gains weight. She smiles. She holds Helena, their beautiful, curly-haired blondie who is the spitting image of Charlie.

Helena gives them purpose. Context. She tethers them to something concrete and important. A hope for them to hang on to.

There are visits. Charlie spends time with Helena at Father Heart. He connects to his boys, still in their adoptive homes with family. He remembers the love their family had.

Things are going well.

But then a friend dies. The estate leaves Charlie a settlement check. It is all he needs to use again. He buys meth. Gets fucked up. Gets everyone at Hiway 80 fucked up.

Hiway 80 kicks him out.

"I get it," Charlie tells me on the Zoom call. "Drug addicts are completely manipulative. They lie. Hiway 80 must enforce the rules."

And when she comes for a visit, he gets Tessie high, too.

He uses and keeps on using until he has no more meth. He wakes up on the floor. Withdrawing, hard.

He hears Tessie's voice.

But he knows it belongs to God.

* * *

At Hiway 80, addicts in recovery take care of unhoused people. The unhoused are called "guests" and Charlie's job was to cook breakfast for 150 guests.

"Some of the guys just reheat and put out pastries," Charlie says on the call.

But not him. The cooking has always saved him.

He goes into the big pantries and refrigerators and looks around for what he can find. He makes biscuits and gravy. Bacon and eggs. He tells me about making dinner with a legally blind man named Dustin.

"I'm making bacon for 150 guys. They'll throw bread at ya, if it isn't any good," he says, laughing and tipping back in his chair.

"I put pans of bacon in the oven. Lay the strips out nicely on the trays."

Dustin can only see colors. Charlie hands Dustin a cleaver and tells him to start chopping.

"You know I'm blind, right?" Dustin asks.

"Shit!" he says, cracking up. "Give me the fucking knife back."

Charlie grabs the cleaver. "You go warm the ovens up."

He shakes his head. Full smile. His time in the Hiway 80 kitchen means something to him.

"Cooking for people, feeding them, teaches you to love people," Charlie tells me. "To love them in the right way."

"You did that for us when we were at our worst," he says to me. "We won't ever forget that hand you stretched across the table to us."

But then he adds: "You know, you didn't mean to, but that cash every day from working on the casita?" he mentions. "That helped us buy drugs."

The lunches created connection. But they also helped fuel their addiction. The comfort with the discomfort.

Then he gives me a little lesson about unhoused folks.

"There are plenty of services offering food," he tells me. "The homeless aren't hungry."

"You can give 'em cold water and boxes of pizza, but they'll stay on the corner 'til they make their drug money," he says in his even more pronounced Southern accent.

He tells me how he used to put Tessie out front with a sign because people were more likely to give her cash.

"Never give the homeless money."

* * *

After he wakes up on the floor of this Texas Roachland, he gets the enormity of what he's done. Tessie is back at Father Heart with Helena.

He is a danger for her. A trigger. It isn't clear they can ever really be together. Charlie is the guy who threw away the only things that mattered, the love of his life and their child.

He signs over to Tessie what he has in his bank account. His SUV. Every dime goes to Tessie.

He is at the end of the road.

He gives every bit of himself to God.

He has been here before.

There is no reason to think this time will be any different.

* * *

"I walked into Hiway 80," he tells me.

He is sitting across from me on Zoom. His Texas kitchen is simple and neat. Sunlight streams in through lacy curtained windows. Tea towels hang neatly on the oven door. Helena bounces around the kitchen while we talk. Sometimes she pops in and sits on his lap. She combs the hair of a Barbie for a while. And then she slides off and runs away to do something else.

". . . me and another guy. We got a ride together in the van. We were waiting for the chaplain to come see us." Charlie stands in the front office, waiting.

This is his chance to get back into rehab at Hiway 80. It's his chance to start over.

"I'm gonna go out for a smoke," the other guy says to Charlie. He leaves.

Charlie is alone in the office for a few minutes. The chaplain comes in.

"You're in luck!" the chaplain says. "There is one bed left."

Charlie considers this an act of God. Proof that he deserves this last chance to be sober. Proof that something miraculous can come out of this.

For Charlie that was his last day on meth.

Tessie's last day is two weeks earlier in Roachland with Charlie.

Charlie and Tessie, newly clean, move back to Vegas. Tessie has family here. But the rifts that were broken open by active addiction have not healed. They might never.

"Vegas was too hard," he tells me.

He alludes to problems with her family. He doesn't want to say more.

When I try to peck away at why this time he is able to quit, there is nothing revelatory. There is no easy answer. No advice to help other people with their sobriety.

"The only way I got sober was trusting God."

He does not wonder why his other attempts to quit didn't work. Or why God didn't help him out earlier. It's all wrapped up in God's plan, which looks more like luck to me than divine intervention.

* * *

Charlie, Tessie, and Helena are doing so well. He works doing what he does best: Plumbing. Building. Fixing. All with his hands. During our conversation, he tells me they have been bank-approved to buy a house. Since then, I read on Facebook they have purchased the house and have moved in.

I am deliriously happy for them.

He is mending relationships with his sons. He has made peace with his father. And gotten forgiveness and grace from his sister.

Charlie and Tessie are making a life for themselves that in the past seemed impossible.

To them and to me.

Charlie is a testament to how far you can fall and still right yourself again.

That there is always, always hope, even in the most braided-up, complex mess of a life.

Charlie is the reason I no longer write off anyone. Even Rosalina and Aaron. Charlie is why I believe someday Becca will show up at our door with her recovery story in hand. Or if not the first time, maybe the second time, or the fifth, or the tenth.

We finish our conversation, sending love to all members of our families.

The next day, I get a message from him.

"By any chance do you have a recipe for fried rice? LOL"

I send him a link to the "Easy Fried Rice" recipe from Kenji López-Alt.

A few hours later, there is a photo waiting for me in texts. It's his fried rice.

"I made teriyaki chicken with it!" he says.

"It's beautiful," I say. And I mean it.

It might be the most beautiful and hard-earned fried rice I've ever seen.

SOME PEOPLE STILL *fight it. They call the heat oppressive, they call it unrelenting. They have not learned how to live within it.*
You must learn to smell the water beneath the surface.
—from the poem "Mojave in July" by Angela M. Brommel,
Clark County Poet Laureate, 2022–2024

AFTERWORD: IN THE WORLD

THE STORIES IN this book taught me so much about what it means to be well and unwell in our culture, supported and not supported, considered and not considered, seen and not seen at all.

This became important to me personally as our family battled our own mental health, trauma, and neurodiversity issues while I wrote this book. I couldn't help but think about how the world would greet and care for my children as they came into adulthood.

For Lucy, isolation and pandemic homeschooling triggered a previously unknown and lurking bipolar disorder. After falling into a dark hole, she had a terrifying manic and fully psychotic episode. She is on meds, in therapy, and stable right now. She is working at Starbucks and finishing school. She is driving. She has moved into the backyard casita, the one Charlie fixed up, kicking David out of his office. She has made it a little home. She has a sweet boyfriend, some good solid friends that require I make them sushi bake or salmon poke when they come over. Nothing makes me happier.

Lucy is in the world.

Edie's ADHD and anxiety became more pronounced as she reached sixteen. But this hasn't stopped her. Edie is learning to drive. She plays AC/DC on her Les Paul. She manages her brain with meds and therapy. She's a film major at Las Vegas Academy, a prestigious arts high school. She has a group of very cool artistic friends who shoot movies together around the city. She is deciding between circus college and circus life, or regular college and regular life.

Edie is in the world.

Desi struggles to stay in school. She is seven, has learning disabilities that make school challenging, and her anxiety makes her uncomfortable even going to school. (It's called school refusal or school can't, a real thing, where kids struggle to go to school because of their extreme anxiety.) Some days, I have to sit in her school, laptop on my knees in a tiny chair, to keep her there. But she goes to a special school with teachers who support her. This makes all the difference. She is learning to read, to do simple math. She is surrounded by friends who love her and welcome her every day.

Desi is in the world.

Puberty has intensified Raffi's developmental delays and behaviors. The transition to middle school was rough. His ability to disrupt a class is nearly legendary, and when he isn't being disruptive, he is masking, pretending to be like everyone else, holding it all inside. He often comes home sapped and brooding. But we recently transferred him to Desi's school with its uniquely patient and accommodating culture. He is learning to manage his anger, his unmet needs. He has support and people who want to see him succeed. It's two steps forward and one step back. But it is still two steps forward.

It's happening. Raffi is in the world.

My take on all this? Nearly everything I've learned about nearly everything comes from parenting my kids through brain-based challenges. They have turned me into a person who thinks differently about, well, nearly everything.

As Andrew Solomon wrote in one of my favorite books ever, *Far from the Tree: Parents, Children and the Search for Identity*: "People who see and acknowledge the darkness in those they love, but whose love is only strengthened by that knowledge, achieve that truest love that is eagle-eyed, even when the views are bleak."

Mostly, I see how easy it is to lose the people we love to the oblivion.

The addict on the street corner.

The elderly woman with the bruised face, hanging out in front of Smith's supermarket.

The man with the wild shouting and his angry talk to the trees.

The floor shitters that do everything to push us away.

The hardest, most difficult people in active, reality-less psychosis.

The stressed-out mom with the five kids to feed, and the dwindling paycheck and CPS on her back.

I am looking for a kinder, more empathic road for my kids and kids like them—so more and more people can be in the world. If you take away anything from this book, I hope you get this: If someone has a disability of the brain, then their behavior is going to be off. That when we, The Well, say "mental health doesn't excuse bad behavior," we are negating the fact that mental illness, addiction, generational trauma, isolation, head trauma, family separation, and the impacts of poverty all create brain issues and disabilities.

It is ableist thinking.

Or as Grammy-nominated rap artist and mental health activist Chika says on Twitter: ". . . someone having a disability of the brain ABSOLUTELY excuses their behavior because BEHAVIOR BEGINS IN THE BRAIN, FOOL."

We need to think with greater complexity, more nuance, less judgment. Fewer knee-jerk reactions to punish and vilify. We need to change how we see people in our communities. It is not on people in crisis, or who are struggling, to bend to us. Our role as a society is to bend for them. To make accommodations.

So they can be in the world, too.

* * *

What does all this mean for us out there in our communities? How do we get started?

For one possible answer, I looked to Stockton, California:

In her book *The Fight to Save the Town: Reimagining Discarded America*, author Michelle Wilde Anderson writes about 2011-era Stockton, California, a small city of over 311,000 people. It was a city ensnared in failed urban policies, high murder rates, street violence, bankruptcy, and corruption.

Stockton felt hopeless.

And this hopelessness trickled down generationally. Over and over. Incident after incident. Stockton's children grew up in a culture of fatigue and negativity. This defined their self-worth.

The media treated the deaths and violence as "social depravity," Anderson writes. "When the homicide rates stopped breaking records, outsiders stopped paying attention at all."

The Stockton police went all in on drug stops. They cracked down on petty crime. The policy was to react to the behaviors of people, not their trauma. Parents stopped sending their kids to parks because the police were ineffectual in protecting the communities. People stayed indoors. Kept to themselves. Stayed low.

But this started to change.

And how it changed and the things that really worked are instructive for the rest of us looking to make our communities stronger and healthier.

Anderson writes about community leaders coming into South Stockton knowing that "bossing families around never worked . . . because it added to their experiences as powerlessness." They knew support and oversight worked when families created their own goals. When they took the lead in creating their own healing.

Churches started "night walks" where they walked door-to-door, holding candles and flashlights, in poverty-ridden neighborhoods. They offered prayer and friendship. They brought the more marginalized citizens out of their homes and into the streets. They brought food and resources when people needed them. They brought friendship and social capital to the elderly, house-bound, and disabled. This helped bring these folks back into their communities.

Their presence signaled change and calm.

The government started buying up drug houses and turning them into affordable homes. Community groups worked to cut through the mistrust that had soaked into the culture of the city, a result of deeply segregated neighborhoods. They used churches, government programs, nonprofits, and hospitals to bring people together, instead of partitioning people off by race, class, and circumstance.

Stockton's people decided what they needed: (1) safe places for kids and teens after school, (2) clinics with mental health resources, and (3) the closing of a liquor store and market that served as a drug hub.

They made these three goals a priority.

The changes began without government funding or intervention. They began with volunteers from churches and nonprofits. Regular folks staffed gyms and rec rooms for kids when no programs existed to hire staff. One running gym, staffed by volunteers, brought pickup games that spilled out into the nearby desolate park, where intramural teams started up. Nonprofits came in later to set up funded youth programs.

That changed the community.

Success created more success. Not policing. Not incarceration. Not fear. Not hopelessness. Not punishment. Not behavior modification.

Anderson writes that "taking back the parks" helped heal the community's trauma.

This success created a domino effect. The city council took notice. It put South Stockton on the map for more funding for programs.

The work that followed focused on—surprisingly enough—intergenerational trauma as the reason behind poor health, early mortality, broken families, neighborhood violence, and chaotic schools. Stockton looked at ACEs as the root cause for violence and poverty. They found that "nine out of ten juveniles convicted of a crime had traumatic events in childhood and up to three in ten met the criteria for PTSD."

Trauma itself was the issue.

Counselors found that in communities with lots of violence, families often parent from that same learned violence. The trauma keeps on giving. The counselors focused on supporting families with therapy, a focus on home cooking, exercise, mindfulness, and lots of sleep. Self-care became a thing in a community that had been all about getting by, day-to-day.

Grants came in that helped counselors work with at-risk kids, like those in foster care or in the juvenile justice system. Healing trauma became the city's antiviolence strategy.

Alfonso Apu, chief behavioral health officer at the time, focused on resilience and making people feel seen and heard.

"When you normalize things and say, 'It makes sense to me that you're struggling,' they say, 'Oh! You're saying I'm not crazy!'"

The therapy and the focus on resilience helped people understand for themselves how their own trauma has impacted their behavior. It's like a missing piece of the puzzle that gets slotted back in. For the most challenging cases, where people's behavior was more severe, the point isn't why are you losing your shit and acting out. For Apu, it's "what has happened to this person acting out and why."

Amazing.

And then a ripple effect: Police began bringing people to Apu's clinic instead of arresting them. The police became part of the solution by working with at-risk youth in their off hours. They created a more connected relationship between the community and the police. And started their own wellness initiatives for officers also impacted by trauma in their own lives and on the job.

If we have police officers who have worked through their own trauma and lived experience with violence, couldn't that translate into more meaningful and peaceful policing in the community?

Stockton is hardly utopia. Politics and the pandemic have dialed back some of the progress. But it's clear that getting to the root of problems, and not just focusing on the symptoms, has substantial merit.

"One day America will be ashamed of the era of making police and prisons our only answer to the toxic chemistry of guns, victimization and chronic economic stress in poor neighborhoods," Anderson writes prophetically.

She's right.

For communities and cities across the country, things might not be as challenging as those in Stockton. It could take much fewer resources to dig down to our own roots, begin to heal our communities, and make people feel worthy of being in our world.

And that is good news. We know the path we need to take.

Nevada, for instance, doesn't even make HUD's (US Department of Housing and Urban Development) top ten list for numbers of unhoused people in the country. Our issues are not as unmanageable as the issues in California, Florida, and New York. We could, if we wanted to, make it our mandate, our promise, to house (independently and in supported housing environments) most of our chronically unhoused community members by building or fixing up homes for people to live in, inside our neighborhoods.

It's doable.

It would be complex. It would not be a success-only journey. It would require resources, capital, time, and labor. And mostly our battle-born, desert ingenuity and tenacity. We Nevadans—yep, I proudly count myself among them now—know how to make good things out of harsh environments.

And anyway, how expensive will it be not to do that?

* * *

Lastly, some thoughts on food and worthiness:

In Anderson's book, a Stockton activist talks about "worthiness." She believes worthiness is "at the center of everything."

Food is an important marker for worthiness.

When we deny people access to choose the food they need.

When we parcel it out to people in pounds and pieces.

When we say, "Sorry, you can't have more of that."

When people are forced to eat shitty institutional food to remind them of their status, their deviance, their unwellness.

When we feed kids that same shitty, packaged, dysfunctional, bullshit food and we wonder why they struggle with brain-based challenges.

When people tell you they need something and are repeatedly denied, the feeling that happens is unworthiness.

But food can also be the simple thing that raises a community.

I'm thinking about the family in North Vegas that has a card table and chairs in their front yard. Every time I pass by on a Friday night—and I do, often—people are always there. They're eating mojarra frita and rice one day. Papusas the next. Music on blast. They have a cooler of iced longnecks. A ratty old couch in the driveway the teens are sitting on and staring into their phones. Kids kick balls in the street as the sky blushes pink and violet. Grownups lean back their chairs and laugh. Voices and delighted screams blast the twilight.

After a few hello waves from across the street, they invited me over.

I'm flirting with the idea of a table in our front yard.

* * *

I'm also thinking about a Tweet thread from Vanessa Guerrero (@nessguerrero), who wrote about what helped reimagine her neighborhood in LA.

She wrote about living in a neighborhood in LA where police helicopters circle all day monitoring, making noise, announcing their surveillance. Guerrero said city planners left her neighborhood in "despair." The streets were filled with trash, and people kept to themselves. Then she goes on to talk about something that improved her neighborhood dramatically. In a matter of a couple weeks.

What was it?

A taco truck.

"Street food vendors on a block mean more pedestrian foot traffic around the clock," Guerrero writes. "If they're open late, that's more eyes on the neighborhood. Additionally in an area with many dark empty store fronts, they literally add light and vitality to the area."

She noticed more of the neighborhood meeting each other while standing in line for tacos.

"I met people three houses down I didn't know. It feels like we're all only now getting to know each other, over a torta and some soda," she wrote in her Tweet thread.

While the city stopped cleaning up the trash in her neighborhood, Guerrero noticed the taqueros were cleaning the block, grabbing trash from the streets around their trucks. The neighborhood quickly started to look better, feel better.

"They [the taqueros] also posted up at a bus stop and are open until 2 a.m. Meaning people waiting at the bus stop are no longer waiting alone in the dark," she wrote. "There's a noticeable air of camaraderie, safety and enthusiasm."

"Any way that people can be knitted into the social fabric is precious," Andrew Solomon writes in *Far from the Tree.*

Sometimes it takes a lot to make that happen. Complex answers to complex challenges.

But sometimes, the answer to bringing people into the world is as simple as a taco truck parked on a corner.

Or an inviting card table in the front yard.

Cooking with and eating alongside your community members is still one of the best ways to start the process of making people feel worthy. Of bringing them into the social fabric. Of smelling the water beneath the surface.

Of keeping all of us in the world together.

ACKNOWLEDGMENTS

ONE OF THE things I tell my kids is that who you pick for your community and your partner is the most important of all the adult decisions. I have messed up some things in this life, but not this.

My community is STRONG.

Thanks to these people for the myriad of ways they supported and nurtured me and the writing of this book.

Lucy, Edie, Raffi, + Desi. Best kids ever

John + Trish

Aunt Lois

Ted, for sending me "the finger" emoji every week until the book was done

Carolyn

Dr. Gwen Mancuso + Megan Thorne Alves, lifesavers

Drew, Scott, Paige, + the Writer's Block Book Shop

Alisha Kerlin, for letting me write at the Barrick Museum

Vegas mafia: Steve Franklin, Steve Evans, Dayvid Figler, + Rae Lathrop

Scott Dickensheets, friend, doodler, editor

Journalists at *Nevada Current, The Nevada Independent, Las Vegas Review-Journal, Desert Companion, Las Vegas Sun,* and *City Cast Las Vegas*

The incredible cooks of Please Send Noodles, especially Noreen, for nailing the tagline

Stacey Glick at Dystel, Goderich + Bourret

The team at St. Martin's Press. Gwen Hawkes, Hannah Philips, Elisa Rivlin, Jennifer Enderlin, Laura Clark, Steven Seighman, Nikolaas Eickelbeck, Hannah Jones, Susannah Noel, Lena Shekhter, Michael McConnell,

Julie Gutin, Allison Ziegler, Paul Hochman, Sara Eslami, Sophia Lauriello, Hannah Tarro, and all the people who are not on my radar who had a hand, even tiny, in the making of this book.

To my husband, David, for all the times you read these chapters, edited my words, made them better, didn't let me off the hook, pushed me, held me up, and made me laugh, just so I could get this done. There is no book without you, my love. You are my everything and always will be. Thank you.

I want to acknowledge the Nuwuvi, Southern Paiute people, traditional owners of our land in southern Nevada, including the Las Vegas Paiute Tribe and the Moapa Band of Paiutes. I pay respects to their elders past and present.

Thank you, mostly, to the people who let me write their stories in this book. I am better for knowing you and being invited into your lives. I hope I do your stories, and your beautiful, important lives, justice.

NOTES

Epigraph

ix *apartment in Las Vegas* Claire Vaye Watkins, *I Love You But I've Chosen Darkness: A Novel* (New York: Riverhead Books, 2022), 234.

Chapter 1: The Care + Feeding of a Drug Addict

6 *as many as 94 percent of them* Luz Gray and Michelle Rindels, "In Vegas, Day Laborers Living on the Fringes Learn to Fight for their Rights," *The Nevada Independent*, January 26, 2018, https://thenevadaindependent.com/article/in-vegas-day-laborers-living-on-the -fringes-learn-to-fight-for-their-rights.

7 *in The Nevada Independent* Ibid.

12 *Black House* Stephen King and Peter Straub, *Black House* (New York: Gallery Books, 2018).

14 *how the old system worked* Sam Quinones, *The Least of Us: True Tales of America and Hope in the Time of Fentanyl and Meth* (New York: Bloomsbury Publishing, 2021).

15 *"from the Mexicans"* Sam Quinones, "'I Don't Know That I Would Even Call It Meth Anymore': Different Chemically Than It Was a Decade Ago, the Drug Is Creating a Wave of Severe Mental Illness and Worsening America's Homelessness Problem," *The Atlantic*, October 18, 2021, https://www.theatlantic.com/magazine/archive/2021/11/the-new-meth/620174/.

15 *according to Quinones* Ibid.

22 *Quinones says* Maer Roshan, "The New Brand of Meth That's Fueling L.A.'s Homelessness Crisis," *Los Angeles Magazine*, March 11, 2022, https://www.lamag.com/citythinkblog /the-new-brand-of-meth-fueling-l-a-s-homelessness-crisis/.

Chapter 2: Surveillance of Humans + Their Food

40 *throughout a given year* Ashley Forest and Heather Mills, "CCDC Raise Awareness about the Growing Population of Mentally Ill Inmates," KSNV, May 16, 2018, https://news3lv .com/news/local/ccdc-raise-awareness-about-growing-population-of-mentally-ill-inmates.

44 *as the general public* "Prison Food Can Be a Sentence for Sickness According to CDC Report," *Correctional News*, March 6, 2018, https://correctionalnews.com/2018/03/06/prison-food-sickness/.

44 *served at the jail* "Complaints, Inspections Expose Unsafe Food at Clark County Detention Center and You Pay for It," *Dirty Dining Jail Edition*, May 8, 2018, https://www.ktnv.com/news/contact-13/dirty-dining-jail-edition.

44 *a litany of infractions* Ibid.

44 *even ketchup* Clare Sestanovich, "Prison Moonshine: How It's Made, How It Smells, and Why Ketchup Is Involved," The Marshall Project, December 30, 2014, https://www.themarshallproject.org/2014/12/30/prison-moonshine.

44 *ready to drink* Greg Hardesty, "Pruno Brew Is the Toast of the O.C. Jail," *Orange County Register*, June 8, 2011, https://www.ocregister.com/2011/06/08/pruno-brew-is-the-toast-of-the-oc-jail/.

45 *in 2006* Scott Hensley, "Botulism Outbreak Tied to Contaminated Prison Hooch," NPR, October 5, 2012, https://www.npr.org/sections/health-shots/2012/10/04/162291607/botulism-outbreak-tied-to-contaminated-prison-hooch.

45 *left over that week* Eliza Barclay, "Food as Punishment: Giving U.S. Inmates 'the Loaf' Persists," NPR, January 2, 2014, https://www.npr.org/sections/thesalt/2014/01/02/256605441/punishing-inmates-with-the-loaf-persists-in-the-u-s.

46 *and shredded cheese* Clifton Collins, Jr., and Gustavo "Goose" Alvarez, *Prison Ramen: Recipes and Stories from Behind Bars* (New York: Workman Publishing, 2015), 21, 97.

48 *"humane attentions"* Amy B. Smoyer, "Hungry on the Inside: Prison Food as Concrete and Symbolic Punishment in a Women's Prison," *Punishment and Society* 19, issue 2 (Sept. 2016): 240–55.

58 *of all CPS cases* US Department of Health and Human Services, "Child Maltreatment 2019: Summary of Key Findings," April 2021, https://www.childwelfare.gov/pubpdfs/canstats.pdf.

59 *sent to jail* Dorothy Roberts, "The Regulation of Black Families," *The Regulatory Review*, https://www.theregreview.org/2022/04/20/roberts-regulation-of-black-families/.

Chapter 3: Hunger, Hoarding + Having Enough

69 *"which is worse"* Andrew Solomon, *Far from the Tree: Parents, Children and the Search for Identity* (New York: Scribner, 2012), 347.

70 *"muscles and organs"* Kay Redfield Jamison, *Night Falls Fast: Understanding Suicide* (New York: Vintage Books, 1999), 119–20.

71 *sense of empathy* Leigh Hopper, "Why Schizophrenia Leads to Social Isolation: Lessons Learned in a Career of Research in Schizophrenia Could Answer Why So Many People Are Disconnected from Family, Friends," *UCLA Health*, October 17, 2017, https://www.uclahealth.org/news/why-schizophrenia-leads-to-social-isolation.

73 *"to build trust"* Katja Rowell, *Love Me, Feed Me: The Adoptive Parent's Guide to Ending the Worry About Weight, Picky Eating, Power Struggles and More* (St. Paul, MN: Family Feeding Dynamics, LLC, 2012), 173.

74 *of the time* Diane Benoit, "Infant-Parent Attachment: Definition, Types, Antecedents, Measurement and Outcome," *Pediatric Child Health* 9, no. 8 (Oct. 2004): 541–45. https://www.ncbi.nlm.nih.gov/pmc/articles/PMC2724160/.

76 *sweet foods* M. Yanina Pepino and Julie A. Mennella, "Sucrose-Induced Analgesia Is Related to Sweet Preferences in Children but Not Adults," *Pain* 119, no. 1–3 (Dec. 15, 2005): 210–18.

77 *Dallas Morning News in 2013* Scott Farwell, "The Girl in the Closet," *The Dallas Morning News*, 2013, http://res.dallasnews.com/ interactives/2013_October/lauren/#.Y0IMpC-97q0.

79 *"Lauren was not mine"* Ibid.

80 *"basically human missing"* Jennifer Emily, "Lauren Kavanaugh's Unrepentant Mother Called 'Girl in the Closet' Victim 'It,' Blamed Her for Abuse," *The Dallas Morning News*, December 20, 2018, https://www.dallasnews.com/news/crime/2018/12/20/lauren-kavanaugh-s-unrepentant-mother-called-girl-in-the-closet-victim-it-blamed-her-for-abuse/.

80 *"to their biology"* Jay Neugeboren, *Imagining Robert: My Brother, Madness and Survival* (New York: Henry Holt, 1997), cited in Solomon, *Far from the Tree*, 347.

Chapter 4: Food That Is Fast + Full of Meaning

103 *"to each other"* Chris Arnade, "McDonald's: You Can Sneer, But It's the Glue That Holds Communities Together," *The Guardian*, June 8, 2016, https://www.theguardian.com/business/2016/jun/08/mcdonalds-community-centers-us-physical-social-networks.

111 *"pivotal life event"* Kelly O'Connor, "What History Teaches Us About Women Forced to Carry Unwanted Pregnancies to Term," *Time*, September 20, 2021, https://time.com/6103001/baby-scoop-era-abortion/.

112 *Scott Carney* Scott Carney, "Meet the Parents: The Dark Side of Overseas Adoption," *Mother Jones*, March–April, 2009, https://www.motherjones.com/politics/2009/03/meet-parents-dark-side-overseas-adoption/.

115 *"higher the bounty"* Elizabeth Brico, "The Government Spends 10 Times More on Foster Care and Adoption Than Reuniting Families," Talk Poverty, August 23, 2019, https://talkpoverty.org/2019/08/23/government-more-foster-adoption-reuniting/.

115 *"in the home"* Richard Wexler, "Confessions of a Caseworker: We Remove Kids to Protect Ourselves," February 22, 2017, https://youthtoday.org/2017/02/confessions-of-a-caseworker-we-remove-kids-to-protect-ourselves/.

116 *"out of poverty"* Kathryn A. Sweeney, "The Culture of Poverty and Adoption: Adoptive Parent Views of Birth Families," *Purdue University Calumet* 16, no. 1 (2012): 22–37, https:// quod.lib.umich.edu/m /mfr/4919087.0016.102/—culture-of-poverty-and-adoption-adoptive-parent-views?rgn=main;view=fulltext.

116 *"care for a child"* Ibid.

Chapter 5: Charity, the Giving + Taking of Food

135 *"been for me"* Bee Wilson, "When My Husband Left Me, I Headed for the Kitchen—Here's How Comfort Food Can Save the Soul," *The Guardian*, May 21, 2022, https:

//www.theguardian.com/food/2022/may/21/husband-left-me-headed-for-kitchen-how -comfort-food-can-save-the-soul.

136 *school lunch* Nadar Issa, "Aramark to Continue Serving Meals to CPS Kids Under New $88.5M Food Contract," *Chicago Sun Times*, May 23, 2022, https://chicago.suntimes.com /education/2022/5/23/23138433/cps-public-school-aramark-food-services-contractor -open-kitchens-lunch-meals.

137 *the word "healthy"* Jennifer E. Gaddis, "The Big Business of School Meals," Kappan, Sep- tember 21, 2020, https://kappanonline.org/big-business-school-meals-food-service-gaddis/.

137 *for breakfast* Brendaliss Gonzalez, "Parents Voice Concerns over Product Served as Fruit in Denver School," 7-Denver, August 24, 2016, https://www.denver7.com/lifestyle /health/parents-voice-concerns-over-product-served-as-fruit-in-denver-school.

147 *in their lives* Katie S. Martin, *Reinventing Food Banks and Pantries: New Tools to End Hunger* (Washington, DC: Island Press, 2021), 10.

147 *"quickly as possible"* Ibid., 4.

148 *"others around you"* Robert M. Sapolsky, *Why Zebras Don't Get Ulcers: The Acclaimed Guide to Stress, Stress-Related Diseases, and Coping* (New York: St. Martin's Griffin, 1994), 372.

149 *social capital* Ibid., 381.

149 *Sapolsky writes* Ibid., 378.

150 *for everyone else* Ibid., 381.

150 *California was 40th* Senator Mike Lee, "Social Capital Project," 2017–2022, https:// www.jec.senate.gov/public/index.cfm/republicans/socialcapitalproject.

150 *"block of democracy"* "Drivers of Trust in Public Institutions in Finland," Organization for Economic Co-operation and Development, May 4, 2021, https://www.oecd-ilibrary.org /sites/83f2a08d-en/index.html?itemId=/content/component/83f2a08d-en.

153 *"spend on food"* Leanne Brown, *Good and Cheap: Eat Well on $4/Day* (New York: Work- man Publishing Company, 2015), viii.

153 *"worth the effort"* Leanne Brown, *Good Enough: A Cookbook: Embracing the Joys of Imperfection and Practicing Self-Care in the Kitchen* (New York: Workman Publishing Company, 2022), 2.

Chapter 6: Food + Housing, Conjoined + Inseparable Twins

163 *whole four years* Census Bureau, *Dynamics of Economic Well-Being: Poverty, 2013–2016*, p. 6, https://www.census.gov/content/dam/Census/library/publications/2021/demo/p70br-172.pdf.

163 *"less than a year"* Ibid., 5.

164 *in 1976* Josh Levin, "The Real Story of Linda Taylor, America's Original Welfare Queen," *Slate*, December 19, 2013, https://www.slate.com/articles/news_and_politics/history/2013/12/linda _taylor_welfare_queen_ronald_reagan_made_her_a_notorious_american_villain.html.

164 *said of Taylor* Ibid.

165 *"remains powerful today"* Bryce Covert, "The Myth of the Welfare Queen," *The New Republic*, July 2, 2019, https://newrepublic.com/article/154404/myth-welfare-queen.

165 *keeping people poor* Ibid.

165 *raise their families up* Cynthia Miller, Manpower Demonstration Research Corporation (MDRC), *New Hope for the Working Poor: Effects After Eight Years for Families and Children*, July 2008, https://www.mdrc.org/publication/new-hope-working-poor.

165 *child development* Greg Duncan, "Refashioning Income Supports for Children in Poverty," podcast, Stanford Center on Poverty and Inequality, https://inequality.stanford .edu/publications/media/details/podcast-refashioning-income-supports-children -poverty.

165 *next generation* Ibid.

166 *for their babies* Jason DeParle, "Cash Aid to Poor Mothers Increases Brain Activity in Babies, Study Finds," *New York Times*, January 24, 2022, https://www.nytimes.com /2022/01/24/us/politics/child-tax-credit-brain-function.html.

167 *left over* Jeff Larrimore, "Assessing the Severity of Rent Burden on Low-Income Families," Board of Governors of the Federal Reserve System, December 22, 2017, https://www .federalreserve.gov/econres/notes/feds-notes/assessing-the-severity-of-rent-burden-on-low -income-families-20171222.html.

167 *things you want* Elizabeth Warren and Amelia Warren Tyagi, *All Your Worth: The Ultimate Lifetime Money Plan* (New York: Free Press, 2005).

168 *considered "unhoused"* Institute for Children, Poverty & Homelessness, "The McKinney-Vento Homeless Assistance Act," September 30, 2022, https://www.icphusa.org/mkv/.

168 *who need them* National Low Income Housing Coalition, "Housing Needs by State 2022," https://nlihc.org/housing-needs-by-state/Nevada.

168 *decisions, by definition* Robert M. Sapolsky, *Why Zebras Don't Get Ulcers: The Acclaimed Guide to Stress, Stress-Related Diseases, and Coping* (New York: St. Martin's Griffin, 1994), 364.

168 *"next stressor"* Ibid., 365.

173 *in The Nevada Independent* Tabitha Mueller, "Indy Explains: How Nevada's Rapid Summary Eviction Process Works," September 9, 2021, https://thenevadaindependent.com /article/indy-explains-how-nevadas-rapid-summary-eviction-process-works.

174 *"to her unit"* Matthew Goldstein, "Falling Behind on Weekly Rent and Afraid of Being Evicted," *New York Times*, December 17, 2020.

174 *piece by Michael Lyle* Michael Lyle, "Congressional Probe Labels Siegel Group's Eviction Practices 'Uniquely Egregious': For Ousted Tenants, Damage Is Already Done," *Nevada Current*, July 22, 2022.

175 *smiley face emoji* Ibid.

Chapter 7: The Limits + Liabilities of Lunch

206 *risk for homelessness* National Health Care for the Homeless Council, "Homelessness & Adverse Childhood Experiences: The Health and Behavioral Health Consequences of Childhood Trauma Fact Sheet," February 2019, https://nhchc.org/wp-content/uploads /2019/08/aces-fact-sheet.pdf.

206 *study in The Lancet* Jesse T. Young and Nathan Hughes, "Traumatic Brain Injury and Homelessness: From Prevalence to Prevention," *The Lancet*, December 2, 2019, https://www.thelancet.com/journals/lanpub/article/PIIS2468–2667(19)30225–7/fulltext.

207 *support mood regulation* Susan Fitzgerald, "Traumatic Brain Injury in Homeless People Is Underrecognized," *Neurology Today*, February 6, 2020, https://journals.lww.com/neurotodayonline/fulltext/2020/02060/traumatic_brain_injury_in_homeless_people_is.4.aspx.

207 *and bipolar disorder* National Coalition for the Homeless, "Mental Illness and Homelessness," July 2009, https://www.nationalhomeless.org/factsheets/Mental_Illness.pdf.

220 *of the program* National Alliance to End Homelessness, "Transgender Homeless Adults & Unsheltered Homelessness: What the Data Tell Us," July 24, 2020, https://endhomelessness.org/resource/transgender-homeless-adults-unsheltered-homelessness-what-the-data-tell-us/.

220 *"or kicked out"* Camille Baker, "The Trump Administration Wants to Make It Harder for Transgender People to Access Homeless Shelters," *The Intercept*, May 23, 2019, https://theintercept.com/2019/05/23/homeless-shelters-transgender-hud/.

Chapter 8: Inconvenient People + the Starving Brain

229 *they could* Blake Erickson, "Deinstitutionalization Through Optimism: The Community Mental Health Act of 1963," *American Journal of Psychiatry*, June 11, 2021, https://ajp.psychiatryonline.org/doi/10.1176/appi.ajp-rj.2021.160404.

230 *Rampant lobotomies* Madeline Bourque Kearin, "Dirty Bread, Forced Feeding, and Tea Parties: The Uses and Abuses of Food in Nineteenth-Century Insane Asylums," *Journal of Medical Humanities*, 43 (2022): 95–116.

230 *"previous meal"* Albert Q. Maisel, "Bedlam 1946," *Life* magazine, May 6, 1946. Reprint: PBS American Experience, https://www.pbs.org/wgbh/americanexperience/features/lobotomist-bedlam-1946.

230 *"only corn meal"* Ibid.

231 *"or milk"* Ibid.

231 *"black coffee"* Ibid.

232 *"of my traumas"* Esmé Weijun Wang, *The Collected Schizophrenias: Essays* (New York: Graywolf Press, 2019), 39.

232 *"human understanding"* Ibid., 48.

232 *other people* Ibid., 46–47.

232 *Lurching or not* Ibid., 39, 96.

233 *"the worker serving"* Penelope Q, "How to Eat Well in the Psych Ward," *Vice*, April 24, 2015, https://www.vice.com/en/article/4xbmjn/how-to-eat-well-in-the-psych-ward.

233 *"feel full"* Ibid.

233 *"to be released"* Wang, *The Collected Schizophrenias: Essays*, 110.

233 *"locked in"* Ibid., 110.

234 *stopped rotting* Penelope Q, "How to Eat Well in the Psych Ward."

235 *"became public policy"* Kay Redfield Jamison, *Night Falls Fast: Understanding Suicide* (New York: Vintage Books, 1999), 158–59.

235 *who are sick* Wang, *The Collected Schizophrenias: Essays*, 40.

236 *debunked, and closed* The World Health Organization, "Special Initiative for Mental Health," 2019–2023, https://www.who.int/publications/i/item/special-initiative-for-mental-health-(2019–2023).

238 *than they are* Sun Young Yum, "The Starved Brain: Eating Behaviors in Schizophrenia," *Psychiatric Annals*, January 1, 2005, https://journals.healio.com/doi/10.3928/00485713-20050101–10.

239 *"inside their underwear"* Ibid.

239 *from 1944 to 1945* David Baker and Natacha Keramidas, "The Psychology of Hunger," *Monitor on Psychology*, 44, no. 9 (October 2013), https://www.apa.org/monitor/2013/10/hunger.

239 *and breathing* Ibid.

239 *"they were given"* Sun Young Yum, Michael Y. Hwang, and Katherine A. Halmi, "Eating Disorders in Schizophrenia," *Psychiatric Times*, 23, no. 7 (June 1, 2006), https://www.psychiatrictimes.com/view/eating-disorders-schizophrenia.

240 *"compensatory effort"* Ibid.

243 *"sense of disability"* Robert Kolker, "Stopping Schizophrenia Before It Starts," *Elemental*, March 12, 2021, https://elemental.medium.com/stopping-schizophrenia-before-it-starts-b53367119c2e.

243 *"processing information"* Ibid.

Chapter 9: Slippage + the Discomfort of Food

247 *"bit of discomfort"* Harry Kloman, "Gursha: Hands Across the Table," Ethiopian Food: Mesob across America, January 1, 2015, https://ethiopianfood.wordpress.com/2015/01/01/gursha-hands-across-the-table.

261 *"only for peasants"* Ken Albaba, *Beans: A History* (New York: Berg Publishers, 2007), 3.

261 *manioc flour* Ibid., 3.

261 *"political beliefs"* Ibid., 2.

262 *bean club* Elena Kadvany, "People Are Frothing at the Mouth: Napa's Rancho Gordo Opens Its Coveted Bean Club Wait List," *San Francisco Chronicle*, March 4, 2022.

262 *"inborn prejudice"* Albaba, *Beans: A History*, 3.

262 *"fudgy texture"* Burkhard Bilger, "The Hunt for Mexico's Heirloom Beans," *The New Yorker*, April 16, 2018.

262 *"hate beans"* Ibid.

Chapter 10: Lunch + the Braided-Up Life

280 *"just as much"* Claire Cain Miller, Josh Katz, Francesca Paris, and Aatish Bhatia, "Vast New Study Shows a Key to Reducing Poverty: More Friendships Between Rich and Poor,"

New York Times, August 1, 2022, https://www.nytimes.com/interactive/2022/08/01/upshot/rich-poor-friendships.html.

283 *Desert Companion* Kim Foster, "The Meth Lunches: The Care and Feeding of a Drug Addict," NPR's *Desert Companion*, July 1, 2017.

289 *2022–2024* Angela M. Brommel, *Mojave in July* (Flagstaff: Tolsun Books, 2019).

Afterword: In the World

292 *"are bleak"* Andrew Solomon, *Far from the Tree: Parents, Children and the Search for Identity* (New York: Scribner, 2012), 587.

293 *"paying attention at all"* Michelle Wilde Anderson, *The Fight to Save the Town: Reimagining Discarded America* (New York: Simon & Schuster, 2022), 48.

294 *"as powerlessness"* Ibid., 75.

294 *into their communities* Ibid., 53.

295 *"criteria for PTSD"* Ibid., 62.

295 *"I'm not crazy"* Ibid., 68.

295 *"out and why"* Ibid., 68.

296 *writes prophetically* Ibid., 78.

296 *in the country* US Department of Housing and Urban Development, "HUD Releases 2021 Annual Homeless Assessment Report Part 1," February 4, 2022, https://www.hud.gov/press/press_releases_media_advisories/hud_no_22_022.

296 *"at the center of everything"* Anderson, *The Fight to Save the Town*, 78.

298 *Far from the Tree* Solomon, *Far from the Tree*, 328.